PRESUMED CRIMINAL

Presumed Criminal

Black Youth and the Justice System
in Postwar New York

Carl Suddler

NEW YORK UNIVERSITY PRESS
New York

NEW YORK UNIVERSITY PRESS
New York
www.nyupress.org

Paperback edition published 2020

References to Internet websites (URLs) were accurate at the time of writing. Neither the author nor New York University Press is responsible for URLs that may have expired or changed since the manuscript was prepared.

Library of Congress Cataloging-in-Publication Data
Names: Suddler, Carl, author.
Title: Presumed criminal : black youth and the justice system in postwar New York / Carl Suddler.
Description: New York : New York University Press, [2019] |
Includes bibliographical references and index.
Identifiers: LCCN 2018042634 | ISBN 9781479847624 (cl : alk. paper) |
ISBN 9781479806751 (pb : alk. paper)
Subjects: LCSH: Juvenile delinquency—New York (State)—New York—History—
20th century. | Youth and violence—New York (State)—New York—History—20th century. |
African American youth—New York (State)—New York—Social conditions—20th century. |
African Americans—New York (State)—New York—Social conditions—20th century. |
Discrimination in criminal justice administration—New York (State)—New York—
History—20th century. | New York (N.Y.)—Race relations—History—20th century.
Classification: LCC HV9106.N6 S83 2019 | DDC 364.36089/9607307471—dc23
LC record available at https://lccn.loc.gov/2018042634

New York University Press books are printed on acid-free paper, and their binding materials are chosen for strength and durability. We strive to use environmentally responsible suppliers and materials to the greatest extent possible in publishing our books.

Manufactured in the United States of America

10 9 8 7 6 5 4 3 2

Also available as an ebook

For "My Life"

CONTENTS

ILLUSTRATIONS

Introduction

"The Way I See It": Reframing Black Youth and Racial Injustice

A man never knows the real importance of fighting juvenile
delinquency until he has to stare it in the face.
—Roy Campanella, "The Way I See It"

"I just got mixed up with some jerky kids," David Campanella told the
police when he was arrested for his role in a Queens brawl. According to
police reports, the fifteen-year-old son of the former Brooklyn Dodger
catcher Roy Campanella, was one of the six boys involved in a fistfight
in the vacant parking lot of a bowling alley as roughly thirty boys from
fourteen to twenty years old looked on. No weapons were involved,
and no injuries were reported. Media coverage of the incident varied
as the young Campanella was subjected to legal proceedings for the
fracas. Still, even with his well-known surname, the black youth faced
tremendous hardship in both the court of justice and the court of public
opinion.[1]

The first public accounts of the parking-lot scuffle were printed by
New York newspapers, the *New York Times* and the *New York Herald
Tribune*, with Campanella's photograph displayed and his name stamped
in the headlines. There was not much discrepancy with regard to what
happened on February 23, 1959; however, the New York dailies' charac-
terization of those who were involved differed. As reported by the *Herald Tribune*, David Campanella entered the Mapleways Bowling Alley
and issued a challenge to a group of white boys to come out and fight.
In accordance with the police report, Campanella was one of the leaders
of the Chaplains, "a Queens gang of Negro and Puerto Rican youths."
The reason for the clash, according to the *Herald Tribune* story, was that
"the Chaplains had been piqued over their 'territorial rights' in Flushing
being taken over by the unidentified rival gang."[2]

The unidentified rival gang was the Champions, a group of white youths who resided in the same neighborhood as the Chaplains. The *New York Times'* coverage of the incident proclaimed that the Champions were said to have called the fight one week earlier "to protest the presence of some of the Negro and Puerto Rican youngsters in a Flushing bowling alley." The Champions considered the bowling alley their "territory" and engaged Campanella and his guys when they entered Mapleways. One of the white boys who fought against the Chaplains, Mike O'Neill, said, "We were lounging around the bowling alley when Campanella and his two friends walked in. Campanella did all the talking. He said he wanted to build up a rep—you know, a reputation in the neighborhood—and he wanted three of us to fight him and his guys. Three of us said we would and we did." Fourteen youths, between the ages of fifteen and twenty, were booked at the Flushing Precinct on charges of disorderly conduct, arraigned in Night Court before Magistrate Edward Chapman, and paroled to their parents' custody—except Campanella.[3]

The police escorted Campanella to the Bronx Youth House but did not release him to the custody of his mother, Ruthe, when she arrived to pick him up. Mrs. Campanella refused to talk to reporters, and the authorities at the Youth House did not immediately disclose why young Campanella was not discharged. Later it was learned that after David was detained for his role in the skirmish, he made damaging admissions concerning a burglary of a drugstore one week prior. Domestic Relations Judge Wilfred A. Waltemade explained to David, "You must understand you have been found a juvenile delinquent and if you get in further trouble and are returned to children's court, you have my word, boy, you will be dealt with very severely." Following a two-and-a-half-hour hearing, David was let go with a warning. His mother told reporters, "This is going to break his father's heart."[4]

Roy Campanella, one of the first black, modern-era major-league baseball players, worked for many years with youngsters, mostly in New York City, to curb juvenile delinquency. In an article published by *Jet* magazine, an African American weekly founded in 1951, Roy Campanella revealed why it was important for him to work with kids around the country when he traveled with the Dodgers. "For years I've been lecturing in YMCAs, boys clubs and to kid groups about walking the straight and narrow," Campanella explained. "Too, I felt I was making

David Campanella, son of the Brooklyn Dodgers'
Roy, 1959. (Courtesy of Queens Borough Public
Library, Archives, *New York Herald-Tribune*
Photograph Morgue Collection)

a contribution towards solving a really serious problem in American life." But like any father, Roy was forced to reexamine the whole picture of juvenile delinquency when he faced the problem firsthand. After his son, David, was released, Roy told *New York Times* reporters dejectedly, "Everything else compared to this is nothing."[5]

The Campanellas scolded their son for his misbehaviors but at the same time understood the role that his reputable status played in the situation. As Mrs. Campanella defended her son in court, she affirmed that the charges were "blown up all out of proportion because of his name." The family's attorney, William O'Hara, agreed. Objecting to the high bail the Campanellas were forced to pay, the lawyer told reporters that he wondered "what would have happened to this boy if his name were Johnny Jones." Though it is difficult to know for certain to what extent David's family name affected the court's response to his wrongdoings, the press openly admitted that its coverage of the Campanella case was indeed influenced by his last name. Objecting to the tacit rule not to publish the names of juvenile offenders, the managing editor of the *New York Times*, Turner Catledge, disclosed, "It is not the purpose of newspapers to prevent crime or to sell any philosophy to the public." Unrelenting in his sentiment that the press was obligated to give the public facts, in reference to the Campanella case, Catledge stated, "We in New York have much less to apologize for than if we had not printed the name. Names do make news."[6]

Ultimately, Magistrate James E. LoPicolo dismissed the charges against the fourteen youths, including David Campanella, for the parking-lot altercation, with a stern warning to the defendants not to participate in any further "gang fights." Young Campanella was, however, judged a juvenile delinquent in Queens Children's Court for his involvement in the drugstore robbery. Justice Sylvia J. Liese of the Domestic Relations Court paroled Campanella in the custody of his mother and a priest. She explained that it was immaterial whether anything had been taken from the store, since breaking into the store itself constituted an act of juvenile delinquency. Campanella's parole conditions prohibited overnight visits to his friends, ordered mandatory school attendance, and enforced a nightly curfew. Deviation from these conditions, Justice Liese implied, would send Campanella to reform school. "I don't expect him to get any special treatment or sympathy as the son of his father," Justice Liese professed. "But I feel he should get the same chance as any other boy."[7]

Justice Liese was right. David Campanella did deserve the same chance as any other boy. And though the coverage of the case exacerbated the particulars, to a certain extent young Campanella's encounter with carceral authorities was, in fact, common—at least compared to other black youth encounters with the carceral state in the mid-twentieth century. Campanella had all the normal interests that boys of his age had, including athletic interests and group interests such as singing. Prior to the Mapleways incident, he had never been in trouble, and Justice Liese confirmed, "The things that got him into trouble [were] not typical of his behavior." Nevertheless, Campanella's attitude toward authority reflected a familiar distrust that many youths of color retained; but as much of the public inquired, why? A *Washington Post* editor wrote, "Even the scars of his race must have been slighter for him since his father was so conspicuous an example of how even deep-rooted prejudice can be overcome by merit and personality." Still, it was difficult for the public to understand how a youth such as Campanella, who did not fit the usually ascribed factors such as parental neglect, an unfavorable environment, and so on, became *delinquent.*[8]

Presumed Criminal: Black Youth and the Justice System in Postwar New York examines how the juvenile justice system and its associated authorities contributed to racialized constructions of youth criminality in New York City from the 1930s to the 1960s. "Criminalization" is broadly defined as the means in which one is criminalized, or prevented from being law-abiding, and its practices and processes extend further than the US criminal and juvenile justice systems. Bridging the historiographical gap between the Great Depression and the War on Crime, I argue that black youths faced a more punitive justice system by the postwar era that restricted their social mobility and categorically branded them as criminal—a stigma they continue to endure.[9]

Cautiously, I use the labels "black," "youth," and "juvenile delinquency" throughout the book. These labels are often defined and understood in particular social settings at any moment on the basis of their relationship with larger structural conditions, social policies, and ideologies, on the one hand, and local practices of everyday life within the contexts of families, peers, and state institutions, on the other. When referring to people, I use "black" much like the proper noun "African American"; however, I employ the term throughout the study in reference to people connected to the African diaspora as well. When referring to age, I use "youth" to refer to young men and women up through their early twenties; however, especially in legal proceedings, there is often variation across race and gender. I use "juvenile delinquency" generally in reference to antisocial behaviors and criminal acts committed by youths that have been categorized by the state. While I have attempted to analyze the complexities of race, class, and gender, young men do constitute the main subjects of the text.[10] By examining the experiences of black youths confined in New York City's expansive carceral systems, *Presumed Criminal* offers timely historical context for contemporary debates surrounding youth, race, and crime in the United States.

Black youth criminality, for all its singularities, continues to resonate as a national concern; however, few people are willing to accept the reality of their plight. Psychologists have determined that "black boys are seen as older and less innocent" than their white counterparts. Economists have found that "race trumps class, at least when it comes to [the] incarceration" of youths in the United States. Even as black youths in the twenty-first century articulate their own experiences with carceral authorities, many people remain surprised by the disparities between black and white youth experiences in the justice system. But these contemporary studies illustrate a much-longer history of policies and strategies that targeted specific communities since the late nineteenth century.[11]

The criminalization of black youth is inseparable from its racialized origins. Because of this connection, much of the historical narrative about crime and delinquency before the 1960s tends to focus on the southern criminal and juvenile justice systems whose racist practices prevailed during the long Jim Crow era. They have been framed as "pre-modern," as noted by historian Khalil Gibran Muhammad, while this history in the North has been more of a "modernizing narrative," which focused largely on the experiences of native-born whites and European immigrants. This approach overlooks the urban North as a critical site of production of modern ideas about race, crime, and punishment, and it gives a false impression that the history of racial criminalization both started and ended in the Jim Crow South—an assertion that scholars continue to debunk.[12] *Presumed Criminal* joins these efforts and makes central the experiences of black youths who faced the expansive justice system in New York City.

For youth crime, or juvenile delinquency, more specifically, these historical narratives have either been framed around the Progressive era and the establishment of the juvenile court system or the post–World War II period, especially the 1950s, when developments of youth culture were tied to the rise of a mass-media society. Like the histories of early criminal justice in the North, histories of youth crime in the Progressive era tend to revolve around the experiences of white youths, generally ethnic immigrants. Progressive reformers believed that "immigrants had to be 'Americanized,' culturally and morally transformed from aliens into citizens." The reformers involved in the establishment of the juvenile court, the "child-savers," believed that a separate justice system for youths could play a role in the Americanization process of its wards.

After all, "the progressive answer to make the state into a parent" quelled national concerns posed by the influx of European immigrants, as the state's power of *parens patriae* accelerated the process of Americanizing their offspring. Thus, the newly established juvenile court system became a protective buffer for white youths that diverted their misbehaviors away from the adult criminal justice system.[13]

Black youths, during the same period, were forced to navigate shifty terrain, where the dominant view characterized any of them whose behaviors deviated from social norms as "an incorrigible, undeserving, and expendable breed of human clay." This was a problem as they became overrepresented in the juvenile court. Black youths encountered a "Jim Crow juvenile justice system" that refused to extend rehabilitative ideals and resources; regularly committed them to adult prisons; and sentenced them to the convict-lease system, prolonged periods of detention, and higher rates of corporal punishment and execution. Therefore, as delinquent white youths benefited from juvenile court interventions under the guise of rehabilitative ideals, black youths were denied such privileges and presumed criminal beyond a doubt—a trend that outlived the Progressive era.[14]

These presumptions of criminality extended beyond the juvenile court, especially by the postwar period. Heightened surveillance of city spaces led to an increase in youth encounters with law enforcement officials that, naturally, inflated crime rates. Further, many of these run-ins with police triggered racial antagonisms in their respective communities and, consequently, caused black youths to view the police as a repressive, untrustworthy authority. To be sure, police brutality and misconduct was not exclusive to black communities, nor was it entirely a postwar phenomenon. And though each city presents its own unique history with police violence, many of the underlying causes and, often, community responses were the same.[15]

Even then, the juvenile justice system and the police are just a part of the criminalization of black youths in the twentieth century. Print media outlets and social scientists, especially with the rise of social psychiatry and social psychology, were also authorities who contributed to the criminalization of the city's black youths. Whether reporting on criminal investigations or stories of uprisings, political organizing, or grassroots activism, media bias reinforced racialized constructions of criminality that intensified public anxieties about black youths. Social scientists continued to rely on crime statistics to substantiate the need for intervention in black communities. Thus, it is imperative to continue to advance our understanding of how criminalization impacted race relations in urban America and vice versa.[16]

* * *

Presumed Criminal not only broadens the burgeoning historiography of carceral studies but also expands the postwar urban narrative that emphasizes the limits of racial liberalism in the North, and it builds on the long-standing efforts to recognize youths as important historical actors. New York City from the Great Depression to the Great Society presents a case study that lends itself well to comparisons with other large US cities. Its demographic makeup from the onset of the twentieth century transformed drastically from decade to decade. The earliest decades of the century witnessed vast European immigration that fueled America's urban growth—a trend that remained from the nineteenth century. By the 1920s, the flow of European immigrants to American cities slowed and was supplanted by migrations of black folks, mainly from the American South and the Caribbean. These demographic changes in America's largest city, combined with technological advances and urban industrialization, sparked many confrontations inspired by societal changes.[17]

To be sure, New York City was one of the many American cities north of the Mason-Dixon line where its citizens confronted, resisted, and challenged the racial status quo, especially after World War II. Historians attest that much of the struggle for civil rights emerged in major northern cities, but because southern movements received more media and national political attention, they tend to dominate the historical narrative and popular memory. Gradually, however, the narrative of the urban North as a utopian melting pot has been exposed. So too has the history of New York City as a "supposed bastion of liberalism." In fact, it has been noted, because of its sizeable black population, "progressive" leadership, and far-reaching print media outlets, New York City became a pivotal battleground in the postwar push for racial equality. This included contests over fair housing, public schools, and the criminal justice system—all spaces that affect the lived experiences of the city's youths.[18]

Even so, youth experiences remain largely omitted from the historical narrative of New York City's postwar struggle toward equality. This, indeed, speaks more to the shortcomings of public records than to their historical significance. *Presumed Criminal* attempts to deal with this dilemma. Teens and young adults often stood "at the vanguard of grassroots mobilizations" in city spaces, and New York City was no exception. Many historians and youth studies scholars continue to develop the analytical frameworks needed to examine not only how ideas about youth have been framed but also how the youths can be studied as agents of change. For example, research on youth gangs in postwar New York reveals that gangs were a product of the confluence of perceptions of masculinity and class in a postindustrial context. However, because the historical sources are generally *about* the youths and not *from* them, the premise relies entirely on the theory that crime is culturally adaptive to economic and social oppression. But what about the many youths who did not join gangs in postwar New York City? Such an approach ignores the majority of the youngsters who were criminalized by association and forced to cope with the unjustified consequences that followed. These are the youths whose experiences make up a bulk of the text that follows.[19]

Presumed Criminal begins in the second half of the 1930s. New York City, like most cities, continued to work its way back to normalcy after the stock market crashed. Harlem, whose renaissance was disrupted by the Great Depression, continued to subsist as the "Negro capital of the world" within the "greatest city in the world."[20] Conversely, the city's youths found themselves at a crossroads. Institutional resources to provide sufficient education, economic, health, and recreational opportunities for youths were drained as the city recovered from the Depression, and this impacted youth behaviors, decisions, and perceptions of authorities. Consequently, many youths, especially black youths, found themselves entering the criminal justice system for the first time—a system that, like the black youths who entered it, found itself at a crossroads.

Chapter 1 focuses on the juvenile justice system and its related efforts to address youth crime in New York City before World War II. Tensions developed among state authorities who vied for position on the way to combat the city's crime problem. On one side, there were those who anticipated a rise in criminal acts and believed it was imperative to increase carceral sovereignty to prevent potential problems. Preventive policing of youth behaviors increased surveillance, which naturally compounded arrests rates and gave reason to become tough on youth crime. On the other side, there were those who made efforts to extend Progressive-era ideas, which emphasized the correction of social ills, to attend to crime and delinquency in the city. This approach offered both promise and perils for black youths in the justice system. For example, Jane Bolin's appointment to New York City's Domestic Relations Court marked promise. The first black woman judge in US history represented a cultural and intellectual tradition that advanced a neo-Progressive ethos that prioritized social influences over race when handling cases of youth crime. Bolin often administered a brand of justice that recognized the racism and structural inequalities that black youths faced, and she joined a handful of black reformers who demanded that whites treat them more fairly. But the Progressive-era logic gave little regard to the demographic changes in the city and, consequently, contributed to its perils. The informality of juvenile justice, combined with absolute judicial authority reaffirmed by the Federal Juvenile Delinquency Act of 1938, made the system a precarious space for countless black youths, who were subjected to a state authority that chose to ignore the character, condition, needs, and welfare of individual cases. Thus, despite the best efforts of Bolin and others, the racialization of youth crime proved too compelling to oppose.

Chapter 2 moves the discussion of youth criminality from the courts to the streets. The chapter examines Harlem's home front during World War II, centered on the 1943 uprising and its lasting impact on police-community relations. The 1943 uprising joined a series of rebellions across the country in response to long-standing racial resentments and animosities. The Harlem uprising, specifically, was a direct response to the system of discrimination, segregation, and police brutality that plagued the community through the 1940s. Incited by the untimely, fatal police shooting of a black soldier, the public protests called attention to the plight of black New Yorkers, especially young Harlemites, as they contested the urban landscape and sought equal access to wartime benefits. The excessive policing employed to quell the uprising agitated any cordial relations the police attempted to cultivate in the 1930s, and it negatively influenced youth perspectives of state authorities, while simultaneously affecting the city's perceptions of its youths.

Chapters 3 and 4 explore postwar constructions, and deconstructions, of youth, race, and crime in New York City. A range of societal forces, such as politicians, print media figures, and social scientists, as well as celebrities and athletes, joined carceral authorities in directing the public discourse on youth crime. This not only influenced theoretical constructions of criminality—that is, reaffirming who was presumed criminal—but also shaped public policies connected to the restored postwar problem. Chapter 3 investigates New York City's postwar crime wave. Crime-wave sensationalism, led mostly by print media outlets, plagued the city after the war, and it launched debates relating to the legitimacy of its rhetoric, its causes, its impact on the community, and prevention plans that were proposed to fight it. It also reconstructed popular crime discourse in ways similar to the Progressive era, when many reformers, both white and black, attributed criminal behaviors to social conditions. In postwar New York City, these reformers included social psychiatrists, criminologists, and politicians committed to stopping crime. These efforts, combined with a fortified police presence in the city, made it difficult for black youths to escape presumptions of criminality. The crime wave was packaged with racial undertones, which were reinforced by disproportionate arrest statistics and crime data, that synonymized New York's crime problem and its black residents, mainly youths.

By the 1950s, the decade of delinquency, there was little doubt that youth crime was a nationwide concern that warranted the attention and resources of all who were willing and able to address the problem. In the 1950s, the United States committed fully to curbing youth crime in a way comparable to the Progressive-era child-saving efforts, leading to the establishment of the juvenile court system. Chapter 4 dissects the effectiveness of antidelinquency efforts that trickled down from the national to the state to the local levels. Of all the dramatic social changes throughout the first half of the twentieth century, shifts in youth behaviors dominated popular discourse at midcentury, and youth crime emerged at the forefront. Considering that youth criminality intersected race, class, gender, and region, as confirmed by the United States Senate Subcommittee on Juvenile Delinquency in 1953, many people took interest in prevention efforts. In New York City, various agencies and organizations, both formal and informal, put forth efforts to combat youth crime as they saw fit—some more successful than others. These ranged from large institutional endeavors to on-the-ground organizing by the youths themselves. For example, the Harlem Young Citizens Council, an enthusiastic group of young Harlemites, called on the adults in the community to accept more responsibility for the unfair branding of black youths as delinquent. In the end, even with all the crime- and delinquency-prevention efforts that emerged, the number of youths arrested, especially black youths, continued to rise, and although this rise was a function of policy and practice as opposed to changes in behavior, it reestablished race as the basis of youth criminality.

The progress made in the decade of delinquency was met by systemic and institutionalized racism in the 1960s. Efforts to create a fair and impartial juvenile justice system became a thing of the past, and black youths in New York City bore the brunt of inordinate police practices and, consequently, endured the stigma of criminality henceforth. Chapter 5 recovers the case of the Harlem Six to attest to the firmness of race as a crucial determinant in American notions of crime and delinquency. With anticrime laws such as "stop-and-frisk" and "no-knock," which contributed to disparate arrest rates and increased police encounters in predominantly black communities, New York City officials established a police state that created a climate for dissension. This tragic tale of criminal injustice—with all its familiarities and uniqueness—reveals the extent to which the community was compelled to go to protect its youths from the overwhelming power of the state.

Before the War on Crime, thousands of black youths in New York City confronted an opponent in the justice system that appeared to be constantly changing, a justice system whose powers derived from its ability to be shaped and reshaped by extension, never revision, and one that prioritized punishment, never prevention. A growing police state that was supported by countless policies to increase surveillance criminalized the behaviors of those who most needed protection, not condemnation. Still, thousands of black youths negotiated their place in the "greatest American city" as different adult social actors proposed their potential solutions to the problems the youngsters faced. But the problems lay in the presumptions: the presumption that black youths elicit a less essential conception of childhood and the presumption of criminality that tethers the lives of black youths to the justice system indefinitely.

1

"The Child Is Never Basically Bad"

Creating Crime through Prevention

Society, the child's home life, environmental influences and other factors influencing him may cause him to rebel, but the child is never basically bad.
—Justice Jane Matilda Bolin, *New York Amsterdam News,* April 9, 1949

As the Depression decade was coming to its end, it seemed like everyone had something to say about crime in Harlem: "But crime in Harlem isn't the weather."[1] It was not a topic of conversation that existed with no effect. To the contrary, the more people talked about it, the more it seemed to influence the everyday lives of Harlem residents.

This was particularly true for Harlemites after the New York State Temporary Commission on the Condition of the Urban Colored Population met in January 1939. The public hearings were set to reveal the findings of a four-month investigation of the community by the commission's research staff. Crime in Harlem was injected into this discussion by Charles Hanson, chairman of the Harlem Public Policy Committee. Hanson accused the police department of "protecting New York City from Harlem" and declared that "more police should be taken off their horses on Seventh avenue and stationed in the side streets where they are needed."[2] The call was reinforced during the hearing by New York City Councilman Joseph Baldwin, who professed, "there's a murder a day in Harlem," and Mayor Fiorello La Guardia, who deplored that he "couldn't stop Harlemites from butchering one another." And though New York City Police Commissioner Lewis Valentine denied such accusations, the diatribe of a crime wave in Harlem was affirmed.[3]

But Commissioner Valentine was right. In fact, at least according to New York Police Department (NYPD) figures, violent crime in

Harlem decreased across the 1930s. At the January hearing, Captain James C. Pritchard cited homicide statistics in Harlem beginning with 1933, when he said there were 124 such cases in the Sixth Detective District, comprising most of Harlem. By 1938, the year under scrutiny, Captain Pritchard testified that there were 71 homicides in the area. Even an independent investigation by Inspector Joseph J. Donovan, at the request of Mayor La Guardia, put the number at 82 in 1938—both totals well under the "murder-a-day" moniker.[4]

Still, it was in the interest of city officials to play up violent crime in Harlem if they wanted to increase the police presence in the community. Therefore, skeptics including Assemblyman William T. Andrews, who jointly presided over the hearing, challenged the accuracy of Captain Pritchard's figures. "It would be impossible for us to fail to report 250 or 300 homicides a year," Captain Pritchard replied to a question from the presiding assemblyman. "We know of them all and we report them all," he said. "Disposing of a body is not so easy." In Pritchard's defense, Deputy Chief Inspector John J. de Martino, in charge of the Manhattan uniformed police, said that he had "the utmost faith in the people of Harlem, with the exception of a small per cent of 1 per cent of agitators and trouble makers." Inspector de Martino testified that he saw no need for increasing the police force in Harlem at this time, and with the exception of the small number of agitators, "everyone in Harlem is wholly satisfied."[5]

What became evident at the two-day hearings at Washington Heights Court was the conflicting schools of thought vying for authoritative position on crime in Harlem. On one side, there were those who believed crime in Harlem was rampant and that an increased carceral sovereignty was critical to reestablish order. On the other side, there were those who rejected such logic and aspired to advance a neo-Progressive rationale that emphasized the correction of social ills contributing to criminal behaviors—regardless of the numbers.

From the 1930s to the onset of World War II, this tension about crime existed at national, state, and local levels. In New York City, this debate had racial, political, and social implications that persisted beyond the period. And though everyone talked about crime, it was primarily black youths in the city who bore the brunt of the new policies, laws, and acts established to quell crime waves and to improve the conditions of the impoverished, idle, and unemployed.

A City within the City: A 1930s Sketch of
New York's City of Negroes

By the 1930s, Harlem established itself as "the Negro capital of the world." There were more blacks in Harlem per square mile than in any other spot on Earth. The renowned Harlem Renaissance writer Alain Locke expounded the all-encompassing community as one that "attracted the African, the West Indian, the Negro American; has brought together the Negro of the North and the Negro of the South; the man from the city and the man from the town and village; the peasant, the student, the business man, the professional man, artist, poet, musician, adventurer and worker, preacher and criminal, exploiter and social outcast." The upsurge of black migrants, and black immigrants, intricately tied a range of peoples in a central location. For the thousands of blacks who trekked north, Harlem marked the consummation of a journey that spanned more than four decades.[6]

To some of these migrants, the outlook for Harlem was hopeful. For example, in 1920 James Weldon Johnson predicted a Harlem future with huge potential. "Have you ever stopped to think what the future Harlem will be?" Johnson wrote. "It will be a city within a city. It will be the greatest Negro city in the world within the greatest city in the world." Johnson's optimism was contagious; however, the problem was that New York City was never an "open city," and the rapid expansion of black people into different neighborhoods intensified racial tensions.[7]

Native black New Yorkers were less optimistic. Prior to the demographic upswing, there were a little more than fifteen thousand self-identified "colored" residents in the Upper East Side of Manhattan, according to the 1920 census. There were black families in the city who traced their ancestry "far back into the Colonial period and who can easily qualify for membership in the Sons or Daughters of the American Revolution, as descendants of the men in the two Negro regiments from New York in the Revolutionary Army." They remembered the 1900 race riot in the Tenderloin district of New York City that "set the tone for the relationships among blacks, whites, and the police in Harlem and the city at large for the remainder of the twentieth century." Thus, the Depression-decade boom of black migrants and immigrants disrupted an already tumultuous racial climate in New York City.[8]

For these new Harlem residents, New York City was supposed to provide a more equal livelihood. In housing, for instance, a federal study showed that these new Harlemites sought "the possibility of escape, with improvement in economic status, in the second generation, to more desirable sections of the city." When compared to the South and the Caribbean islands, to which the new Harlem residents were accustomed, Harlem was different but not perfect. In fact, they quickly realized that the same racial attitude that favored residential segregation elsewhere "was carried on here in New York and has been promoted with unwavering effectiveness."[9]

Certainly, residential segregation in New York City was a multifaceted problem with a history that predates the Depression decade; however, it was exacerbated when the stock market crashed. By the end of the 1920s, blacks lived as far south as 110th Street—the northern boundary of Central Park—and most white residents had moved away. Even the Russian-Jewish and Italian sections of Harlem, founded a generation earlier, "were being rapidly depopulated." This mattered, because it not only shifted Harlem's demographics but changed dramatically the government aid that Harlem received as its residents fought their way out of the Depression.[10]

In New York City, one in six residents were out of work in the first year after the market crashed; in Harlem, the figure was one in four. Even the small middle class of Harlem suffered from a wave of layoffs and business failures. Police reports showed that "more than 1,000 Negro families . . . [were] in want, and hundreds of men other than heads of homes [were] walking the street vainly in search of work and money to buy food." As federal aid slowed, various local groups organized relief for the jobless and plans for the hungry. Soup kitchens opened across the city. The Harlem branch of the Salvation Army opened an emergency depot, and "within a short time after the initial sign was placed in front of the building 35 hungry men filed into the kitchen and were given huge bowls of hot beef stew." By the weekend's end, more than five hundred persons were fed at the Salvation Army on 135th Street.[11]

In addition to organizational efforts, there were countless instances in which Harlem residents traded goods or provided temporary shelter for each other. There were even individuals who took it upon themselves to supply the entire neighborhood with food and clothing. For example, Sister Minnie Bedell, "a kind-faced woman with a battered baby carriage," roamed the streets of Harlem serving those who were in need. Popularly known as the "angel of the streets," Sister Minnie canvassed shops in the city on foot, requested store owners to contribute "anything they were willing to give to the poor," placed the items in baskets, and distributed them free of charge to needy families. Attributing her urge to serve to her "religious impulses," the "angel of the streets" saw the days of the Depression as "a new opportunity to mend a broken home, to do a good turn, and give a word of cheer."[12]

Community organizing in Harlem to relieve the desolation of the Depression spoke directly to the gravity of unemployment in the city. Unskilled workers experienced the sharpest cuts in employment and wages—"first fired, last hired." Because of this, most civic leaders agreed that it would take a paradigmatic shift in *both* wages earned and hiring practices to alleviate the economic crisis. Samuel Allen, the industrial secretary of the New York Urban League, spoke to the way the severity of unemployment impacted black families in Harlem, while offering potential solutions. "The home is determined by the wage received," Allen explained. "Health and housing are determined by the economic status of a people." At a meeting sponsored by the Brotherhood of Sleeping Car Porters at the Abyssinian Community Forum in Harlem, Allen called for a "two-job man" as one way to abolish the unemployment problem that blacks faced. The problem, though, as Allen acknowledged, was that black men were "always employed in addition to, but never in place of, the white man." This was why Allen advised black Harlemites to prepare themselves for more than one job: "this second job will serve as a 'spare tire' in an industrial crisis."[13]

The call for a second job seemed far-fetched for Harlem residents, especially since most found themselves without one at all. And even for those who did, they earned well under a living wage. This was cause for concern for various community leaders in the city. Reverend Adam Clayton Powell voiced his worry that "no man can be moral in Harlem on $15 a week." Further, Powell was concerned that the "tragic and pathetic" rates of unemployment would increase crime rates in the city. "The conditions of vice," Powell indicated, "which exist in Harlem may all be traced to the low economic status of the people." Powell was not wrong. Because such wages did not adequately meet living standards in Harlem, there was a rise in crimes, mostly nonviolent crimes such as bootlegging, the sale of "hot" goods, and numbers running; the latter "seized Harlem like a form of madness."[14]

In the first half of the 1930s, over half of all black arrests in Harlem were for possession of policy slips. An arrest for possession of a policy slip was "hardly a major crime, [yet] nearly all of the people brought into court were Negroes arrested in connection with the daily lottery called policy, or the numbers game." For many Harlemites, the risk was worth the reward; the chance to win your way out of poverty, even for a short while, was enticing to men and women who pursued economic survival amid the economic turmoil. Harlem's youths coveted the same, although, aside from placing the occasional bet for their parents, Harlem youths were not firmly tied to the elaborate illegal gambling world. Still, they were impacted by the war against the policy game as it increased police presence throughout the city.[15]

The heightened police presence upset community relations in Harlem. As residents fought to stay afloat in the sea of poverty, their encounters with law enforcement escalated. Police vigorously pursued policy slips, and consequently, reports of brutality and illegal searches emerged. Testimonies of homes being subjected to illegal searches for policy slips surfaced, and follow-up reports with similar experiences were printed in local newspapers. For example, in a letter to Mayor La Guardia printed in the *New York Amsterdam News*, a Harlem resident reported that three men "in civilian clothes" entered his home "to search without showing shields or search warrant" and with no explanation. The intrusive nature of the search detailed in the letter caused the Harlem couple "quite a little worry, especially as there is no assurance that it will not happen again." Such insecurities about police aggression became a common cause for hostility toward carceral authorities, among all age groups.[16]

The Depression Decade and *The Negro Children of New York*

For Harlem's youth, the Depression decade was ripe for a spike in delinquent behaviors. It is important to note, however, that when analyzing crime and delinquency in Harlem, one must keep in mind the social and economic setting in which the behaviors occur; otherwise the insight will be valueless either as a means of understanding the factors involved or as a guide in establishing potential solutions. Owen Lovejoy, the secretary of the Children's Aid Society in New York, disclosed the effects of the Great Depression on black youths in the five boroughs in his study. Lovejoy asserted in *The Negro Children of New York* that the chief needs of this particular population were education, economic security, health, and recreation. More specifically, the study of black youth in New York City articulated that the lack of sufficient educational opportunities, inadequate recreational spaces, the instability of economic security, and substandard living conditions impacted youth behaviors, decisions, and perceptions of the authoritative figures in their lives.[17]

Inevitably, the Great Depression disrupted family life in the city, and as the decade proceeded, the strains on nuclear families worsened. As many adults immediately felt the impact of the Depression in their work lives, Harlem youths felt it in their school lives. Education problems were worsened by the low incomes and high living costs of New York City. "It's a vicious circle in a city of such color segregation," the assistant housing director at the Young Women's Christian Association (YWCA) told a *New York Herald Tribune* reporter. High rents were difficult to sustain without two working incomes; as a result, many mothers had to go out to work, and "the children [would] come to school with the keys of their house around their necks." Harlem kids encountered overcrowded classrooms that doubled, sometimes tripled, in size from their pre-Depression numbers, making the "usual class size" range from forty to fifty students. While many parents expressed their discomfort sending their children to such congested schools, their options were limited, and they were forced to make the most out of what they were given.[18]

After school, kids' efforts to find play opportunities waned in the 1930s. "There is no one there when they go home," Lovejoy explained, "and so they simply play around in alleys." Inadequate recreational spaces proved critical in the rise of juvenile delinquency rates throughout the nation, especially for those who were confined to city spaces. "Picking apples is a useful and pleasant occupation"; unfortunately for city kids, "picking them off a push cart, the only place [they] can see them grow is a misdemeanor." Various social service agencies presumed that an increase in recreational facilities would, at least, reduce the number of youths arrested and brought to courts for petty crimes. In a 1936 report on "the problem of education and recreation" in Harlem, a reporter for the *New York Amsterdam News* emphasized that the schools lacked adequate recreational facilities and that "children [were] forced to use the streets for playgrounds and thereby [were] thrown in contact with the vicious elements in the community." For these youngsters, much of their time was spent unsupervised and idle—an equation for trouble.[19]

Discussions of how to improve these problems, educational and recreational, to lessen the chances of youths running afoul were happening throughout the country. However, Harlem presented its own alternatives to recreation that attracted youths and contributed to heightened juvenile delinquency rates in the city. Inadequate education, lack of recreational spaces, and financial hardships led many people to take advantage of Harlem's sought-after nightlife. Through the 1930s, Harlem's nightlife "remain[ed] on the 'must' list of most New York visitors." For the visitors, especially the "people whose faces are white, people whose pocketbooks never get dusty and people who don't know any better than to believe what they see," Harlem was different. "It is the home of happy feet—gusty, swing-crazy, happy-go-lucky, [and] wide open," one visitor described. This was not exactly false, but it was a long way from being the truth. For most Harlem residents, they recognized that policy shops, pool rooms, gambling houses, speakeasies, and other underground institutions thrived in their city. And though these spaces were designated for adults, they became sites of activity for young people. More specifically, for black youths, these spaces, in addition to the numerous theaters, dance halls, and music halls, offered them "an opportunity to exploit their artistic talents for self-expression or as a means of livelihood." It also exposed them to more frequent interactions with the police. City police observed the elevated presence of black youths wandering the streets, and consequently, the number of arrests increased, thus increasing the numbers of black youths who entered the criminal justice system.[20]

The criminal acts that these youths were being arrested for covered a wide range. But whether they were arrested for stealing rides on the subway, shining shoes on the street, or burglary and unlawful entry, black youths' encounters with the police led to a rise in their court appearances. If the proportion of black youths arraigned in New York City courts told the tale, it appeared that juvenile delinquency among black youths steadily increased through the 1930s. Once these black youths were taken to court, a much-larger percentage of them compared to their white counterparts were either jailed or placed in workhouses or reformatories. This was largely due to the offenders' inability to pay fines. On the other hand, various authoritative figures declared that they "could not find suitable homes for black youths." On the living conditions of black youths in Harlem, a representative from the Children's Aid Society wrote, "Their parents are poor; their mothers are employed away from home, unless barred by the worse condition of unemployment." Reinforcing the findings of Lovejoy's study, it was often held that institutionalizing these youths served their benefit because in their current circumstances, they were "without recreational facilities; their tenements [were] congested." That is, the economic instability that many Harlemites experienced through the Depression decade and that impacted family life was cited as reason enough to remove youths from their homes. But incarceration did not resolve the problems these youngsters faced, and the delinquent stigma they bore carried a lasting impact as the state worked through its alternative means of rehabilitation.[21]

Potential Delinquents: The Juvenile Aid Bureau and the Problems of Preventive Policing

In December 1934, New York City's police commissioner, Lewis J. Valentine, told the Women's City Club, "You can't prevent child crime by arresting youngsters and taking them to the station house." In a talk titled "The Police Department as I Know It," Commissioner Valentine outlined the principal features of the newly established Juvenile Aid Bureau (JAB) to about one hundred women at a public forum. The new name for the bureau, formerly the Crime Prevention Bureau of the Police Department, came with new emphases and changes in both size and scope on the tasks undertaken by the department. With the support of Mayor La Guardia, though with the dissent of others, Commissioner Valentine opposed the former Crime Prevention Bureau and stated, "its cost of $500,000 a year was not justified by the results its obtained." The new bureau "constituted a better description of the work the bureau would do in the future than the old name did," and according to the police commissioner, the "chief reason" JAB was designed was to place direct responsibility for juvenile crime on police inspectors, not officers.[22]

In the 1930s, women's clubs were not the only groups interested in curbing juvenile delinquency. Efforts to combat and prevent juvenile

Mayor Fiorello H. La Guardia with Police Commissioner Lewis
J. Valentine, 1941. (AP Photo / Robert Kradin)

crime occupied various organization agendas throughout New York
City. Projects of various kinds, and in various fields, came into being,
and though most were well intended, nearly all were operationally ineffective. "The subject of juvenile delinquency should be approached
on a common-sense basis," Dudley P. Gilbert, president of the Catholic Boys Clubs of the Archdiocese of New York, wrote to the editors of the *New York Times*. "Those who are filled with prejudice and
pseudo-scientific ideas," Gilbert continued, "are totally unqualified to
pass judgment on this problem." Unfortunately, this was not the case.
Everyone had their beliefs as to how the problem of delinquency ought

to be approached and resolved. For example, there were medical experts who advocated for the sterilization of "persons who have shown themselves unfit to be parents" as a way "to protect society and children themselves from the depredations of criminals." Social scientists, such as the progressive Frederic M. Thrasher, defended their assertions that to prevent crime, one must propose "the elimination of the conditions which are known to foster crime and criminals." No matter how extreme the methods presented to help control juvenile delinquency appeared, the reality prevailed that the problem of delinquency needed to be addressed.[23]

In New York City, JAB readily fit the bill. The preceding Crime Prevention Bureau had been set up on an experimental basis. It was responding to public concern about the numbers of youths apprehended by police and studies of criminality in the 1920s, which emphasized that "anti-social careers" were detectable early in life. As these observations developed in the city, the police commissioner called into being an Advisory Committee on Crime Prevention with a focus on juvenile delinquency. This committee was made up of citizens and consultants whose primary responsibility was "to survey the crime situation and existing social resources" for offenders. They prepared a report that featured a comprehensive plan for the Crime Prevention Bureau. In it, the committee defined prevention as "determent, adjustment, [and] treatment of the vulnerable and the delinquent." Further, they articulated that both prevention and the apprehension of delinquents were police responsibilities, and as a result, it was critical for the Crime Prevention Bureau not only to be staffed by police officers but also to be a function of the police department.[24]

By 1931, an amendment was made to the Greater New York Charter, and the Crime Prevention Bureau became an official part of the New York Police Department. Led by Henrietta Additon, the initial staff assigned as crime prevention investigators consisted of police officers appointed from the uniformed force—130 men and 44 women—and 25 social workers, all women. The declared intention of the program was twofold: (1) to control crime-contributing community conditions and (2) to treat *potential* delinquents. In order to achieve these goals, it was suggested for the staff to extend their surveillance of community conditions, with particular reference to "high-delinquency areas"; to conduct social investigations of reported cases; to increase their efforts to instill a "respect for law and an appreciation of good citizenship"; and to produce a publication of studies that shed light on the causes and nature of delinquency. Combined, it was presumed, these strategies would shift the perception of police from repressive to protective and, in doing so, nip the crime problem in the bud.[25]

In the first three years of the Crime Prevention Bureau, its caseload expanded by 50 percent. These cases varied in significance and severity—from armed robberies to truancy—as well as in those who reported the delinquent behaviors. In fact, though some cases were brought forth by the Crime Prevention Bureau's patrolmen and women, parents and relatives of youths, schools, social agencies, and other individuals in the community, most were referred by the police. Consequently, on the one hand, it was believed that, according to Police Commissioner Edward Mulrooney, "although the full effects of its work cannot yet be known, the bureau's report shows that the value of having a unit in the department devoted to the prevention of delinquency is already being demonstrated." On the other, there were critics, such as Mayor La Guardia, who were skeptical of how the allocated funds were being used if the city's police were handling a bulk of the legwork.[26]

Those who defended the Crime Prevention Bureau did so largely on the Progressive-era premise that the approach to crime prevention must be through the individual, and each boy and girl presents his or her own problem. Thus, it was determined that "it takes time to establish good relations, and knowledge of the way a youngster's mind works to bring him into a more wholesome relation with society." Additon and her staff produced several reports, replete with statistics in line with national trends, to defend this logic and proclaimed, "It will be years before the full effect of its work can be measured." But Mayor La Guardia did not want to wait years; he preferred to overhaul the Crime Prevention Bureau.[27]

In 1934, the Crime Prevention Bureau was reorganized under a new director and renamed the Juvenile Aid Bureau. For Mayor La Guardia, it was vital that this new division justified its expenses. To do so, it seemed as if JAB needed to demonstrate a higher demand. At its peak, the Crime Prevention Bureau reported roughly fifteen thousand cases in a year. In JAB's first year, there were more than seventeen thousand cases—and that number increased to more than sixty-six thousand by the end of the decade.

This number did not reflect a spike in youth crime per se. Like national trends in juvenile delinquency, New York City experienced a steady climb through the 1930s; however, the exponential growth of cases reported to JAB can be attributed to its decision to compile a list of "potential delinquents." This referral-based list included any youths who engaged in acts that could "ultimately bring them into conflict with the law." These *potential* delinquents made up almost 90 percent of the bureau's caseload.[28]

The economic aspects of crime prevention remained a point of contention; therefore, the ability to acquire real dollars for theoretical problems needed these potential delinquents to boost the defense. Because the JAB numbers were so great, appropriating more funds and resources from the city became a priority. An increase to the bureau's budget was requested, and various committees around the city compiled data to show the costs and effects of long-standing crime prevention programs. For example, a model recreational program to break up juvenile gangs and reduce delinquency was presented to Mayor La Guardia and the new police commissioner, John F. O'Ryan. One of the cases presented was built around Harry Murch, a fifteen-year-old Queens native and "leader of a juvenile gang," who killed a playmate, William Bender. The data showed that the cost of Murch's trial and the cost of holding him for the duration of a sentence, "twenty years to life," would approximate $30,000. This was compared to the cost of "a play class" of 175 children that could be held two nights a week in a public school, at a cost of $300 for a thirty-week season. The police commissioner agreed to set up a model of the recreational program "in some section, probably the lower East Side," as an opportunity to study the costs and effects of such a program, "with a view to a more general application if proved worthwhile."[29]

JAB continued to develop programs to utilize vacant public and private spaces, empty buildings, and school and church playgrounds as recreational spaces. It established centers "in areas where delinquency rates were high, emphasizing the importance of facilities for recreation, art, music, science, [and] crafts."[30] JAB also cooperated with community resources such as the Works Projects Administration (WPA) to increase play facilities throughout the city. The Progressive-era belief in recreation as a means of deterrence to delinquency extended through the 1930s, and perhaps JAB's most important contribution in New York City was the promotion of its Police Athletic League.

The Friendly Policemen: Athletics, Recreation, and the Police Athletic League

Almost every large city in the United States had some kind of crime prevention bureau in its police department. Most had personnel who performed preventive investigations; others had police who actively supervised predelinquent youths or referred them to recreational agencies in the community. In many instances, the crime prevention bureaus organized their own recreation groups. This meant that those potential delinquents faced heightened surveillance through means other than courts and juvenile institutions under the guise of prevention. Perhaps the best known of these was New York City's Police Athletic League (PAL).[31]

"The occupation of leisure time is one answer to the crime problem" was the slogan and immediate objective to be carried out after the Leisure Time Conference in 1932, and in cooperation with the Crime Prevention Bureau, PAL was formed. Initial interest centered mainly around an organized stickball tournament in the Lower West Side district; then, in collaboration with the Police Department, seven blocks in the district were set aside and organized into play areas. It had been reported that a systematic organization of the Police Athletic League "provides a means of enrolling each boy by name and keeping records of his attendance, behavior conduct, etc., and furnishes a way of learning something about his social and family background." This form of surveillance was incentivized in various ways. Each boy was given a score or rating card, and "boys attaining the highest rating in attendance and attainments were taken to the American and National League games." During the summer, these youths had a chance to attend games at the Polo Grounds, under supervision, and to take trips to the Bronx Zoo, Botanical Gardens, city swimming pools, and gymnasiums. As PAL continued to grow, it developed a well-rounded program of games and activities. By the end of its first full year, the daily attendance at play areas totaled approximately one thousand youths.[32]

When the Crime Prevention Bureau was overhauled for the establishment of the Juvenile Aid Bureau, PAL became a critical component of the reorganization. Recreational centers expanded to different parts of the city, and by 1936, the police commissioner received a list of five thousand "truants" enrolled in PAL. Even the nonorganized spaces of youth congregation, such as playgrounds and poolrooms, were informally frequented by patrol officers in an attempt to build relations with the youngsters and to reshape their attitudes toward authority. "The Police Athletic League has developed a new respect and confidence among the youth of the city for the police," Police Commissioner Lewis J. Valentine reported, "and has materially assisted in reducing their anti-social behaviors." Though subjective, this assessment may have very well been accurate.[33]

"It was policemen who started P.A.L.," PAL president William M. Kent wrote. "Policemen are leading the way in its resurgence at a time when opportunities for youths are most needed." And it was Henrietta Additon, the deputy commissioner of the Crime Prevention Bureau, to first call them "PALs." In any case, the work of the Police Athletic League was being praised from above. New York's Governor Thomas H. Dewey and New York City's Mayor Fiorello La Guardia appeared to be in full support. "The people of New York owe a real debt of gratitude to the members of the New York Police Department who organized P.A.L.," Governor Dewey proclaimed. Mayor La Guardia, who was skeptical of the Crime Prevention Bureau and still somewhat unconvinced of JAB's work, was all in on PAL. "I believe in crime prevention just as I believe in preventive medicine," the New York City mayor expressed. "The Police Athletic League is taking a great step in that direction." Such accolades, combined with the shift to appeal to youths through recreation, with an undercurrent of treatment directed toward potential delinquents and delinquents alike, propelled New York City through a rapid expansion of youngsters under surveillance in the late 1930s.[34]

While these services were making efforts toward creating amicable relations between youth and authority, abuses of police power reminded the public of why such services were ever needed in the first place. In September 1938, for example, a fifteen-year-old Harlem youth reported that he was struck in the face by a police officer. Though the alleged officer emphatically denied the accusation, the investigation was turned over to the Juvenile Aid Bureau, while the boy's mother gave the case to the National Association for the Advancement of Colored People (NAACP). Eventually, the case worked its way up to Police Commissioner Valentine, though no charges were filed. Similar occurrences emerged throughout the city. On the one hand, they served as a reminder to the public about police misconduct. On the other, they exposed an internal tension between the social service element of crime prevention and the behaviors of the police in the street.[35]

Over time, this tension recurred, and some uniformed police personnel took issue with the oversight of the prevention bureaus. Though JAB and PAL services prioritized crime prevention and working with youths directly, they did intervene with police responsibilities—especially in the more serious delinquent cases. This caused some high-ranking police officers to voice their disproval. "Police officers have every requisite to perform the services required in a crime prevention program," Police Lieutenant James J. Brennan declared. "The professional worker [does] bring academic knowledge and social work experience, but work that is intimately related to police activity [is] best performed by the police." Establishing a balance proved crucial to the continued success of the crime prevention efforts, as handling young "criminals" became not only a city priority but also a national concern.[36]

Parent of the Nation: Progressive Logic and the Federal Juvenile Delinquency Act of 1938

Each state faced its own problems relating to juvenile delinquency; however, by the latter half of the 1930s, it was clear that there would need to be some kind of federal legislation that reinforced state laws in the event that a youth committed a federal offense. But in comparison to state governments, the federal government lagged in establishing policy on how to address youth crime. By 1925, nearly two-thirds of the states, in some form, had adopted a separate legal system for youths; by 1932, all but two states—Maine and Wyoming—established juvenile court legislation to handle cases of youth crime. The presumption, to a great extent, was that juvenile delinquency did not warrant jurisdiction of the federal courts, because young people did not commit federal offenses. Still, the federal government followed the states' lead, and on June 16, 1938, the Federal Juvenile Delinquency Act (FJDA) was approved.[37]

The primary purpose of the FJDA was to ensure that all persons under eighteen years old charged with violating federal law, not punishable by death or life imprisonment, were to be charged as delinquent and not tried as an adult. Subsequently, the youth would either be placed on probation "for a period not exceeding his minority" or committed to the custody of the attorney general, who could place the youth in "any public or private agency or foster home for . . . custody, care, subsistence, education, [or] training." This was an important shift, because prior to the 1938 act, juvenile offenders who broke federal laws had the same legal status as an adult offender. Thus, the FJDA and its provision marked a rather significant departure from the routine of criminal procedure.[38]

But the growing concern about youth crime at the end of the 1930s forced lawmakers at the state and national levels to revisit their established statutes. Many juvenile courts were established during the Progressive era—some functioning better than other—by reformers who focused on juvenile delinquency and methods of rehabilitation. They asserted that criminal acts committed by youths were not signs of an inherently flawed character and that separate courts with "judges that were cognizant of the malleable nature of children" were critical for this reason. Accordingly, "open-ended, informal, and highly flexible policies" were put in place to grant total discretion to the adjudicating criminal justice professional, commonly the judge overseeing the case. The state, then, attained authority and responsibility for those youths whose "natural parents were not providing appropriate care or supervision." The goal was to ensure that youths were protected and treated instead of detained and punished for their misbehaviors.[39]

Because Congress merely adopted state practices at the federal level, the 1938 act contained informal and flexible policies in proceedings involving juveniles. For example, because cases in juvenile court were considered civil and not criminal, regular criminal procedures and due process protections did not apply. This meant that juries were not used, and the established statutes did not require courts to provide "defense attorneys, appeals, or even formal procedures." Instead, an informal dialogue would take place between the youth, the judge, and any attorneys involved. Then, per the judge's discretion, the juvenile was arraigned. The judge, therefore, decided the youth's fate—from a dismissal of the case to expulsion to the adult system. The logic was that such informality allowed youths to avoid "the stigma of a criminal conviction."[40]

The Federal Juvenile Delinquency Act of 1938 signaled the federal government's first attempt at juvenile law. Though minor in a practical sense, because most juvenile cases fell under state jurisdiction, the

1938 act reestablished judicial authority over youth offenders. From arrest to judgment, the provisions of the act affirmed that the nature of the youth carceral experience was to be determined not so much by the nature of the offense as "by the character, condition, needs, and welfare of the juvenile himself." This optimistic thought was an extension from the Progressive era; however, the judges and, perhaps more importantly, the youths who found themselves ensnared in the juvenile justice system at the end of the 1930s were not of the Progressive era.[41]

"There's No Such Thing as a Bad Child": The Lady Judge and Judicial Authority in Harlem

For black youths who found themselves living under such expansive surveillance and at the total discretion of an authoritative judge, the informality of juvenile justice was precarious. Similarly situated youths received different sentences based on mood, temperament, or the personal philosophy of individual judges. The powers that be carried the Progressive-era practice on the way delinquent youths ought to be disciplined into the 1940s with little regard—or perhaps full regard—for the demographic changes in their respective cities. By the turn of the decade in New York City, roughly 37 percent of cases brought to the Children's Court involved black youths. Unfortunately, neither the representation of nor the allotted resources for young offenders matched this disparity. Black judges were rare; black judges who were assigned juvenile cases were even more so, and the resources available to white youths, such as access to reform schools, were often denied to youths of color. What this meant, in New York City specifically, was that the fate of delinquent youths lay in the hands of white judges who did not always display empathy. Though most juvenile court judges in the late 1930s into the 1940s tended to promote "progressive" politics from their bench, this did not imply racial equality.[42]

Then, on July 22, 1939, Jane Matilda Bolin appeared before Mayor La Guardia at the New York City Building at the world's fair. Uncertain as to why the mayor requested her presence, Bolin "got one of the surprises of her life" when the New York City mayor swore her in as the first African American woman judge in the nation's history. Described as "the finest appointment that La Guardia [had] given to Negroes," Bolin

Justice Jane M. Bolin, 1942. (Library of Congress, Prints & Photographs Division)

was appointed to the Domestic Relations Court in New York City. She remembered feeling "naturally pleased," accompanied by her husband, Ralph E. Mizelle, as the oath was administered in the mayor's office. Entering a world in which she would be the only African American woman for the next two decades, Bolin's 1939 appointment marked a pivotal moment that connected the diminishing Progressive-era child-saving efforts with an emerging civil rights movement.[43]

Bolin's upbringing prepared her to be the first African American woman judge in US history. After graduating from Wellesley College in 1928, she embarked on a series of remarkable firsts. Bolin was the first black woman to graduate from Yale Law School in 1931. Upon graduation, she became the first black woman to be admitted to the Bar Association of the City of New York in 1932. Bolin received honorary LLDs from Morgan State College, Tuskegee University, Hampton University,

Western College for Women, and Williams College. She practiced law privately until 1937, before becoming an assistant corporation counsel of the City of New York. Through it all, Bolin confronted critique from supporters and naysayers alike who believed a black woman judge was too far-fetched.[44]

The cynicism started early. As an undergraduate at Wellesley, Bolin— one of only two black students in her class—was forced to live off campus with the other black student and described her college days as "mostly sad and lonely." When she told a career adviser in college that she wanted to study law at Yale, she was advised to "aim lower." Thankfully, Bolin ignored the advice and went on to be one of the three women in her cohort at Yale; however, she was the "lone pepper pod[. . .] in all that sea of salt." Following graduation, one of her main supporters through it all, her father, Gaius, became disparaging of his daughter's ambition. Gaius Bolin, the first African American graduate of Williams College and a practicing attorney in Poughkeepsie, New York, worried about the high-level stress involved in the type of work attorneys pursued. Though Jane Bolin remembered her days as a child, hanging around her father's law office "soaking up the ambiance" and intrigued by "those leather-bound" books, she admitted that her father assumed she would "be a schoolteacher." Jane Bolin also knew that her father's skepticism, as much as it was fatherly instinct, was also gendered. "He didn't think that women should hear the unpleasant things that lawyers have to hear," Bolin recalled. When she was appointed to bench of the Domestic Relations Court as a thirty-one-year-old African American woman, Gaius Bolin was once again concerned. "Judges have so much tension in their lives, they die early of heart attacks," he told his daughter. On this point, he was less convincing.[45]

When Bolin was inducted as "the first Negro woman ever appointed to any court of the United States" on July 24, 1939, she knew that she had little room for error and that she would be forced to defend her new post because of not only her race and gender but also her age. At her induction, the senior justice of the same court, Jacob Panken, commended Bolin for her qualifications and assured her that the position was earned "on the basis of merit and achievement." "You are quite young," Justice Panken remarked, "but this is an age of youth anyhow." Her bench-mate acknowledged the challenges that Bolin faced but stated confidently, in front of a mostly white audience, that he believed in her abilities to excel. "I am gratified by your elevation to the bench," Justice Panken continued, "first, because of your sterling qualities; because of your ability; and, more so, because of your humaneness." It is difficult to decipher how genuine Justice Panken's induction remarks were toward the incoming Bolin, but the change of guard was evident. "If the world is to be made better it will not be made so by us of the last generation, it will be made so by your generation," the senior justice proclaimed. This mattered immensely for the Domestic Relations Court in New York City.[46]

Established in 1933, the Domestic Relations Court of the City of New York was given "a name which connotes functions more inclusive than its jurisdiction covers." In addition to Family Court jurisdiction that was part of the Magistrates' Court system, the 1933 act provided that the Domestic Relations Court thereby established should succeed to all the powers and jurisdiction of the Children's Court of the City of New York, which had been functioning as a separately organized court since 1924. New York's Children's Court was in line with the fundamental juvenile court philosophy—it "inaugurated the concept of the court as a social rather than a penal or police agency." The main purpose of the Children's Court was to help, not to punish, even those who were found to be delinquent. It was to reach out beyond the police system and formalize the efforts of the various social agencies in the community. The Children's Court, ideally, represented what the journalist Albert Deutsch described as "the socialization of justice," and others have called it "a symbol of personalized justice." Thus, Bolin's appointment to the Domestic Relations Court was pivotal for the city's youths—especially its black youths.[47]

Justice Bolin presided over hearings in New York City that involved the total spectrum of the Domestic Relations Court, which included homicides and other crimes committed by juveniles, nonsupport of wives and children, battered spouses, neglected children, children in need of supervision, adoptions, and paternity suits. She had prior experience with the Domestic Relations Court from her years as an assistant corporation counsel assigned to the Family Court. Still, without much guidance, Bolin's judicial responsibilities began almost immediately following her induction. On her first Monday morning, Justice Bolin heard six routine cases in the Brooklyn court, and in the afternoon, she took up her work more formally at the Manhattan family court on the Upper East Side. Though Bolin had been on the record stating her belief that a lawyer should know the law before accepting a judiciary position, she voiced her preference for more time to learn the specialized laws pertaining to specific courts. "No lawyer should be thrown cold into court," Bolin suggested. But if anyone were up for the challenge, it was "the lady judge."[48]

The humaneness of Justice Bolin, about which Panken spoke at her induction, was evident as her career from the bench started. Still, she knew that "humaneness alone does not do the job." Bolin identified points of interests to address that challenged the racial discrimination and segregation in New York City's judicial system. This included the race of the workers who made up the courtroom staff as well as the employees in the city's various youth institutions and social agencies. "One could count on one's fingers the number of minorities on our staff—with me the lone one on the bench," Bolin recalled. Unabashed, she often asked, "Where are the black law assistants?" This racial disparity in authoritative figures associated with the Domestic Relations Court, according to Bolin, called for a resolution beyond her control. But it was imperative for Bolin, and black youths in the city, to advocate for change and bring their concerns within the sight of city responsibility.[49]

Like many black leaders in the first half of the twentieth century, Bolin's efforts to attain racial progress for people in the community were laden with race-neutral rhetoric. To make change from her judicial position, Bolin contended for a better balance of representation without direct regard to any racial parameters. "I am a judge, not of Harlem, nor the children of Harlem," Bolin stated publicly, "but for the whole city and for all children who are in trouble." She continued, "Every child who comes before the court needs attention and his case must be heard and judgment made in view of all the factors of personality and environment entering into the particular child's life." But as the demographics of those who found themselves more often in the former Children's Court shifted from white youths, mostly immigrant, to black, the representation of authoritative figures mattered, if only in principle.[50]

In practice, perhaps Bolin's most significant achievement regarding youth crime involved the assignment of probation officers to cases without regard to race or religion, and another involved private child-care agencies accepting youths without regard to racial or ethnic background. Another carryover practice from Progressive-era juvenile legislation was that probation officers served as the judge's right hand in the juvenile court at both the state and the federal levels. They played a significant role in all phases of detainment of the youth offenders—investigation, detention, hearing, and treatment. Not only were probation officers assigned to the juvenile courts as investigators of the offending youth's past, but they also served as liaisons between the judges and the social service agencies involved. The chief of probation, Richard A. Chappell, described the role of the probation officer as "a challenging and delicate responsibility," "a delicate task, an interesting and enlightening experience." Chappell continued, "the manner in which the probation officer meets this responsibility in each individual case will profoundly affect the future of a young life." Thus, for Bolin and the other justices of the Domestic Relations Court, the Department of Probation was critical in determining and distributing equal treatment.[51]

Only a few years into the position, Bolin noticed that the Domestic Relation Court's administrative judge, John Warren Hill, routinely assigned cases that involved black youths to black probation officers and cases that involved white youths to white probation officers. On the one hand, it was believed that black probation officers would be more sympathetic toward black youth offenders. On the other, because there were only "one or two" black probation officers, black youth offenders received less than half the probation attention they warranted. Black probation officers were overwhelmed in their positions, and Bolin was appalled by the court's silence on the issue. She confronted Judge Hill on the matter and argued that because probation officers were public servants, they should not be assigned cases by race. Judge Hill, annoyed with her stance, replied that there was "nothing he would do about it." Subsequently, Bolin called on a lawyer friend, who threatened with a lawsuit if Judge Hill continued the practice. The threat of court action forced Judge Hill "to discontinue requiring racial and religious disclosures on court petitions." This was one of the first major victories for Justice Bolin.[52]

After Bolin managed to reform the court's policy on how probation officers were assigned, the next step was to reassure those assigned probation officers put forth equal effort in providing the support and resources to the youths whom they represented. To do so, Bolin made efforts to address the "Jim Crow juvenile justice" practices that plagued child-placement facilities throughout New York City. Nonwhite youths were regularly denied access to private reform schools and other institutions on the basis of their race. And to address this, according to Justice Bolin, the first step needed to take place in-house. The probation department filed face sheets to placement facilities for the offending youths they represented. On them, "they used to put a big N or PR on the front of every petition," Bolin recalled, "to indicate if the family was black or Puerto Rican." Barring this policy, it was believed, would force the placement agencies to request information regarding the youth's race or religion. At this point, a case could be built against the institution to show a pattern of discrimination, and this would then allow the withholding of public funds—which eventually caused the eradication of segregation in placement facilities.[53]

But there were too many variables to integrating child-placement facilities, and Bolin soon realized that the path to do so was long and complex. Most of the reform schools and rehabilitation centers in New York City, as elsewhere, were established during the Progressive era, and nearly all of them were segregated along racial and religious lines. Facilities for nonwhite youths often lacked significant financial support, and as a result, the services provided were poor in comparison. Places in New York designated for black youths, such as the Colored Orphan Asylum and the Wiltwyck School for Boys, struggled to accommodate many youths, and the youths were often sent back to their homes. The Wiltwyck School, for example, was established in 1936 under the leadership of the Episcopal City Mission society, and it was "the only institution in the metropolitan area for the treatment of delinquent Negro Protestant boys." But six years after opening its door, the school was in danger of closing because of a severe lack of funds. Thereafter, Justice Bolin and "some other forward thinking people," such as First Lady Eleanor Roosevelt, seized the opportunity to restore the Wiltwyck School as "an interracial treatment facility for court-involved boys." These efforts, as the renowned Harlemite James Baldwin pointed out, deserved great praise. "The handful of extraordinary people . . . and staff of Wiltwyck have done something more remarkable, at least in my eyes, than they know," Baldwin penned in an essay on the Wiltwyck School, because "whatever differences one may imagine to exist between one-self and these children, between these children and children who seem luckier, in fact, these are all our children and we are responsible for them all." The shift in policy and in language led to a broader success for the reform school just outside Poughkeepsie, and it caused similar institutions to follow suit.[54]

Bolin was persistent in her efforts to desegregate these facilities throughout New York City, and she appeared before the City Council and the Board of Estimate as the chief spokesperson against the seg-regation of youths and "especially against public funds being used to sustain any institution or agency that discriminated on the basis of race." Her work toward this cause proved crucial in helping in 1942 to enact the Brown-Isaacs amendment to the city charter, which "prohibited segregation by race in the private child care agencies receiving public funds." Unfortunately, segregation prevailed. In a 1950 letter to Justice Bolin, Madelyn E. Turner, an African American woman member of the Protestant Big Sisters of New York, expressed her frustrations with the organization and resigned because it continued to condone de facto segregation. Turner described that in her time with the Protestant Big Sisters of New York, she had never been assigned to work with a white youth. She believed that the organization felt she "could not work with white children, because white people did not want colored people going into their homes." Bolin continued to protest discrimination in case pro-cessing and segregated court services well into her career—a tenure that spanned five decades.[55]

Bolin's victories proved to be meaningful for the black youths who benefited from the support that these policy changes in New York City's justice system provided at the end of the 1930s, but they held significant ramifications as the black population of the city grew in the early years of the 1940s and beyond. As the city gained strength after an era of de-pression, the wartime period provided its own challenges regarding crime and punishment. The next decade witnessed an increase in juve-nile delinquency rates across the country, and even though in New York City the largest hike took place chiefly among white boys and girls in Brooklyn and the Bronx, a study conducted by the City-Wide Citizens Committee pinpointed "Negro juvenile delinquency" as "the most im-portant crime problem in New York."[56]

The published report claimed, "Negro crime and juvenile delinquency cannot be substantially decreased by any remedies short of large-scale social reconstruction." The members of the committee, which included Justice Bolin, recommended a seven-step campaign to mitigate the coming "crime wave," and it seemed to be their final effort at retaining any semblance of the child-saving movement from the Progressive era. The report recommended a campaign to

(1) reduce discrimination in employment; (2) construct more low-rent housing; (3) provide additional social services for black children, such as family case work, foster homes, and institutions for problem children. If private charitable institutions cannot provide these services, the city and State must shoulder the burden without delay; (4) provide more adequate probationary and psychiatric care in the courts and schools for black youths at the beginning of their delinquency careers; (5) keep playgrounds, parks, and community centers open, war or no war Harlem needs them; (6) provide a new type of correctional institution for first-offender adolescent girls, which will be operated without race discrimination; and (7) increase police force, especially in the vicinity of Central Park, adding Negro plain-clothes officers who can circulate in Harlem without easy identification.

If these campaign recommendations were any indication of what was to come in wartime Harlem regarding youth crime, then black youths faced a revamped juvenile justice system that would be more punitive than ever before. Justice Bolin had her hands full as preventive organizations such as JAB and PAL suffered from city budget cuts and staff shortages related to the war—though their increased surveillance tactics loomed. This, combined with the scarcity of black probation officers and discriminatory placement facilities positioned New York City's black youths in a precarious state as Harlem became the focal point for authorities and their efforts to control "communities ridden with vice and crime."[57]

2

"Margie's Day"

Youth, Race, and Uprisings in Wartime Harlem

Cause everything that Hitler and Mussolini do, Negroes get
the same treatment from you.
—Langston Hughes, "Beaumont to Detroit: 1943"

"A hoodlum is a hoodlum," a *New York Amsterdam News* contributor
opined, "and the sooner we stop calling them by any other name and
regarding them as something else, the sooner we will be on our way
toward bringing to a halt the numerous outbursts of violence." The
dogged stance printed in the African American weekly reflected a popular viewpoint in wartime Harlem as segments of the community grew
frustrated by the shifts in behavior that its young people were showing.
On the one hand, these "outbursts of violence" did take place, and when
they did, it validated the criticism. On the other hand, this "hoodlum"
designation condemned black youths in New York City in a very particular way to create the backdrop of the 1943 Harlem uprising. More
specifically, the hoodlum premise was employed to criminalize black
protestors and conflated their behaviors with the racialized discourse
surrounding wartime crime and delinquency.[1]

The 1943 Harlem uprising joined a series of revolts across the nation in
response to long-standing racial resentments and animosities. For many
Americans on the World War II home front, the wartime conditions
improved their economic standing. But still, though the Depression decade was over, millions of Americans remained unemployed and lived
in dismal conditions. Unfortunately, most blacks in New York, and those
new to the city, fell in the latter category. As the country poured funds
into war-related industries and training programs expanded, many
blacks expected better living conditions and a fair share in the new economic boom. Others enlisted in the armed forces to serve their country

and make a living while doing so. And they were both reminded that racial discrimination and segregation limited those opportunities. "This blockage of a normal response to a general stimulation," Kenneth B. Clark described, "plus the Negro's inability to understand such obvious inconsistency between democratic principle and democratic practice, build up in him feelings of despair, futility, and frustration." Such experiences and emotions provoked protest.[2]

The 1943 Harlem uprising was a direct response to the system of discrimination, segregation, and police brutality that plagued the community up through the 1940s. The upheaval called public attention to the plight of black Harlemites, especially its youths, as they contested the urban landscape and sought equal access to wartime benefits. A reexamination of Harlem's home front during World War II, centered on the 1943 uprising and its lasting impact on the community, reveals a noticeable shift in police-communal relations. The excessive policing employed to quell the uprising in Harlem agitated the relations that were built in the community in the 1930s and negatively influenced youth perspectives of state authority and carceral sovereignty.

"When the Forces of Progress Meet the Forces of Reaction": Harlem at War

The United States' entry into World War II triggered an industrial mobilization that provided an upsurge in jobs.[3] Around the time of the attack on Pearl Harbor, the US Employment Service learned of more than 280,000 new jobs that would be made available in the coming months. For an economy attempting to recover from the Great Depression, this was enormous relief. Most African Americans had high hopes of bettering their economic standing because of the plethora of jobs anticipated; others were skeptical because of the all-too-familiar circumstances that surrounded the new positions. Unfortunately, barriers to equal economic opportunity prevailed, and more than half of the expected jobs "were absolutely barred to Negroes." This applied to both skilled and unskilled workers in both northern and southern states.[4]

The expectation that the war industry would improve the economic status of all workers, regardless of race, proved to be illusory. For white workers, progress was almost immediate, and access to wartime industries provided them a boost in wages and entry into labor unions. Black workers were not as fortunate. At the onset of the National Defense Program in 1940, it was apparent that employment discrimination against black workers raised barriers against the use of the available labor power. According to Lester B. Granger, the executive secretary of the National Urban League, the reasons given for the nonemployment of black workers varied and were often "mutually contradictory." The most common reasons for nonemployment, Granger stated, were, "Negroes never applied; whites and blacks can't mix on the same job; haven't time or money to build separate toilets; no trained Negroes are available; they are racially unequipped for skilled work; the union won't have them; don't like Negroes and don't want them around; this is a rush job and we haven't time for experiments." But the unprecedented drain on labor reserves caused by the war demanded industries that held defense contract to reexamine their hiring practices. The Advisory Commission to the Council of National Defense urged these companies to consider training and employing black workers in all occupations for which they could be used. They advised holders of defense contracts that in the congressional bill that appropriated funds for vocational training and employment, there was a "provision that the benefits of such training must not be denied to any worker because of his race, religion, or place of birth." Even so, neither the government's insistence nor the war was strong enough to convince many employers at home to drop old habits.[5]

The black press and organizations representing social welfare came out against the racial discrimination that blacks experienced throughout the country, as they were constantly denied opportunities to obtain gainful employment. Committees were formed in most black communities, providing the masses with a platform to express their resentment, and as Granger declared, "the more angry Negroes became, the longer grew the names of their 'co-ordinating committees.'" Surveys and offhand investigations supported the claims that blacks were being denied jobs and that the few exceptions were in unskilled work. One summary of the national situation was that "only about 1.3 percent of all workers in war industries in any capacity are colored and most of them are in unskilled jobs." These alarming numbers and the steady pressure applied by national organizations forced the president of the United States to get involved.[6]

Once word got around that various black organizations were preparing to march on Washington, led by A. Philip Randolph and the Brotherhood of Sleeping Car Porters, President Franklin D. Roosevelt took immediate action to mitigate the potential protest. He requested that Randolph and the members of his committee come to Washington to meet to discuss alternatives, and upon their agreement to cancel the march on June 25, 1941, President Roosevelt issued Executive Order 8802, which prohibited racial discrimination in the national defense industry. The march was canceled, and, seemingly, the long fight for equal employment opportunities was over. Many blacks soon learned, however, that though the executive order was a step in the right direction, it did not produce immediate change, as employers took their time to make the change.[7]

It was not until the latter half of 1942 and the early parts of 1943 that most blacks who entered war work gained employment in varying industries, some more so than others. For example, shipbuilding experienced a 10 percent gain, compared to a 2 percent increase in electrical work; and war industries in Pennsylvania, New Jersey, and Delaware increased from 4 to 7 percent, while Los Angeles's nonwhite employment increased almost fourfold. Nationally, black employment in defense industries almost tripled within a two-year span, and the total number of black workers in the United States increased by a third, from 4.4 million to 5.9 million employed. These employment gains for black workers, as stated in an annual report issued by the president of the Tuskegee Institute, F. D. Patterson, marked a "definite improvement [and] have given new impetus and hope to the educational and training efforts of Negro youth." As young people watched their adult relatives obtain gainful employment, it signaled a step in the right direction.[8]

For black New Yorkers, the economic gains being made elsewhere from wartime industries were not as abundant in the Big Apple. The National Urban League estimated that 2 percent of the war workers in the New York area were black, compared to the 6 percent of the city's population who were black, and many were in menial work. The City-Wide Citizens' Committee on Harlem also reported that "war production has had little influence on the Negro's economic status in this city." Surely there were exceptions, for example, a small factory on the west side of the city that rewired and repaired shrapnel-riddled instrument panels and sometimes the damaged bodies of B-29 bombers. Doris Saunders, a black woman Harlemite, was a solderer who obtained employment, along with her two sisters, in the plant. It is important to note, however, that a part of the reason that blacks in the city generally struggled to obtain wartime employment was the lack of manufacturing positions *in* the city. The city paled in comparison to other parts of the state and other states around the country, but some blacks, such as the Saunders sisters, took advantage of the defense industry in New York City. Still, despite New York being one of two states that matched the federal government in passing legislation forbidding racial discrimination in war industries, the economic advances were relatively minor and did not meet the expectations of black New Yorkers, especially in Harlem, and their frustrations began to grow.[9]

Black youths, again, bore the brunt of the frustrations caused by this collision—the promise of jobs with a lack of opportunities. The American Council on Education conducted a study in 1940 on the attitude of black youths toward race relations. They found that "lower-class, middle-class, and, in some cases, upper-class youth place an equal chance with whites for jobs first among the changes which they would like to see in race relations." The war seemed to accelerate the pace toward this economic democracy. However, since vocational schools took their cues from other wartime industries, black youths were often denied the opportunity for adequate training for industrial occupations. Employers who were unwilling to hire black workers in production jobs were doubly resistant to admitting them into the training classes established in their factories. Thus, a circle of defense discrimination against black workers emerged: "no training and therefore no jobs; no jobs and therefore no union memberships; employer and union opposition and therefore no training."[10]

All in all, the war industry and economic improvements did not drastically change the social fabric of Harlem. Employment opportunities expanded, somewhat; however, racial discrimination remained the standard, and black Harlemites' economic standing and access to educational resources did not match their expectations. Especially, school-age youths were critical of the education system and the preparation it provided for employment opportunities. Most believed "school was a waste of time," and only a small minority thought attending school regularly would result in landing gainful employment. Even those who were attending school frequently had their reasons for becoming disengaged. In the master's thesis that Steven Ross wrote on Harlem during the Second World War, he found that overcrowded school conditions and dated textbooks that "painted an unfavorable picture of the black man" discouraged everyday attendance and diminished youngsters' faith in what they were being taught. This was among several reasons, such as economic hardship, that many Harlem youths dropped out.[11]

But at home, more often than not, these black youths would find that their families were fighting to make ends meet. Some relied on government relief well into 1940s, and though job prospects improved, more so for whites than blacks, black families' income remained substandard. Even with a lower cost of living in Harlem than in other parts of New York City, black families' incomes did not cover their basic necessities, and their living conditions remained dire. Segregation and discrimination continued to limit blacks' access to wartime benefits, and the optimism was dwindling—a combination that historically prompted grassroots activism.[12]

The Kindling of an Uprising: Local Organizing and Activism before Unrest

As the war progressed, political programs aimed toward improving the living conditions of African Americans on the home front were slowing or ending, especially for black Harlemites. Most government and public attention was turned away from domestic problems and concentrated on the war abroad and international relations. New Deal agencies that were once helpful to blacks were being cut. The threat of a march on Washington was "successful" in attaining its major goal—a national ban on racial discrimination in the defense industry—but ended with just that. Adam Clayton Powell Jr., the "darling of most black New Yorkers," focused most of his energy on his upcoming congressional campaign. And Mayor La Guardia, who had appointed "more Negroes to big, responsible jobs . . . than all the other mayors of the city combined," including Justice Jane Bolin, was losing his footing with black New Yorkers as he prioritized the war effort over the problems of his city.[13]

Mayor La Guardia—who was not too far removed from being at a political rally at Colonial Park in Harlem where over twenty thousand black supporters chanted, "That's our mayor!"—found himself being publicly referred to as "one of the most pathetic figures on the current American scene," who no longer needed the black vote and, therefore, ignored black concerns.[14]

Mayor La Guardia was arguably the most polarizing politician among black New Yorkers in wartime Harlem, and his mayoral tenure became more volatile over time. When he was appointed in 1933, La Guardia marked the end of the Tammany Hall corruption that had previously run the city. Two years later, an uprising swept Harlem as the frustrations that had been intensified by the Depression exploded when a youth, Lino Rivera, was involved in a violent altercation with a store owner who accused him of stealing a penknife. A woman who witnessed the fracas, as accounted by the historian Cheryl Greenberg, "screamed that the boy had been hurt or killed." As a crowd gathered shortly after, a hearse pulled up, and the crowd concluded that the young boy had been killed. Once the police arrived, they arrested the woman who screamed for disorderly conduct, attempted to disperse the crowd, and shut down the store. Another crowd assembled afterward, except this time holding signs and giving speeches, to protest racial violence in the city. Then "a rock hurtled through the store window and the riot began." The numbers of those who participated reached the thousands, spreading along 125th Street, from Fifth to Eight Avenues, and when it was all said and done, seventy-five people were arrested, fifty-seven civilians and seven police officers were injured, and more than six hundred windows were broken.[15]

Upon a return to normalcy, Mayor La Guardia appointed an interracial Mayor's Commission on Conditions in Harlem, to be led by the Howard University sociologist E. Franklin Frazier, to investigate the 1935 uprising. The commission produced a thorough study that documented the social and economic conditions that black Harlemites faced that contributed to the March 19 incident. This was a step in the right direction, it was surmised, for La Guardia to improve race relations in the city, and his efforts were highlighted by black leaders around the city. Still, once the war started, the mayor continually made contradictory decisions that thwarted his efforts to appease black New Yorkers.[16]

It was not surprising that the New York City mayor preferred a gradualist approach to racial politics—better than some but not perfect. "A mayor who cannot look fifty or seventy-five years into the future," Mayor La Guardia expressed, "is not worthy of being in City Hall." Thus, while he made progressive decisions such as the Bolin appointment, his gradualist philosophy frustrated many of the city's black leaders and residents. Mayor La Guardia believed that racial barriers would eventually break down not by force but by "practiced goodwill . . . and good, human qualities." His job, as he explained, was to make impactful appointments, and he "expected blacks to take advantage of existing opportunities." A series of events and decisions during the war, however, drove a deep divide between City Hall and black New Yorkers.[17]

Three decisions, in particular, stand out as driving this rift between Mayor La Guardia and black New Yorkers in the wartime period: the WAVES choice, the closing of the Savoy Ballroom, and the Stuyvesant Town controversy. First, in late 1942, the Navy requested La Guardia's permission to use Hunter College in Manhattan's Upper East Side and Walton High School in the Bronx as part of a training center for enlisted women. The United States Naval Reserve, Women's Reserve, better known as Women Accepted for Volunteer Emergency Service (WAVES), excluded black women. This issue was not raised in the negotiations for the use of the space; however, according to Adam Clayton Powell Jr. and the City Council, the segregation policy was well known, and they urged Mayor La Guardia to request an end to the practice in return for use of the space. He did not. By January 1943, WAVES was using the facilities. Mayor La Guardia denied having authority over "any activity of the United States Navy," and he was adamant that his city "must cooperate with the U.S. Navy in every possible way." Small protests surfaced, but La Guardia disassociated himself by insisting that under the War Powers Act, "the City has absolutely no jurisdiction or power over . . . the United States Navy."[18]

The next incident happened four months later when the NYPD closed the Savoy Ballroom, a nondiscriminatory dance hall in Harlem, because of alleged prostitution practices. Black leaders, including Powell and the NAACP's Roy Wilkins, and the black press, led by the *New York Amsterdam News* and the *People's Voice*, disputed the allegations and were insistent that the decision to shut down the Savoy Ballroom was prompted by "race-mixing on the dance floor rather than by sexual solicitation." Supporters of the Harlem landmark, both black and white, were denied any opportunity to be heard in a formal hearing and were irate that Mayor La Guardia did not call for a more thorough investigation. They denied the accusations of sexual solicitations and believed the charges were inflated. A poet, Andy Razaf, wrote on the closing of the dance hall in the *People's Voice* and expressed that the Savoy was "guilty of national unity, of practicing real Democracy, by allowing the races, openly, to dance and mingle in Harlem." Still, the allegations were degrading, and black Harlemites were upset by the lack of support from their mayor. Though Mayor La Guardia's position on the matter was not clear, the closing of the Savoy Ballroom was unjust, and it continued to damage the relationship between him and black New York. In this wartime context, it appeared that the Savoy Ballroom was guilty of nothing except being in Harlem.[19]

By April 1943, with the closing of the Savoy Ballroom, Mayor La Guardia's good standing with black New Yorkers, especially in Harlem, had essentially disappeared. Formerly viewed as an ardent defender of civil rights and black equality, the mayor made wartime decisions that provoked a sense of distrust that he had not previously encountered. For the mayor, he felt that some of the city's black leaders, especially Powell, were largely responsible for instigating this rift. Mayor La Guardia received some support from some black constituents. For example, Warren Brown, a black contributor to the *Saturday Review of Literature*, agreed that Powell and "other sensational-mongering black leaders" were problematic and that the mayor's gradualist approach to civil rights was appropriate "for future race problems." The evidence proved otherwise, however, and amid the wartime atmosphere and as racial conflicts around the country emerged, the coup de grâce happened when Mayor La Guardia publicly supported the decision to build Stuyvesant Town, a white-only housing project in New York City.[20]

The Stuyvesant Town controversy upset countless black, and some white, New Yorkers as Mayor La Guardia openly supported the city's decision to build a "walled city for [the] privileged." The president of Metropolitan Life Insurance Company, Frederick H. Ecker, submitted to the mayor and the Board of Estimate plans to build a postwar housing project on the Lower East Side of Manhattan. The insurance company, though burdened with a history of residential segregation, was given control of tenant selection. When asked whether black families would be permitted to apply for residency, Ecker responded, bluntly, "Negroes and whites don't mix. Perhaps they will in a hundred years, but they don't now." He continued, "If we brought them into this development, it would be to the detriment of the city, too, because it would depress all the surrounding property." At the end of a three-and-a-half-hour hearing, the city approved the housing plan.[21]

By the end of the week, a rally was scheduled to take place at New York's famous Madison Square Garden to protest the decision. It was expected that roughly twenty thousand persons, "about equally divided between white and Negro," were to assemble and demand that the City Council revisit the decision. Some attendees, including Adam Clayton Powell Jr., went as far as to call for Mayor La Guardia's impeachment—leading a chant that received a standing ovation. But, according to the voices at the rally, the Stuyvesant Town decision marked the culmination of a series of domestic issues in wartime New York that were marred by racial discrimination. Combined with the experiences of black soldiers abroad who fought "to help all people be free," New York's home front voiced its opposition and pleaded to Mayor La Guardia and other city officials not to let their sons and loved ones return home to find "Hitler's police right here in dear old New York." Such sentiment struck a chord nationwide as it echoed the Double V campaign—"victory over our enemies at home and abroad"—that black newspapers promoted from the onset of the war. After the rally in Madison Square Garden, La Guardia was forced to prioritize race relations in New York City.[22]

Heightened racial tensions were evident, in New York City and elsewhere. Cities in the Jim Crow South such as Beaumont, Texas, and Mobile, Alabama, witnessed uprisings as wartime conditions intensified racial animosity. So too did northern and more liberal cities, such as Detroit and Los Angeles, which experienced upheaval as black servicemen clashed with white soldiers, civilians, and local law enforcement. Competition over employment opportunities and equal living conditions that were promised by wartime industries ignited conflict—a scenario that was all too familiar to observers in New York City. Even still, Mayor La Guardia fought to convince himself that there was "no

Detroit here." This was wishful thinking, because others knew very well of the "Negro problem in New York."[23]

"Hoodlums' Holiday": Reexamining the 1943 Harlem Uprising

The start of a summer Sunday was routine for most New Yorkers, black and white.[24] The weather continued to warm with late showers in the forecast, though they never occurred. Local newspapers printed articles that updated their readers on the war, briefed them on the president's budget plans for fiscal year 1944, and reported that all three professional baseball teams sporting the city on their uniforms lost games the day before. In Harlem, well into the early evening, people gathered on sidewalks and stoops and sat on windowsills; it appeared to be the end of a typical summer day. "It was a reassuring picture" amid what had been an intense summer. Within a few hours, however, Walter White recalled being awakened by an NAACP staff member asking if he knew about the "riot . . . in Harlem."[25]

On August 1, 1943, Marjorie (Margie) Polite was cited and arrested for disorderly conduct in Hotel Braddock in New York City's Upper West Side. Popular accounts of what followed vary and have changed over time. General consensus remains, however, that the interaction between Polite and the arresting police officer, James Collins, became quarrelsome and attracted the attention of Robert Bandy, a black military police (MP) officer who was on leave from the Army's 703rd MP Battalion in Jersey City, and his mother, Florine Roberts, a domestic from Middletown, Connecticut, who were checking out of the hotel that night. Most reports indicate that Bandy and his mother protested the arrest and demanded that Officer Collins release Polite. The demand was perceived as threatening, according to the official police report, and a physical altercation ensued between Bandy and Collins. During the altercation, Bandy swiped Officer Collins's nightstick, struck him with it, and attempted to flee. Bandy ignored Officer Collins's request to halt, and Collins fired his revolver, striking Bandy in the upper body. Per Private Bandy's report, however, when the arresting officer shoved Margie Polite to the ground, he and his mother insisted that she be released, at which point Collins threw his nightstick at them. When Bandy refused to return the weapon, Officer Collins drew his pistol and shot him in the shoulder. Police reinforcements arrived on the scene, and Private Bandy and Officer Collins were both admitted to hospitals—Collins to Sydenham Hospital and Bandy to the prison ward of Bellevue Hospital.[26]

A small crowd gathered in the hotel lobby as the incident transpired. Within minutes of the altercation, though Private Bandy sustained only a minor wound from the gunshot, word spread around Harlem that a white policeman had killed a black solider, who, some people said, had been protecting his mother. Crowds of Harlemites, mostly black, moved from the hotel to the hospital and then to the Twenty-Eighth Police Precinct. By 9:00 p.m., it was reported that the crowd grew to almost three thousand Harlemites, including "soldiers, respectably dressed men with jackets and ties, men and boys with open collars or polo shirts, youth in 'zoot suits,' women, girls, and children." They demanded to see Private Bandy's body and strongly urged the police department to take immediate action against the officer who was responsible for Bandy's alleged death. For the next two hours, the crowd and tension increased, as mostly everyone believed that "the cop had killed Bandy." One bottle was thrown. Other bottles followed.[27]

The shooting of Private Bandy by Officer Collins was more than an isolated event. The incident embodied a greater conflict that was national in scope. The built-up frustration that blacks experienced, underlined by the unmet expectations of wartime industry, helped clarify the significance of the incident that sparked the uprising. For Harlem, Bandy's shooting symbolized government support and approval of authoritative oppression—Bandy was not shot by a white civilian but by a white police officer. Naturally, such an incident, magnified by rumor, garnered an immense response. Even in its exaggerated form, "rumor represents the psychological truth to those who tell it." Thus, it was those who told it, those who believed it, and perhaps most importantly, those who identified with Private Bandy who took to the streets.[28]

Around 10:30 p.m., it was reported, groups of individuals began breaking windows. Crowds continued to develop, and a chain reaction of disturbances spread quickly. Within the first hour, storefronts from 110th to 145th Streets were wrecked. The acclaimed author Claude Brown, then six years old, recalled being awakened by loud noises that he thought were German or Japanese bombs but turned out to be the "crashing sound of falling plate-glass windows." After midnight, several shootings were reported, including one of a policeman, Meyer Berkman of the Clinton Street station, who was seriously wounded and taken to Harlem Hospital. In the early reports of the uprising, it was proclaimed, "No organized disorder occurred but in some streets there were disturbances when youths, mostly in their teens, began throwing stones and milk bottles, breaking windows." Later reports revealed that some of these youths took up shop in stores and doled out goods to some of the perusing adults. "Come on in auntie, and get something for nothing," a teenage Harlemite told an elderly woman who had just left church and was passing a grocery store in the process of being ransacked by a dozen or so teenaged youths. By 3:00 a.m., the difficulties of the patrolling authorities were increased. Persons started to pull fire alarms throughout the city, and fire companies were forced to respond to nonexistent fires. Mayor La Guardia ordered traffic diverted from the area from Fifth to Eighth Avenues, which included the entire section of West Harlem. All patrol officers in the city were held on duty, Army reserves were sent in by the truckload, and even the subway police were called in and assigned to ride all subways serving Harlem, one patrol officer per car, to quell what the mayor emphasized was not a race riot.[29]

By 9:00 a.m. Monday morning, a pretense of order returned to Harlem. Small crowds continued to roam the streets, and sporadic incidents occurred. But despite the obvious tension, the upheaval from the night before seemed to be over. "I want to assure you if conditions can keep as calmly as they are now," Mayor La Guardia charged New York City residents, "it will not be necessary to maintain this order very long." On August 2, 1943, the mayor, via radio broadcast, issued a curfew in response to the upheaval in Harlem from the night before. The New York City mayor lauded the residents who aided the efforts of the NYPD and assured them that with complete cooperation, the order, "which was brought about [because of] a few rowdies and hoodlums," would be lifted.[30]

The physical damage was done, however, and the streets of Harlem "looked as if they had been swept by a hurricane or an invading army." Store windows were smashed, and sidewalks were littered with broken glass, foodstuffs, clothing, and other debris. Reports of looting were recorded, and according to Police Commissioner Valentine, "all types of stores were plundered." Markets and food stores suffered the most, followed by liquor stores and pawnshops. Of 500 food stores in Harlem, 150 reported severe damage that forced them to remain closed for the day after, and 50 of those store owners "did not think they could open again." Chain stores and supermarkets, according to *New York Times* reporting, fared the worst of all. One account claimed, "Every article of merchandise was taken from the shelves of a large supermarket at Eight Avenue and 134th Street," and whatever the crowd did not want, or could not use, was thrown into the street. For some black writers, such as Dan Burley, it would be a mistake to assume that these targets were random and that the goods plundered were arbitrary. "The symbols of exploitation that felt the weight of the mob's ire were the drugstores that sell pills that make one more sick instead of better," Burley wrote, "the groceries which short change and short weight poor, over-burdened people." He continued, "it was a tangible demonstration of the result of herding people into one area, pressing them against the wall until the only thing they can do is explode." In addition to storefront properties, a number of automobiles were damaged, with some being overturned and at least one burned. The early estimates of reported damages and losses ranged from $225,000 to $5 million—making the uprising the most destructive in New York City since the turn of the century.[31]

Still, for city officials, matters could have been much worse. Contrary to what Harlemites expected, Mayor La Guardia was prepared for the uprising. The day after Detroit's uprising, Adam Clayton Powell Jr. wired the mayor and expressed his concern about similar sentiments existing in their city. The mayor did not respond directly to Powell's message; however, he had been engaged in extensive behind-the-scenes preparations in the event that there was such an occurrence in his city. Having governed through the 1935 Harlem uprising, the mayor was confident in his abilities, mainly his resources, to quell an uprising with minimal consequences. Following the 1935 uprising, Mayor La Guardia found himself in good stead with black New Yorkers; it appeared that his handling of the 1943 "social explosion" was also, as Powell described, "wise and effective." And the New York City mayor interpreted this as an opportunity to improve contentious race relations in the city.[32]

Mayor La Guardia learned of the disturbance around 9:00 p.m. on August 1. Soon thereafter, the mayor, accompanied by several black leaders such as White of the NAACP; Max Yergan, president of the National Negro Congress and director of the Council on African Affairs; and Myles A. Paige, the first black New York City magistrate, who was appointed by La Guardia in 1936—three years before Bolin—conferred with the police and fire commissioners at the Twenty-Eighth Precinct and proceeded to travel the "riot district." Jeered and booed by many passersby, Mayor La Guardia advised people to empty the streets and go to their homes. He mounted the steps outside the station house and made an effort to assure the demonstrators that he and the police "would look after the welfare of all, regardless of color." These words, however, were easy to ignore, as the countless patrol officers "in white-steel air-raid helmets patrolled the streets," creating a militaristic mood in the New York City neighborhood.[33]

Following the suggestions of supporters, Mayor La Guardia took to the radio for his first of five broadcasts to New York City residents. Around 1:00 a.m., he moved to dismiss the rumor of Private Bandy's death that had sparked the uprising in Harlem. Embittered by the scene throughout the city, the mayor asked all its residents to "please get off the streets and go home to bed." Asserting his commitment to maintain order, Mayor La Guardia instructed his listeners, "go downstairs and call the members of your family and your friends and get them off the street." Not wanting the disturbance to escalate any further, he warned, "unless you do that we may have serious trouble." After the mayor, Max Yergan spoke briefly "as a citizen of Harlem," and he tried to convince Harlemites "to leave it to the officials of the city to take care of the situation." Together they closed the broadcast affirming that there would be a thorough investigation of the incident that sparked the upheaval and emphasizing a priority to protect lives and property.[34]

The following morning, Mayor La Guardia implemented the preventive measures to ensure there would be no further incidents, no further violence. Print media across the country, and even abroad, ran their versions of "Black Sunday," and the mayor was now faced with the daunting task of defending his city and its image to people around the world. In his third radio broadcast, Mayor La Guardia declared, "Shame has come to our city and sorrow to the large number of our fellow citizens . . . who live in Harlem." Judicious in his word choice, the mayor avoided condemning Harlem in its entirety as he described the

New York City police officers wear steel helmets and carry nightsticks in Harlem to prevent rioting, 1943. (AP Photo)

uprising and explained the actions to be taken to restore order. These actions included restricting traffic to and from Harlem, denying non-residents entrance to the New York City neighborhood, ordering a strict ban to be issued by the Alcoholic Beverage Control Board on the sale or dispensing of liquor or alcoholic drinks, disallowing pedestrians to assemble in the streets, and enforcing a curfew applied to gatherings of four or more persons walking the streets. Following the broadcast, Mayor La Guardia met with city justices including Jane Bolin, police inspectors, and military officials, in addition to more than fifteen hundred volunteers, most of whom were black, and roughly six thousand city police officers "to secure the riot area." These measures, according to the mayor, were absolutely necessary because "law and order must and will be maintained in this city."[35]

It was not until Tuesday morning, after the uprising, that the mayor announced that the situation "at this moment [was] definitely under control." All signs of upheaval died out, and at least among Harlemites, it appeared to be back to normal. Mayor La Guardia took another "tour" of the district and noted that "Negroes from Harlem and other Negro districts traveled to and for their work in other parts of the city . . . without molestation." Even in Midtown Manhattan, black New Yorkers were able to go about their work as usual, unbothered. That night, many persons were on the streets throughout Harlem, and many more peered out their windows; but quiet and order was maintained. By 11:00 p.m., the streets were nearly deserted, and the mayor finally headed home, "after an almost unbroken vigil that began Sunday night." Street patrol officer remained on duty, and among the civilian volunteers who patrolled Harlem streets with the police were "300 Negro women armed with clubs wearing armbands to identify them as upholders of law and order." Over time, the curfew was pushed back, the traffic ban was relaxed, stores reopened, and the liquor ban was eventually lifted. The police force, however, did not return to its pre-uprising size for weeks, as the police commissioner proclaimed that extra detectives were needed to search for "riot loot" in Harlem residences. Despite the outward appearance of normalcy in the everyday life, the immediate after of the 1943 Harlem uprising stirred racial politics in the city as its shift in police practices appeared to become permanent thereafter.[36]

"They Just Don't Give a Damn about Negroes": The Aftermath of a Social Explosion

On September 11, Margie Polite was sentenced to a year's probation for her role in the Harlem uprising.[37] Designated "the riot starter," Polite was charged with disorderly conduct instead of the more serious assault charges she faced; Private Bandy, who survived the gunshot, was turned over to Army authorities for disciplinary action. Having spent about six weeks in jail, Polite stood before Magistrate Charles E. Ramsgate, who doled out the decision and remarked, "The probation officer's report shows you had borne an excellent reputation up to your arrest that night. I agree with the police and District Attorney's office, however, that your disturbance actually was responsible for that rioting. I hope you realize you were responsible for that rioting." In a separate hearing, eleven youths watched their sentences be suspended in exchange for a plea deal. "I feel that what you boys have been through should be a lesson to you," Magistrate Leonard McGee announced. "In the future you should behave yourself, be a credit to the community and not heap upon the Negro race the criticism you have. Hereafter act as decent citizens." For Magistrate Ramsgate, Magistrate McGee, and the corresponding authorities, their want to pinpoint the cause of the 1943 uprising to an individual happening was critical for them to redirect responsibility. Harlemites knew otherwise. "It serves no purpose to stress that a disorderly woman being arrested" caused the riot; "'twas Jim Crow."[38]

The numbers of reported arrests, injuries, and causalities from the uprising were significant. Polite was one of over five hundred arrested that Sunday night whose fate lay in the hands of the city's justice system, a group of which included one hundred women and many youths. Even several soldiers were taken into custody for their involvement. Private James Logwood, for example, a twenty-one-year-old California native, was arrested and held on $10,000 bail on a charge of inciting a riot. It is important to note that a majority of those who were arrested, some reports claim as high as 98 percent, were accused of suspicion of burglary. The rest mostly received charges of criminally receiving stolen property, assault, inciting a riot, and disorderly conduct. Very few received jail sentences, as most were held on varying amounts of bail for later hearings and trials. Newspapers reported roughly six hundred injuries, including forty-four police officers, most of whom sought medical attention for glass cuts. Most significantly, six men were killed the night of the uprising. In totality, these figures were alarming as the city shifted its attention to search for the underlying motives and conditions that led to the 1943 uprising.[39]

Political leaders, city authorities, social agencies, and New York City residents, mostly from Harlem, debated the causes and potential cures for the disturbance that occurred on August 1. For Mayor La Guardia, whose response to the uprising was both cheered and jeered from all sides, preventing "Detroit from occurring in our own city" was always the priority and, arguably, one that he attained. The New York City mayor continued to contend that no race riot transpired. Instead, he believed, it was "thoughtless hoodlums [who] had no one to fight with [who] gave vent to their activity by breaking store windows and looting many of these stores belonging to people who live in Harlem." On the one hand, many people concurred with the hoodlum premise, a popular rationale employed after urban uprisings, and defended their claims by drawing on wartime crime and delinquency assertions and statistics.

This argument was loaded with stereotypes that connected youth and criminality to blackness. On the other hand, "the Harlem riot was the direct result of the American system of discrimination, segregation and police brutality against the Negro people." In other words, systemic racism rather than hoodlumism was what warranted public attention.[40]

On hoodlumism, Mayor La Guardia and other supporters, white and black, insisted the uprising in Harlem was not racially driven. This stance was based on two premises. First, the uprising in Harlem was relatively free of physical violence between blacks and whites; second, those who participated in the uprising damaged black as well as white property. "Misrepresenting the situation as a race riot," La Guardia told the Newspaper Guild's president, "may have a serious effect in inciting disturbances in other mixed areas in Greater New York." This, again, disassociated Harlem from New York City, while simultaneously allowing the mayor to evade responsibility for any subsequent happenings. For black leaders who concurred, they presumed that a "race riot" label would increase tensions and deter sympathetic whites away from the city's struggle for civil rights. Elmer A. Carter, a state official and Urban League representative, for example, proclaimed that branding the uprising as a "race riot" would make it "infinitely more difficult for colored people to live in decent neighborhoods and to secure improvements in Harlem." Consequently, this allowed the discussion to evade addressing systemic inequalities and instead to focus on addressing individual hoodlum elements to prevent further disorders.[41]

Print media coverage of the 1943 Harlem uprising also eluded the "race riot" narrative, and not just the mainstream coverage. Columnists and reporters alike cited detailed reports from varying sources, and most early coverage of the uprising reinforced the hoodlum theory. Roughly 25 percent of those who were arrested carried prior charges, and "among the others were delinquents, rowdies, street corner toughs and other underworld characters and irresponsibles who are always ready to loot and destroy when the opportunity presents itself." The arrested youths, mostly teenagers and young men, were characterized as "irresponsible and misguided."[42]

For the like-minded black leaders who supported the hoodlum theory, it was argued, they did so with future race relations in mind. For many, even those who agreed with the underlying reasons, they deemed such methods of protest as unfit. "It cannot be stressed too often that colored people are not going to get anywhere at all without the goodwill, sympathetic understanding and co-operation of white Americans," a *Pittsburgh Courier* columnist wrote, "and smashing and looting stores to the extent of $5,000,000 damages, injuring law officers and otherwise confirming Negrophobist propaganda is emphatically not the way to win friends and influence people." Their interpretation was largely based on protesters who appeared to be "looting and vandalizing" property in Harlem. Elmer Carter, an African American journalist who had a regular column in the *New York Amsterdam News* and was often featured in other black newspapers, was one of the more vocal of the black hoodlum theorists to take to print. "New York is the fairest city in America to its Negro minority," Carter wrote after the uprising, and "this progress has not been due to hoodlums, to lawbreakers, or to demagogues." For Carter, the participation in the "outbreaks in Harlem on Sunday night . . . are a disgrace to their race, a disgrace to the city and a disgrace and a shame to the nation of which they are citizens." He continued, "There can be no excuse for them and they should be dealt with not by half-hearted measures such as has been reported were taken by the police during the disturbances, but by swift, stern and relentless enforcement of the law." Even the president of the New York chapter of the NAACP, Lionel C. Barrow, maintained, "We who fight to advance the cause of the Negro and all minority groups have nothing but censure for those who participated in this deplorable event." From this, the presumption was clear that the motivation for protesters was inadequate, and they must have been criminal; however, this was in no way the reality.[43]

Did a criminal element exist? Based rigidly on the letter of the law, yes. Still, the hoodlum theory oversimplifies the complex reasons as to why folks participated in the uprising. For example, Adam Clayton Powell Sr. remembered a friend who was standing on a street corner by the side of a policeman. The two were discussing the happenings when "a colored man resembling an athlete with a club in his hand and looking mad as a Bashan bull dashed by them shouting, 'Shoot me, I would rather die here for my people than in Germany,'" Powell recalled. This individual represented the spirit and psychology of the protestors. He did not stop to steal anything, but he did destroy store windows. But to

Powell, these actions reflected "an avalanche of accumulated injustices and discriminations." He was not alone.[44]

Crime was part and parcel of the oppression that blacks faced in wartime Harlem. On the uprisings happening throughout the country, the prominent W. E. B. DuBois explained, "The black folk in this land have developed a dangerous criminal class," but this was not unusual. "Any group of disadvantaged people forced into and kept in poverty," DuBois continued, "insulted beyond self-respect, given but partial and limited education, exposed to disease without adequate medical care—such a group will develop dangerous criminal classes." Contrary to what some black leaders believed, the 1943 Harlem uprising was no attempt to cry discrimination "whenever he [the Negro] is charged with anti-social behavior." The struggle matched the experience of most Harlemites, and although blacks did not attack whites directly and exclusively, "it was a RACE RIOT."[45]

It was not the actions but the motivations that confirmed the race riot in Harlem. To be sure, the pattern of property destruction was color blind, though white property sustained more damage in the city. The motivations, for those involved, were directly connected to race and racism in New York City. In a letter to the *New York Amsterdam News*, a Brooklyn resident insisted that the paper's readers not lose sight of the series of events that led to the uprising in Harlem. "The incident which precipitates a riot is not the cause of a riot," Wilfred H. Kerr explained, and what happened in Beaumont, Mobile, Los Angeles, and Detroit all added up to Harlem. "Let no fine-drawn distinctions between these other riots and Harlem be made," Kerr suggested. Contrary to what others may have proposed about those who participated in the uprising, "they were not all hoodlums." They did share, however, lived experiences that were plagued with discrimination, segregation, and police brutality. It was learned, for example, that of the people who ran into the streets of Harlem, "among them were many good people fed up to the core with the cheating and robbery of the Harlem storekeepers, the laxity and inefficiency of the O.P.A. [Office of Price Administration], discrimination in employment, discrimination in the Army, lack of recreational facilities and hypocrisy of the ruling group who do these things while ostensibly waging a war for democracy." Kerr was not alone in these observations. Others, including the likes of Roy Wilkins, interpreted Harlem's uprising this way. For Wilkins, what happened in Harlem marked "the boiling over of pent-up resentment in the breasts of millions of American Negroes all over this country."[46]

For those who did not elude the facts, the 1943 Harlem uprising presented an opportunity to discuss racial inequalities in New York City and in the nation at large. The executive secretary of the National Urban League, Lester Granger, went as far as to regard "race riots" as preferable. It was "better than quitting [the] fight for equal rights," Granger asserted, and "to prevent the development of race riots in the postwar period we must provide opportunities for full American living for all our citizens." He continued, "We must get the bogey of fear and insecurity out of the background. It may be necessary to reduce profits in some cases and increase rewards in others. It may mean changing our caste system. We must cease thinking that our security can be obtained only at the expense of someone else." Similar to how the 1930s witnessed efforts to confront racism with interracial committees dedicated to racial equality, the aftermath of the uprising saw the same.[47]

Ranging from national to local in scope, these committees materialized across New York City. Residents used multiple platforms to offer their opinions and potential solutions to the social ills faced by Harlemites. Some individuals wrote letters published by the black press, while others joined like-minded organizations and committees. Several of the letters printed called on religious leaders to assume more active roles in the community. "Where is their faith?" one Harlemite questioned. "Just how can these ministers of Harlem, or any other place for all that, justify their position when they go into hiding when something frightful happens." Other letters included calls for federal action, because "the outbreak in our midst was not a single isolated incident, not merely a local affair." This rhetoric reaffirmed the agendas of different groups across the city. Groups such as the Citizens' Committee on Better Race Relations, the Council Against Intolerance, and several socialist groups met to discuss the Harlem uprising and to offer suggestions relative to improving the dire conditions black New Yorkers faced.[48]

As these committees worked toward formulating their recommendations to prevent the likelihood of further uprisings in Harlem, whether Harlem had experienced a "race riot" became a digressing issue. They focused largely on the social issues impacting the neighborhood, and each group had its own vision for the direction of Harlem. The overall interest of Harlem lay at the heart of their objectives—if no more than to publicize its many issues in the right way. For example, the Citizens' Committee on Better Race Relations, which organized its efforts alongside A. Philip Randolph and the Brotherhood of Sleeping Car Porters, prioritized its investigation of the causes behind the Harlem uprising and developed a ten-point program as a solution. These included,

(1) a demand to the Mayor to call upon the President to issue a national proclamation abolishing segregation, discrimination and Jim Crowism in the armed forces and throughout the government; (2) a plea to the President to issue an order calling on the Red Cross to discontinue its Jim Crow blood bank forthwith; (3) a demand that the Mayor appoint two blacks, one as a member of the Board of Education, the other to serve on the Executive Administration staff of the Board of Education; (4) a call on the Mayor to appoint an African American as one of his ranking secretaries; (5) a call on the Mayor to appoint a black Deputy Police Commissioner; (6) a call on the Mayor to confer with the merchants of Harlem, the Markets Department and the Office of Price Administration on correcting the wide differential existing in quality and quantity of foodstuffs and other commodities sold in Harlem; (7) a call on the Mayor to appoint a black person to the Administrative staff of the City War council to coordinate the Civilian Defense activities of the Council in Relation to Negro Participation; (8) a call on the Mayor to appoint a Commission on Race Relations consisting of representatives of all races, creeds, colors and nationalities, and that this commission be empowered to accept and consider recommendations to better race relations in the city; (9) a call to increase the number of play streets and playgrounds in Harlem; and (10) a call on the city to acquire buildings in Harlem for indoor musical concerts, skating rinks, dance halls and other recreational activities.

The Citizens' Committee on Better Race Relations was convinced that the "social explosion" in Harlem was caused by the ever-present problems of segregation and discrimination, similar to those faced by black people in every section of the country. Thus, they declared, "In the distressed imaginations of Negroes who know the humiliation of second-class citizenship, all of the inequalities imposed by the Federal

Government in the armed services, in political, civil and social life, burst forth with what was not just hooliganism and vandalism, but a violent and surging protest—actually a sort of revolution of the common man."⁴⁹

Some of these demands, per Mayor La Guardia's acceptance, were taken into consideration to alleviate some of the immediate problems in the city. The OPA, for example, announced that it was opening an office in the basement of a branch library on 135th Street, and its first order of business was to address the high food costs believed to have contributed to the uprising. Also, in cooperation with a local charity foundation, the Board of Education started a two-year program in three Harlem schools in an effort to provide an improved curriculum for elementary and junior high school students. NAACP's Walter White and Algernon Black, the latter a teacher and leader of the New York Society for Ethical Culture, formed a special committee to help black New Yorkers obtain jobs and to keep the public aware of the plight of blacks throughout the city. In a direct attempt to reconcile the Stuyvesant Town deal, Mayor La Guardia announced a plan to develop new housing in Harlem. Even the Savoy Ballroom was permitted to renew its license and reopened in late October. Still, the changes in policing that the mayor called for to quell the uprising and prevent further disturbance remained.⁵⁰

"Simple Looks for Justice": Black Youth and Wartime Police Brutality

Long before the Harlem uprising, Mayor La Guardia was mindful of the role police could play in both aggravating and pacifying race-related troubles in his city.⁵¹ Police brutality was a topic of discussion since the turn of the century, and black New Yorkers often found themselves at the center of the debate—and at the wrong end of the encounters. As "race riots" flared across the country in wartime America, La Guardia knew he needed to be prepared to have the police force ready to be aggressive, while under extreme scrutiny. The New York City mayor looked to Detroit as a template for what not to do. He received Walter White's report "What Caused the Detroit Race Riots?," which White described the brutality perpetrated by the Detroit Police Department as "one of the most disgraceful episodes of American history." White disclosed appalling details of black persons who were shot by the police, "a number of them in the back," and reported that for years the police department in Detroit "permitted racists to operate without check or hindrance." The NAACP leader blamed Detroit's lack of leadership and the absence of superior officers for the police officers' misbehaviors. White sent this report to the New York City mayor not just to disclose what happened in Detroit but to challenge him to be better prepared.[52]

To do so, Mayor La Guardia met with countless city officials, including some black leaders, to discuss and devise a protocol for policing racial disturbances. Suggestions included requiring patrol officers to operate in numbers, at least in twos; if possible, to arrest looters and only to use force "when necessary" and to shoot only as "the last resort"; to employ tear gas "as a last measure"; to close all the bars; to ban the sale of intoxicants; to guard pawnshops, gun stores, fire-alarm boxes, and schools; and to divert all traffic from the designated "riot area." Perhaps most importantly, the mayor emphasized that he would not tolerate any form of police brutality and expressed to black New Yorkers that "police . . . [would] protect all citizens regardless of race or color."[53]

Charges of police brutality plagued the 1935 Harlem uprising, and for Mayor La Guardia, it was critical not to have a repeat occurrence. It is too difficult to know how often between the 1935 uprising and the Detroit race riot that New York City police officers were reminded to practice restraint in the event that a racial incident happened in their city. Patrol officers were advised that "their language and actions, if not proper, will be subject to much criticism," and Police Commissioner Valentine regularly instructed them to "remain calm, cool and collected; act firmly but courteously." On the basis of White's account, the police officers involved in quelling the uprising did just that. "During all those troubled hours," White recalled, "I heard not one word about 'niggers,' as I had heard so frequently in Detroit, nor was there any other manifestation of racial animosity." The police officers were out to do a job of restoring order, and as reported by White, "it was all in a day's work."[54]

For all that, there were reports that challenged White's telling of the 1943 Harlem uprising, particularly from the city's youths. For example, a young black male recalled attempting to cross Seventh Avenue during the uprising and a policeman lunging in front of this car. "Do I have to get out of the way for you?" the officer challenged. "You black bastard."

There was also police officer Benjamin Wallace, who was responsible for two of the six causalities from the August 1 uprising. It remains unclear whether Officer Wallace acted irresponsibly, but his actions clashed with Mayor La Guardia's requests and Commissioner Valentine's orders. There was no evidence to prove if "the looters had been attempting to escape" or if their behaviors "threatened his [Officer Wallace's] personal safety or that of others"; however, there were two dead bodies pinned to Wallace's record. In addition to these accounts, there were several instances in which patrol officers and detectives kept the confiscated stolen goods they recovered. While these happenings may very well represent the exception, they were the cases that resonated with Harlemites, especially its young ones, well after the uprising settled.[55]

For young Harlemites, police brutality remained a serious concern and was exacerbated by the uprising. They never bought into any of the praise police officers received after the 1943 uprising—it was a façade. Almost two weeks after the disturbance, several black youths reminded a black reporter from *The Call* that if it were not for the actions of a policeman at Hotel Braddock, the uprising may have never happened. These young boys, who still held that Private Bandy had been killed, told the reporter, "That cop shot a soldier in the back, and we ain't satisfied." The reporter tried to convince the youths that Bandy had suffered only a flesh wound and was alive and that the NAACP conducted an investigation to inform the public that "the soldier was all right." They remained unconvinced. "That ain't true. That soldier was shot five times in the back. And he's dead," the youths asserted. "That don't come out in the papers, because they're scared to let it be known." They remained adamant: "Mayor LaGuardier [*sic*] is lying." The reporter challenged the youths for proof, evidence of where their account stemmed from, and one boy shouted, "How do we know it! Because my brother was right there when it happened. They killed that soldier, and they've killed a lot more people—but they ain't letting that out yet." Such impassioned feelings were cause for concern for city officials and community leaders. These young Harlemites embodied a sentiment that demonstrated a raised consciousness and awareness of contemporary race relations, as well as a distrust of authorities.[56]

As the debate shifted from what happened in Harlem on August 1, 1943, to why it happened in Harlem and then, ultimately, to what needed

Boys wearing their "looted" suits, 1943. (Bettmann / Getty Images)

to take place to prevent another happening of this magnitude in Harlem, black youths bore the brunt of the responsibility and sustained the most enduring effect. The hoodlum premise now combined with New York City's efforts to control juvenile delinquency and crime. Because many of the protestors were teenagers and young adults who "appeared to fit the general concept of lower-class types and hoodlums," the catchall term instinctively attached itself to black youths—though none of the proponents of the hoodlum theory, including Mayor La Guardia, ever attempted to define it. Still, they continued to use details from the uprising weeks after it passed to preserve the hoodlum theory. For example, a commanding officer of the Fifth Division police unit reported to the police commissioner an occurrence that included a small number of white pedestrians and trolley passengers who were "attacked by black youths." This took place outside the "riot area" and in "a contested neighborhood that the Young Citizens' Committee on Race Relations identified as a spawning ground for white 'conflict gangs.'" Still, it was filed under the city's cases connected to the August 1 incident, and it was used to justify a call to control youth behaviors following the uprising.[57]

This mattered, because though crime rates across the nation generally declined, especially violent crimes, juvenile delinquency rates increased through wartime. In 1942, the Federal Bureau of Investigation (FBI) categorized nineteen-year-olds as the predominant age group for those who were arrested in the nation's major cities. In 1943, the age fell by two years for boys and one year for girls. The arrest rates of male youths under eighteen rose by roughly 24 percent. In all, over one hundred thousand youths under eighteen were arrested in 1943—approximately one in every five arrests in the entire country. In New York City, specifically, the arrest rates and subsequent court rates mirrored national trends. The Domestic Relations Court showed an increase of nearly 11 percent in juvenile delinquency cases and about a 12 percent increase in the number of neglected children cases. A disproportionate number of these youths, nearly half, who were arrested and brought into court in New York City were black.[58]

Thus, in Harlem after the uprising, as energies shifted toward uncovering ways to resolve the social ills that youths faced, black youths became the target of attention from city authorities and civic organizations. As groups such as the Citizens' Committee on Better Race Relations called for an increase in the number of playgrounds in Harlem and called on the city to acquire more buildings for skating rinks, dance halls, and other recreational activities, doing so with good intentions, they reinforced the idea that in the interim, black youths may turn to alternative vices. This gave city authorities, especially the police, reason to be on the lookout for idle youths. Combined with the enhanced prevention efforts that preceded the uprising, the police state that these youngsters faced in postwar Harlem was unlike that of any previous generation. But this postwar generation of black youths was also unlike that of any previous generation, especially in their perspective on democracy.[59]

Maybelle Carey, a black woman from Harlem, wrote a letter to the *New York Amsterdam News* predicting more uprisings unless city officials across the United States "get it together." Carey conveyed distress about what happened in Harlem, "not only for Negroes, but other Americans as well." She argued that so long as the present setup of things continued and unless a sound solution were found, the tumult would happen again, "be it five, ten or twenty years hence, it is inevitable." The most disgruntled segment of the protesters were teenagers and those in their early twenties, Carey pointed out, and she asked, "Is there any wonder? Do you think these youths are fools? What sort of future lies head for them under a system—a democratic system—which contradicts its own constitution?" This reasoning was echoed by the NAACP's Walter White, who revealingly conveyed, "Young hoodlums in Bedford-Stuyvesant, Harlem, Atlanta, or Los Angeles are in part the inevitable product of the depression when they saw no hope for themselves or parents for living decent, secure lives." White continued, "These youngsters hear all the ballyhoo for winning the war for freedom doubting cynically that any of that freedom will be theirs." To make amends with these youths who continued to view state authorities with such animosity presented a daunting task that required total cooperation from political figures, city authorities, social agencies, and community leaders—a combination that was more often "still divided, still ineffective." Until and unless these leaders became known by youths, worked with youths, and gained the confidence of the youths, little could be done to guarantee a better future for them in Harlem.[60]

"Every Generation Has Had the Habit of Going to the Devil"

Constructions of a Postwar Delinquent

All over Harlem, Negro boys and girls are growing into
stunted maturity, trying desperately to find a place to stand;
and the wonder is not that so many are ruined but that so
many survive.
—James Baldwin, "The Harlem Ghetto"

On a moderately warm Saturday in the city as the summer of 1945
came to an end, *New York Amsterdam News* readers were greeted with
a front-page headline that read, "Kid Gang Shoots Lad Five Times." The
account that followed was of a seventeen-year-old Harlemite, Joseph
Mitchell, who was shot by a group of youngsters before being rushed
to Harlem Hospital. As reported, Mitchell was aggressively approached
by five youths, who police declared were members of "a club called the
Slicksters." This club was reported to have a membership of "at least 100
Harlem teen-age youths," and after questioning more than fifty boys
in the New York City neighborhood, the police arrested three of the
offenders within a day of the incident. Mitchell, who interestingly was
the first cousin of the famous jazz pianist Eddie Heywood, survived the
attack, as the doctors revealed he was shot three times in the back and
once in each leg. Witnesses confirmed the report and described "five
tough-looking boys, each armed with a revolver [who] took turns at
shooting the victim," before Mitchell scampered away to a bar and
grill on Bradhurst Avenue. Mitchell's mother, Mamie, disclosed to an
Amsterdam News reporter that "the mothers of some of the boys under
arrest had visited the hospital to see her son and had begged him not
to press charges." The motive for the shooting remained unsolved; one
report suggested that the incident was sparked over a stolen bicycle,

and another report claimed that Mitchell was attacked for not paying a five-dollar debt to the Slicksters. Still, the melee happened, and for the African American weekly, it was front page worthy.[1]

Joseph Mitchell's story was just one of the captivating front-page headliners on that Saturday. Under the headline was an image of an elementary-school-age black boy waving good-bye to his mother, who "affectionately watche[d] him trudge off for a great adventure, the first day of school." This image was juxtaposed with an image that captured the "Tragedy of a Broken Home in Harlem Told through the Eyes of a News Camera" and the accompanying article that described a broken home "as acute a Harlem problem as are jobs and housing." Succinctly, and not coincidentally, this front page of the *New York Amsterdam News* captured the "growing tragedy" of Harlem in the postwar period. Since July 1, the African American weekly carried at least five front-page stories of youth gang shootings and stabbings similar to the Mitchell headline, because "every mother and father, every school, every community agency, [was] revolted at the cold-blooded youths who shot Joseph Mitchell lying helpless on the side-walk, because the community needs [a] waking up." This was a deliberate tactic by those who ran the *Amsterdam News*, because they were convinced that the larger community either "slumber[ed] on in lethargy or is annoyed that [their] headliners disturb their complacency." Thus, they accepted the challenge to use their platform in a way that tackled the postwar crime and delinquency problem.[2]

Compared to the state and city authorities who enforced the laws and policies regarding crime and delinquency in New York City, the media held a distinct power that influenced public discourse and behaviors. Their power to control the narrative affected disparate societal forces that vied for authoritative position as well as the everyday perceptions of presumed culprits. For example, as predictions of a postwar crime wave saturated the headlines of newspapers across the country, law enforcement officers were advised to be "very much on the alert against an undoubted rise in offenses." Debates about who would be the main cause for concern shifted from returning veterans to war-industry employees, especially youths, who were forced back to prewar salaries and opportunities; however, once wartime crime statistics were accounted for, the consensus eventually settled on the young.[3]

As the crime-wave sensationalism plagued New York City after the war, debates surrounding the legitimacy of its rhetoric, its causes, its impact on the community, and prevention plans transpired. In this moment, black crime discourse reestablished itself in ways similar to the Progressive era, when many northern, white and black, reformers attributed social conditions to criminal behaviors. This included the efforts of criminologists such as Edwin J. Lukas and the Society for the Prevention of Crime as well as social psychiatrists such as Frederic Wertham and the Lafargue Mental Hygiene Clinic in Harlem. The stakes, however, were different for the black youths who were presumed delinquent in the urban North, especially when they encountered the police. Carceral authorities continued to feed on their quelling of the Harlem uprisings, and police extended their punitive tactics and strategies into the postwar period. Consequently, police arrested black youths in higher numbers, which reinforced the perception of the crime wave; the discourse of the crime wave, led by New York City's print media outlets, mutually reinforced the racialized perceptions of crime held by the larger public.[4]

"Go In Shooting": Police Responses to the Postwar Crime Wave

"We know it is one of war's aftermaths," the newly appointed police commissioner, Arthur W. Wallander, announced to his chief subordinates at the Police Headquarters. "We shall do all within our power to cope with it."[5] Police Commissioner Wallander continued, "We'll use every damned thing we can get to down this crime movement. We fully realize the situation is bad." The new police commissioner was appointed by old mayor La Guardia, who believed Wallander to be a "worthy successor to Commissioner Valentine."[6]

Shortly after Commissioner Wallander's appointment, he brazenly outlined his plans to address New York City's crime problem. He sought to redistribute police responsibilities by surveying the police department to see how many men were assigned deskwork or other nonpatrol duties who could be put on the streets. The police commissioner turned to the military to alleviate the work-force shortage and informed respective branches that "not only the rank and file but lieutenants and sergeants engaged in lesser tasks [were] to be put out on beats or on motor patrol until the wide gap in the force can be filled." The former deputy chief inspector was forward about his "warlike preparations" for the "war on crime" in New York City. Commissioner Wallander reassigned the department's "top-flight pistol marksmen" to radio car and cruiser patrols; he replaced night-cruiser patrol cars with radio-equipped cars borrowed from other city departments, which carried machine guns and rifles. "We do not hesitate to recognize that crime has increased," the police commissioner proclaimed, and he was determined to strengthen the police force, if only in presence, to control the crime rise in the city.[7]

"The crime growth may be traced to several causes," according to Commissioner Wallander: "the police manpower shortage and lack of parental control over the city's restless adolescents." To the former, most reports indicated that the police shortage in New York City, and similar in US cities, was a direct result of the war. Returning veterans' efforts to join or rejoin the police force were delayed for different, mainly bureaucratic, reasons. In November 1945, there were more than four thousand unfilled vacancies in the New York Police Department. Many accounts suggest that this void was because of the men who enrolled in the armed forces and were still on leave; however, there were also those who inferred that Mayor La Guardia's push toward aggressive police tactics discouraged many to rejoin after returning from war. The shortage in the department was "not because of the war," a special issue published by the Chicago Defender reported, "because only 780 of its personnel [were] still in the service." Instead, the blame was placed on the New York City mayor for overworking police officers with more menial tasks. "Under La Guardia's control," the writer explained, "policemen in 1943 were detailed to 24 hour duty watching homes where persons had been found playing cards." Reports exposed some police officers being camped at homes for seven weeks and in one case for a month, raiding poker and bridge games, and ransacking guarded stores where race bets were taken. Before the war, the police force was then "hundreds of men short of its authorized complement," and the suggestion that similar policing tactics were employed to combat this postwar crime wave discouraged some officers from returning to their positions.[8]

The New York City mayor denied these allegations and declared his commitment to provide a suitable police department. Mayor La Guardia proclaimed he was responding to citizens' demands for an adequate police force, and he was "ready to appoint to the police department any man coming out of the army who passed an examination but was called into the army before taking a final physical examination." These citizens included Joseph Goldstein, for example, the president of the Taxpayers Union of New York City, who affirmed in a letter to the mayor that if the demand was not met within a reasonable time, he would be forced to call on Governor Dewey to remove the mayor and the police commissioner on charges that they were neglectful of their duties. "Criminals are marching thru the streets of our city unmolested by the police," Goldstein wrote, "and it is your duty to make safe the streets of our city and properly protect the lives and property of our citizens." Within days, Mayor La Guardia announced that his plan of action was in place to suppress the "growing wave of violence in the city."[9]

But Mayor La Guardia held no qualms administering aggressive police tactics. In fact, after the war, he encouraged patrol officers to be more assertive in their war on crime in New York City. In his address to police rookies being sworn in for duty on December 1, 1945, the mayor advised the provisional police officers to be forceful when they faced situations in which a firearm may be being used in the commission of a crime. "Be quick on the trigger," Mayor La Guardia insisted. "You've got a nightstick. You've got a gun. They're not meant to be ornamental." He continued, "When you know there's a crime being committed and there's a criminal in the place, go in with your gun in your hand. Go in shooting." Mayor La Guardia closed his address reminding the newly minted officers that their life on the force would be "no bed of roses," because the department was short-handed. He encouraged the war veterans, some who were holders of combat citations and battle ribbons, to boast that identity for "every bum in town to know that." While the address faced some criticism, Mayor La Guardia's message was clear.[10]

Commissioner Wallander was hardly a critic. In fact, he was in full support of Mayor La Guardia's message to the newly minted police officers, and the two met to discuss a plan of attack. "We have more plans for meeting this situation which we'll put into operation," Mayor La Guardia informed reporters, without revealing too much of said plans. He did disclose, however, that the plan of attack involved an increase in the police force. "I am making my second appeal for the release of 750 policemen still in the armed forces," Mayor La Guardia explained. "I made the first after V-J Day. Apparently, it was ignored." He continued,

"I'd like to have these men released as quickly as possible to bolster up the force." This demonstrated a shift in priority for the mayor. At first, Mayor La Guardia showed signs of prioritizing the war's efforts over his city's issues; such was the case in the WAVES decision. With the war being over, the mayor was determined to refocus his priorities, and the number-one priority was to quell the crime wave that alarmed city officials. Mayor La Guardia urged Washington to release all former New York City police officers who still served in the armed forces. The secretary of war, Robert P. Patterson, said of the mayor's plea, "I don't know the details of the New York City situation, but if the need of separation from the service of people needed by the City of New York is shown to us, it will receive our most careful attention."[11]

Thus, it became critical for the city to prove that the crime wave existed. For those who were close to Mayor La Guardia, it was hardly a question. Revised figures, "obtained from an authoritative police source," showed the number of violent deaths rising exponentially, including seventy-eight in eighty-six days in the last months of 1945—not including vehicular homicides. The Correction Department's statistical director, Paul D. McCann, reported in New York City, "the number of fingerprints received by the department in connection with arrests for serious crimes increased from 3,350 in June to 3,750 in October, or approximately 12 percent." McCann continued, "the November figures [were] showing a continued rise." And these numbers confirmed what Commissioner Wallander speculated about the city's "restless adolescents," as the officials cited an increase in criminal activity in the twenty-year-old and teenage groups as the "cause of the crime wave."[12]

"The Mounting Tide of Lawlessness": Combating an Armed Crime Wave

The rise in criminal activity among youth in New York City was not exceptional. In the years after the war, the highest crime rates nationwide were in large cities, and young people made up roughly 50 percent of the documented arrests in both 1945 and 1946. As the nation furthered itself from the immediate aftermath of the war, arrest rates continued to rise, while the ages of those who were arrested continued to drop. According to the 1946 Uniform Crime Report, "more persons were arrested during

1946 than during any year of the past decade." Of the more than 645,000 arrests recorded by the Federal Bureau of Investigation, most fell around the twenty-one-year-old age group. Because of this, the numbers alone did not bolster Mayor La Guardia's demand for the release of New York City police officers enlisted in the service, because the city's crime rates hovered around the national average.[13]

Consequently, the secretary of war turned down the mayor's request. "While the need of the City of New York for uniformed police is recognized," Secretary Patterson wrote in a letter to La Guardia, "the War Department is unable to comply with your request for the immediate mass release of these individuals." On the one hand, this may have indicated that the urgency expressed by the mayor and other city authorities was exaggerated, at least in the opinion of the secretary of war. On the other, as Patterson attempted to convey in the letter, to release these service members from duty was a bureaucratic nightmare and made for an intricate personnel problem. "Some ninety other professional and occupational groups," Secretary Patterson wrote, were "distributed all over the United States, [that] have also requested priority in release from the Army." The truth probably lay somewhere in between, as many expected that crime-wave arrests would steadily decrease gradually "with the ever-increasing number of veterans returning to civilian life" and that "the nation's need for manpower in all categories [would] be shortly met." But Mayor La Guardia and other city officials were less optimistic, and the crime wave evoked a public debate with broader social implications beyond the wood-paneled walls of City Hall.[14]

Thus, the effort to arouse public support through fear became the next tactic employed by city officials. In La Guardia's last month as mayor, before William O'Dwyer was to take office, he moved on "the mounting tide of lawlessness" that ravaged New York City. Property crimes are one thing, but the real fear was inspired by a lawlessness involving violent crime. Though the popular narrative shifted from a postwar crime wave with war veterans as the culprits, it was believed that they still did add to the cause. According to Commissioner Wallander, discharged war veterans did not add "materially to criminal ranks," but their weapons may have. That was confirmed by numerous reports that indicated that weapons once belonging to war veterans, including guns, were confiscated in street crimes. When pressed on how this happens, City Council district attorney Frank S. Hogan pointed partial blame toward the War Department. "In order to improve the morale of soldiers overseas," an official bulletin circulated by the War Department expressed, "troops may be permitted to bring home as souvenirs rifles, small arms, swords, bayonets, slingshots, billies, bludgeons, metal knuckles and the like." These weapons were sometimes brought back in GIs' personal luggage; other times they were mailed home. Regardless of how they got into the country, the concern was how they got into the streets. District Attorney Hogan reported that between September and November, "sixty-seven foreign-make guns have shown up in criminal cases in Manhattan," and he was convinced that an underground market had developed a "sinister new strategy" to arm the crime wave. It would be up to the police commissioner, whether he was convinced or not, to establish a practical policy to rid the city of these excess weapons.[15]

"I am not proposing a drive of any kind," Commissioner Wallander told the three hundred or so law enforcement officials who attended the annual FBI conference at Fordham University, "but the establishment of a sensible policy and the sustained application of that policy" was needed to combat the rising wave of crime and delinquency in New York City. The police commissioner encouraged the conference attendees to return to their communities and to be more active in their efforts to remove firearms from their residents. "They should be picked up regardless of who owns them," Wallander said, referring to veterans and "any other respected member of society." He closed his address with a call for integrated and coordinated efforts by city authorities and the community to reduce the numbers of firearms in the streets.[16]

To be sure, the street crimes involving the confiscated war weapons were committed by a range of offenders; however, Commissioner Wallander worried a great deal about the "many souvenir war weapons coming into the possession of misguided youth." Because the increase in crime, according to the police commissioner, stemmed from the police-force shortage and the lack of parental control over juveniles, the combination of youth culprits and access to weapons was distressing. Be that as it may, such was a concern for the nation at large. Even FBI director J. Edgar Hoover warned of the "mounting crime" problem, and he declared that the country was "facing a potential army of 6,000,000 criminals and an ever-increasing wave of lawlessness which is feeding the criminal ranks with a never-ending supply of recruits." Like New York City officials, the FBI director cited arrest statistics to defend his stance and further argued that youths composed the "vast army" of criminals, as their numbers trended toward a figure "ten times greater than the number of students in our colleges and universities." Beyond this, Hoover reinforced Wallander's reasoning on lack of parental control. For the FBI director, there was little doubt that the postwar crime wave was a direct consequence of "a recession of moral fortitude, laxity in parental control, lowered moral standards, social and economic conditions, and abuses and maladministration of the penal system." Hoover further underscored the point of parental neglect, suggesting that the postwar generation of youths were not receiving adequate rearing from their parents. "If all parents fulfill their obligations to their children we would soon experience a sharp decline in crime," Hoover posited. Such a claim was laden with racial implications connected to a longer history of the state's function as a "surrogate parent."[17]

Accordingly, in New York City, authorities moved forward with their efforts to avoid the national trend as much as possible—at times with extreme measures. For example, Commissioner Wallander invoked the powers of a rarely used statute in which he ordered police officers to "haul parents into court when there is a definite indication that parental neglect is a contributing cause to the delinquency of a juvenile." Admitting that this was not "a complete cure-all," the police commissioner unveiled this order to an audience of Queens Rotary Club members in Long Island. "We do feel that making parents realize their responsibility will materially help in cutting down juvenile delinquency," Wallander pledged. The order reaffirmed what many juvenile judges advanced for years: juvenile delinquency was traced to home life. Consequently, the police commissioner combined the new directive with older tactics designed to prevent crime. These included calls for the police to break up "corner gangs and groups of youngsters before they can be tempted by their solidarity to engage in disorderly acts," to keep a sharp eye on pool parlors where "potential young offenders might resort or be encouraged and developed," and to prevent "the loitering of thieves, criminals and other suspicious persons in cabarets, dance halls and night clubs." The same level of diligence was given to bars and grills that were known to be "hangouts of degenerates, prostitutes and disorderly persons."[18]

As city officials continued to devise and revise tactics to address the postwar crime wave, they recognized their responsibility to mitigate the crime-wave discourse from a policy standpoint. In other words, while the calls for increased surveillance to cope with the shortage of officers and the directives to extend police power over youths to include their family, it gave the impression that crime was rampant in New York City, and this could mean something drastically different for different New Yorkers. For example, the perception of a crime wave was used as a defense technique for attorneys defending "reputable" criminal offenders, such as the sixty-two-year-old Catherine Jefferson, who was visiting New York City from Ohio and arrested for the possession of a pistol. "When I told my friends I was going to New York, they told me that I ought to take the gun along to protect myself," Jefferson explained to judicial authorities. "They pointed out to me what a wild place New York was and told me about crime waves in the city." The prosecution did not buy the account and attempted to convict Jefferson after she jokingly admitted that she was "going to use the gun for some sort of revenge" on a man who was her suitor in the past. In any event, Jefferson and her attorney used the perception of a crime wave and the need for protection as a reason, to which the courts gave credence.[19]

The use of New York's crime wave as a defense strategy to protect specific offenders suggests a troublesome element that reveals a different truth of who exactly was being implicated in the discourse. It is one thing for an elderly woman to rely on the fear sparked by the crime wave as defense, but the defense also covered those who were considered reputable. Such was the case for Charles Hopkins Vejvoda and Hugh R. Thomas, two youths arrested for a melee on Thanksgiving night 1945. Vejvoda and Thomas, "two seventeen-year-old honor students," were charged with a violation of the Sullivan law, a misdemeanor weapons charge, for carrying homemade brass knuckles during their "noisy argument with four naval officers." Vejvoda, the son of a surgeon, and Thomas, the son of an attorney, were arrested around 1:00 a.m. by Patrolman Robert Baron. Patrolman Baron informed the adjudicating authority, Chief Magistrate Edgar Bromberger, that Vejvoda kept his hand in his pocket, and when demanded to show his hands, he brandished the concealed "knuckles." The teenager told the arresting officer that he received the brass knuckles from a sailor a year before the incident and that he "carried them for protection." Vejvoda's father, Charles Vejvoda, defended his son and his son's friend, and he attributed the arrest to the "overzealousness" of the arresting officer, who was "making a mountain out of a mole hill." Chief Magistrate Bromberger immediately dismissed the charges against Thomas, who was determined to be "merely accompanying the other boy," though he held his decision on Vejvoda for a later date. The judge decided that he needed to review additional briefs to determine if Vejvoda's intent to use the brass knuckles had been enough to entail a violation of the Sullivan law—it is presumed that the charges were dropped, and Vejvoda eventually joined the Navy.[20]

The Vejvoda case was telling. The fact that two youths were arrested for the possession of a deadly weapon—two predominant descriptors of the postwar crime wave—and escaped culpability because of the same crime wave demonstrates the protection that privilege can buy and suggests that the new policies had different subjects in mind. Also, the favorable media portrayal of Charles Vejvoda and Hugh Thomas suppressed public scrutiny of the two youths and played down any potential guilt. They were two of four persons arrested that Thanksgiving night in New York City who were charged with violating the Sullivan law, but they were the only ones to receive media coverage. Also, the two "honor students" benefited from their parents' status and were described as fearful youngsters who were protecting themselves from "New York's crime." The possessive nature of the coverage conveyed to the public that Vejvoda and Thomas were not representative of whom "New York" personified. Hence, New York City's media outlets joined the attack to fight crime by utilizing their platform to define who was the city's crime problem.[21]

Whose New York? Black Crime and the New York Press

Print media coverage of New York's crime wave became the driving force behind how it was experienced and who sustained the long-term effects. Unfortunately for black New Yorkers, coverage of the postwar crime wave was usually spearheaded by crimes committed in predominantly black neighborhoods and was usually the cause for the application of repressive responses by the police. Regardless of what the crime and delinquency statistics revealed, the press routinely emphasized crimes committed by blacks in preference to white crimes. By accentuating the words "Negro" and "Harlem," they contributed to the public perception of the postwar crime wave by stimulating a phobic apprehension with which uninformed persons viewed the crime wave in New York City. "New York's crime" became synonymous with "black crime," and it was the most influential media outlet in the world that led the charge.

In the *New York Times*, for example, crime reports were laden with racial markers, some more glaring than others, that did more than cover the incidents under investigation. For example, in November 1943, a front-page article on a second-offense robbery, adjacent to "War News Summarized," bore the headline, "Ex-Convict Gets 40 to 60 Years as a Lesson for Brooklyn Thugs." The coverage included "the tongue lashing" imposed by King County Judge Louis Goldstein to Jack Morgan, "a Negro," for his offense. "Let the punishment I mete out to you," Judge Goldstein told Morgan, "be a warning to those of your criminal element who have infested the Bedford-Stuyvesant section that when they commit vicious crimes no consideration whatsoever will be given to them." Of course, Bedford-Stuyvesant is a neighborhood in the Brooklyn borough; however, coverage of the crime and sentencing in the *Times* regularly referred to the neighborhood as "Brooklyn's 'Little Harlem' because of its large Negro population." The same article also included superfluous updates on the state of the Juvenile Aid Bureau, the successes of police increases "to curb lawlessness in that area," the "much too lenient" Adolescent Court and its "youthful hoodlum offenders"— two-thirds of whom were white—and admissions of crime increases in the city from notable black residents.[22]

But the commentary provided by black residents to reporters was rarely an admission to having an inherent crime problem as much as it, generally, reflected an effort to address neighborhood social conditions that may lead to crime. For instance, the Reverend Thomas Harten of Holy Trinity Baptist in Brooklyn told the *Times* reporter on the Morgan case, "I do not deny that crime has increased here, but the increase is national." For the African American pastor in "Brooklyn's Little Harlem," crime was "due largely to bad economic conditions, bad housing, exorbitant rents and the fact that, until Pearl Harbor very many of our people were out of

Benjamin Davis Jr. at the Hotel Theresa discussing policing in Harlem, 1949.
(AP Photo / John Lent)

work and on relief." Rev. Harten believed that reports were "exaggerated and the result of pressure by persons who have long been making 'vicious attacks' on Brooklyn's Negro population." And Brooklyn was not alone.[23]

At a convention of the Young Communist League, the prominent Harlemite Benjamin Davis Jr. told an audience of roughly a hundred young men and women that the postwar emphasis on "muggings by Negroes" in the news was "exaggerated crime wave slander." The executive secretary of the Harlem division of the Communist Party denied the accusations of a postwar crime wave and expounded on how "mugging [was] a new handle of slander and libel to be used against the Negro people to exaggerate and to create the impression that the Negro people are a criminal element and that the white population should regard them as such." Davis, like Harten, did not dismiss the fact that crimes were being committed in Harlem; similarly, he associated the crimes with neighborhood social problems that "existed there for a long time," while emphasizing that the postwar crime-wave sensationalism was fabricated by the print media.[24]

Many black leaders discerned the media's tendency to conflate New York's crime problem with its black residents. In 1945, a staff of researchers and writers led by Duane Robinson published their study on "mugging" and the New York press in *Phylon*, a quarterly journal founded by W. E. B. DuBois. The study sought to respond directly to the media's attempt to "create a Negro crime wave." The researchers interviewed an editor or staff representative from their respective newspapers, who interpreted their paper's policies on handling crime news. In doing so, they sought to answer the following: (1) Do the readers of *PM* and the *Post* and the readers of the more conservative newspapers differ in the degree of acceptance of the "mugging" stereotype and differ in their views of the policy of the press? and (2) Do important differences of opinion exist between black and white groups, between economic groups with different levels of education, and between different religious groups in regard to the problem? The results proved, according to Robinson, that "the New York press has a long-established practise of giving crimes among the city's half-million Negroes excessive prominence," and after World War II, "the press proceeded to create a fictional and exciting picture of this new brand of Negro crime, 'mugging.'" The data indicated that the newspapers examined could be divided into two groups. One group followed the "conservative" and traditional policy of sensationalizing reports of black crimes without regard for the misinformation and prejudice that these reports created. The other group of papers exercised varying degrees of caution in their reporting of black crimes. Both defended their stances with varying reasons.[25]

One representative from a "conservative," traditional newspaper declared, "It [Negro crime] all goes back to religion and sex." The representative insisted that black people in the North have too much freedom, and because of this, "they get away with murder in New York City." The unnamed representative concluded the interview declaring, quite frankly, "I hate them." A representative from the second group, whose newspapers were described as cautious in their crime reporting, told the interviewer that though his or her newspaper used the race tag "Negro," it also used the term "Harlem" synonymously, and it was doing "everything possible to improve the position of the Negro in the public's mind." This mattered, because the prejudices and personal feelings of the editors carried into the reporting and the news coverage, which influenced strongly the opinions of their audience.[26]

Following these interviews with newspaper representatives, the researchers shifted their attention to public opinion. They used a questionnaire seeking information about the respondents' attitudes toward crime in general, toward "Negro crime," and toward the press's handling of "Negro crime." The questions ranged from "Do you think that there has been a greater increase in crimes in Harlem than in other parts of the city?" to "Do you think that Negro crimes are reported by the newspapers with too little emphasis, or by and large fairly and correctly, or with too much emphasis?" There were considerable differences in opinion between black and white respondents on the questions. On the first question, roughly two-thirds of the white respondents believed yes, there was a greater increase in crimes in Harlem; 80 percent of blacks said no. On the second question, roughly half of the white respondents believed that "Negro crimes" were reported fairly; 79 percent of black respondents believed there was too much emphasis. By and large, the evidence from the study indicated that the press played a vital role, either as a liberal influence or a conservative influence, in the development of public opinion on crime.[27]

For many black newspaper writers and readers, this information did not come as a surprise. Earl Conrad, who served as the Harlem bureau chief for the *Chicago Defender*, printed a report that affirmed that two New York City newspapers, the *World-Telegram* and the *Times*, made no apologies for how their coverage of the crime wave led to a "smear attack on the New York Negro communities." Lee B. Wood, executive editor of the *World-Telegram*, confirmed his newspaper's use of the word "Negro" to describe crimes connected to black people; Richard Joseph, city editor of the *Times*, "bombastically refused" to discuss the situation. It was the *World-Telegram*'s policy, according to Wood, to designate the race of the culprit when a black person was arrested or charged with a crime, but it did not specify national or ethnic origins of others. "I haven't heard of anything yet which would convince me of a need for changing that policy," Wood explained. "I've talked with Negro groups before about that, and they know our position." He continued, "Our policy is to use the word 'Negro' when we think a story is sufficiently important to indicate its need." When asked why other ethnic groups were not identified, Wood countered, "Their names would identify them: that is, if Italian, Jewish, Polish, or other, their names would indicate what they were." The

Defender representative challenged Wood and informed him that it was a matter of group relations, of understanding between black and white, and that the *World-Telegram*'s policy injured the black community each time the word was used. Wood acknowledged, "It might have this kind of effect," but the specification was needed.[28]

But most black New Yorkers knew there was no "might" about it. Black journalists, in particular, believed that since the war ended, news media outlets were running low on newsworthy events, and "the papers now return[ed] to their original scapegoat, the Negro, to spotlight him as a criminal to the nation." In New York City, the crime wave was built by lumping routine crimes together to make it appear as though a great increase in violence had occurred. "When repeating these sensational stories of lawbreaking," according to the *Chicago Defender*, "the word Negro was used profusely creating the opinion that the upward trend of crime was directly traceable to Harlem." To be sure, black journalists did not completely reject the idea that there was a natural upswing in crimes committed after the war; however, they did not believe the rates put forth by mainstream media outlets and did not presume it was a solely a black problem. The racial identification of black persons as offenders in every possible case created the impression that they were the main culprits, and presentation as much as content contributed to this belief. For example, when eighteen black waiters were accused of defrauding the railroads and the passengers of large sums of money in a meal-check scheme, the story was covered by most newspapers with large front-page stories, and the waiters were "belabored as leeches preying upon poor servicemen and their families." But after the trial, when the waiters were exonerated, those same papers printed the outcomes in much smaller articles, buried in the depths of the newspaper. This practice, according to many black journalists, was a custom that print media outlets had followed since the Emancipation; that is, "Negroes are not news unless connected with crime."[29]

At times, black journalists made use of their platforms to counter the crime-wave sensationalism. For example, Carl Lawrence of the *New York Amsterdam News* wrote a piece that denied the crime wave's existence and divulged an ulterior motive. According to Lawrence, "serious" crimes were decreasing in Harlem, and rumors of a crime wave were being applied to get more police in the city. "The downtown papers have decided that we need some more help," an unnamed detective from the 135th Street Station told Lawrence, "so I guess they figured that's the best way to get it." Another police officer from the Thirty-Second Street Station disclosed to the black weekly reporter that "even teen-age gang brawls, the community's most serious crime problem in the opinion of some police officials," were cut to a minimum. Still, countless headlines continued to be printed across New York City newspapers that reported otherwise.[30]

"Can Crime Preventive Efforts by Police Be Helpful?": Prevention beyond Policing

Black journalists were not alone in their efforts to combat the sensationalized, racialized crime wave being spread by the New York City press after the war. Crime-wave opponents included a new surge of reformers who worked through various organizations to expose their truths. This included the Society for the Prevention of Crime, which was founded in 1877 and continued to promote "temperance for judicial and legislative reform and for public and legal education" into the postwar years. The executive director, Edwin J. Lukas, was adamant that there was "no genuine crime wave—yet." Lukas admitted that some crimes, mainly property crimes, increased; however, Lukas expounded, "What we are now experiencing appears on analysis to be nothing more than the expected upsurge of those types of criminal behaviors which during the war diminished for a variety of reasons." Further, the unpaid director of the Society for the Prevention of Crime did concede that the potential for a crime wave existed. Lukas's reasoning echoed many of the early predictions of a crime wave happening, and he acknowledged one would come about "if and when the incidence of crime surges above average rates; if and when idle teenagers remain idle for a protracted time, and in greater numbers; if and when displaced war workers remain unabsorbed into industry; and if and when returning GI's with unresolved personal problems and emotional disturbances do not receive appropriate guidance and jobs."[31]

Lukas also advocated for revised and refurbished prewar programs such as the Juvenile Aid Bureau, athletic leagues, and summer camps that had been reduced or cut. These kinds of programs, according to

Lukas, needed to be readjusted for the times if they were to be successful. The Society for the Prevention of Crime director acknowledged that the programs used before the war were "gravely emasculated" and needed to be revived to be effective. For example, the Juvenile Aid Bureau in New York City lost many caseworkers who were either released from their duties or transferred to other city departments. "The activities of the unit," Lukas wrote, "gradually deteriorated into fairly routine and mundane matters varied only by the thus far unspectacularly effective Coordinating Councils established in precincts scattered throughout the city." Thus, Lukas used his platform to address the needs to prevent a crime wave from happening, because it seemed to be on the horizon, and his concern was that many prevention programs were being suppressed and replaced by more punitive police-selected directives.[32]

Another opponent of the "fabricated" crime wave was Frederick A. Moran, chairman of the New York State Board of Parole. At the forty-seventh annual New York State Conference on Social Work at the Pennsylvania Hotel, Moran announced that the predictions of a postwar crime increase were based on "incomplete statistics" concerning juvenile delinquency. In fact, the Board of Parole chairman affirmed, "every generation, in the opinion of the older one, has had the habit of going to the devil." In other words, there was a generational tension. The postwar crime wave received undue attention because the older generation misinterpreted the shifts in youth behaviors as they took over positions of power.[33]

These positions included the judges and lawyers who worked the juvenile courts. Moran recommended changes in the court procedures to adjust to the times. "It is the contention of many that the failure of so large a percentage of the courts to function effectively is due to a misconception, willful or otherwise, of the purposes of these courts not only on the part of laymen," Moran opined at the National Conference of Social Work, "but of lawyers and judges as well, and that the greatest part of the responsibility for the present condition of affairs rests with the legalists." That is, judges and lawyers needed to use their discretion better to determine the fate of youth offenders by individualizing their cases—a founding component of the juvenile court that postwar reformers believed the courts no longer understood or accepted.[34]

In New York City, most juvenile judges were pressured to consider revising their court standards. In a letter to Justice Justine W. Polier, Bolin's colleague at the Domestic Relations Court, Lukas expressed his discontent with why the courts were still combined. "In my opinion," Lukas wrote, "it is no longer arguable that a juvenile court should also be a domestic relations court; the integration of these two functions has been inordinately delayed in most places." Further, he argued that this separation did not make much difference in practice; however, the change in terminology would promote a shift of the fundamental principles. "Many of us have reached the point in our discussions concerning the adjustments of youngsters' problems at which mere words begin to take on disproportionate significance." Perhaps this was a lesson learned from the press's role in perpetuating the crime: words mattered and held consequences.[35]

The trouble remained, though. Everyone had something to say about crime in Harlem, and its youths continued to bear the burden. Amid the postwar crime-wave sensationalism, these debates reignited conversations on the role of state authorities in controlling youth behaviors. Questions emerged such as whether police should be agents of repression, of correction, of prevention, or where possible, of all three. New York City youths admitted that they were unclear about police roles in their neighborhoods, but they objected to having their teachers "act as policemen." Others raised questions concerning the influence of the police in meeting the problems of delinquency but noted "the good influence of the Police Athletic League" and urged that it be advertised more widely. They made efforts to navigate the carceral terrain laid out by different authorities in the city. And before they knew it, another one intervened by way of science.[36]

Psychiatry Comes to Harlem: Social Scientific Constructions of Youth Criminality

By the last years of the 1940s, crime and delinquency had "been studied 'to death.'" The time had come "for some forthright work to be done not only to get the facts, but to do something about them." In the midst of the New York City media touting the postwar crime wave and state authorities becoming increasingly tough on crime, many social scientists, particularly psychologists, psychiatrists, and sociologists, came forth as authoritative participants in public debates dealing with crime and delinquency. Their affirmation reinforced preconceived notions of criminality that were politicized and racialized. In a domineering sweep, many of these scientists sought to "cure" delinquency, and they believed science was the missing piece in efforts to prevent crime and, potentially, purge it altogether.[37]

For resident New Yorkers, there was some skepticism as medical science entered crime and delinquency discourse. Mistrust in medical practices, especially for black New Yorkers, was long established in the community because of the racist history of being misdiagnosed, dismissed, denied treatment altogether, or worse. Thus, suspicions emerged as scientists—from within and from outside the community—concurrently joined crime-prevention efforts when the idea of "black crime" saturated public opinion.

Of the numerous scientists in New York City to enter the assault on crime in Harlem was Frederic Wertham, a German-Jewish émigré who opened the Lafargue Mental Hygiene Clinic in the basement of St. Philip's Episcopal Church on 133rd Street near Seventh Avenue. Wertham was trained in psychiatry in Vienna, Paris, London, and Munich before he joined the prominent psychiatrist Adolf Meyer at the Phipps Psychiatric Clinic at Johns Hopkins University in 1922. From there, Wertham moved to New York City in the 1930s and worked in various capacities before he started the Lafargue Clinic. Insistent that the clinic was not "a racial or interracial project," Wertham avowed that he set up in Harlem "merely because the need here [was] greater." And with hardly any money and no sponsorships from any significant reformers, he organized a staff that shared his belief in bringing psychiatry to the people.[38]

"There must be some way to bring psychiatry to the penniless urban masses," Wertham proclaimed after years of unsuccessful pleading for the extension of a psychiatry clinic in Harlem. For more than a decade, jurists, social reformers, doctors, and the clergy requested a state or city mental-hygiene clinic in Harlem. Many proposals were considered; however, it was not until a Children's Court magistrate stressed that the community's juvenile-delinquency statistics demonstrate the severity of the call that progress was made. Noting that 53 percent of Manhattan's juvenile delinquency occurred in Harlem, the Children's Court justice

believed "a competent, easy-to-reach mental-health clinic could reduce that figure tremendously." But the lack of finances or sponsorships
proved too significant of a barrier, and the advancements were shelved.[39]

Refusing to accept that only the wealthy coveted mental health, Wertham and a staff of fifteen opened the Lafargue Clinic and started to
work in the community. The staff included four black social workers; a
black psychiatrist, André Tweed, who joined immediately after getting
out of the Army; three white psychiatrists; and several pediatricians. The
African American writer and poet Richard Wright, an ardent supporter
of Wertham and the clinic, declared that the clinic's staff was "composed
of the best technical talent in the city, medical people and social workers of so high a standing in their respective fields that no one would
dare question their qualifications." Together, under Wertham's lead, they
attempted to address what they understood to be the interior and in-
tangible effects of racial discrimination; a problem that the renowned
African American novelist Ralph Ellison described as "the sickness of
the social order."[40]

The upsurge in the fields of psychiatry and psychology in the postwar years led to an increase in public and private institutions dedicated
to mental health that promoted a growing interest in the psychological roots of prejudice and discrimination. Even so, many of the medical
practitioners, social scientists, policy makers, and institutions responsible for those developments often ignored African Americans who
experienced the grim realities of the late 1940s. Harlemites, specifically,
continued to face limited employment opportunities, overcrowded
housing conditions, and limited access to equal education and health
care. It was determined that these conditions were detrimental to the
development of the psychological character of a person—"a character
that arises from the impact between urban slum conditions and folk
sensibilities." Thus, it was diagnosed that inadequate social conditions
held the ability to alter biological behaviors. Behavioral and medical scientists alike agreed that elevated frustrations caused by social circumstances led to neuroses, a mild mental illness that was often induced by
stress; and neuroses too often engendered crimes. As a result, practicing
psychiatrists and psychologists developed "social psychiatry" and "social psychology"—which held that all neuroses and psychoses, the latter
being the more severe mental disorder, do not necessarily result from in-

herent problems but that many can be attributed to society—to focus on cultural contexts of well-being. Still, African Americans were denied access to services and "treatments" in the capital of the Jim Crow North.[41]

The Lafargue Clinic targeted that population "to provide psychotherapy for those who need it and cannot get it"; however, it encountered numerous obstacles from its inception forward. The New York State Department of Social Welfare, for example, denied its early attempts to obtain a license. "We've decided that there's just no need for a psychiatric clinic in Harlem," a department representative explained to Wertham. "Well if there's no need for our clinic," Wertham refuted, "can you please give me the names and addresses of all the other places where I can send my Negro patients?" Wertham's query, though sarcastic, was an explicit shot at the discriminatory practices of the field.[42]

Before the Lafargue Clinic opened its doors in 1946, a team of social workers surveyed Harlem and its existing mental hospitals. They revealed that high rates of discrimination in practically all clinics was the rule and "that the few Negroes ever examined were treated with such contempt and sometimes brutality that they were afraid to go back." This alone, for Wertham, justified the clinic's existence. The year Lafargue opened for business, there were roughly twenty black psychiatrists in the entire country, and most practicing white psychiatrists rejected black patients who sought their services. In New York City, Bellevue Hospital did not discriminate against its patients; however, very few blacks voluntarily went because of the boilerplate diagnosis they received. Black patients seeking mental help were usually determined to be "just unhappy, or they need[ed] housing, or they [felt] downtrodden." Even black veterans were denied services. Wertham and his staff aimed to correct this. They knew that African Americans were not "a happy-go-lucky race with natural immunity to stress and neuroses." In fact, they believed because African Americans endured the most disadvantaged and ill-fitting circumstances, they needed it the most.[43]

But the problem that everyone was aware of but no one wanted to discuss was whether black folks would trust Wertham and his staff enough to give their confidence. Even potential financial supporters questioned Wertham's ability to sway this population. Wertham recalled the hesitations of "supposedly liberal rich man" about the clinic when Wertham was delivering his sales pitch: "My good Dr. Wertham, yours is a *magnificent* plan, but everyone knows that Negroes don't need any psychiatry." The man continued, "There are 400,000 Negroes in Harlem. A tiny clinic like yours won't even make a dent. And, my dear Dr. Wertham, do you honestly expect the Negroes to come to you, to trust you? One other thing, by placing your clinic in Harlem, aren't you actually practicing segregation?" Wertham slammed the door and proceeded to leave.[44]

Wertham was discouraged with the lack of financial support he received, but he continued to believe his clinic could successfully reach black patients. One night in 1945, the story goes, Wertham, Richard Wright, and Earl Brown, the latter a staff writer for *Life* magazine, were reviewing their failures to raise funds when the doctor looked at Wright and said, "If we can't get the money, let's do it without money. All we really need is talent, and I can get that." Wright and Brown introduced Wertham to the Reverend Shelton Hale Bishop, who offered them free use of his basement at St. Philip's Episcopal Church, and without any formal opening announcement, even with the space "dirty and empty, except for a small red table and some benches," two patients sat and waited to be examined.[45]

Whether Harlemites trusted Wertham and his staff was tough to know for sure; however, between 1946 and 1958, the Lafargue Clinic, which was only open two nights a week from 6:00 to 8:00 p.m., did treat as many patients as it could handle. In its first eighteen months of operation, the clinic examined more than two thousand patients—children and adults. Those who visited the clinic ranged from those who needed someone to talk to about their problems to those who "suffered from mild forms of neuroses" to the extreme cases in which a patient was considered psychotic and referred to a hospital. This was a lot of work for a staff that worked largely on a volunteer basis. The Lafargue Clinic generated limited income from small financial contributions from individual, private donors. It also charged patients who could afford to pay twenty-five cents per visit and fifty cents to testify in court on their behalf; it was free for those who could not afford to pay anything. Still, for Wertham and his staff, they were doing the work for people in need.[46]

These psychiatrists and social workers were regularly visited in their screened-off cubicles by "war veteran[s] who can't settle in a job; a young woman in love but afraid of marriage; a boy who disobeys his parents; a girl barred from her home because she is to bear an illegitimate baby; a man who is scared of people; a woman who simply 'feels queer' and wants to be told why." But not all patients sought medical attention voluntarily. For example, the Veterans Administration, the State Department of Social Welfare, and a number of private agencies sent soldiers who returned from the war to the clinic to be treated for "war neuroses." Also, many youths treated at the Lafargue Clinic were either accompanied by their parents who wanted to suppress early signs of delinquent behaviors or by police officers who presumed that "the kids ought to have a chance before they get into serious trouble." This was highly encouraged by Wertham and the Lafargue Clinic staff.[47]

"The big thing is to get the kids here," an unnamed social worker in charge of youth casework at the Lafargue Clinic told a reporter from the *New Republic*. In an article chronicling Wertham's "dream" institution, this social worker detailed why it was critical for concerned parents or arresting police officers to bring youths into the clinic instead of the precinct and explained how the clinic served as a constructive intermediary that could precede legal action. "Because once they're delinquent," the Lafargue staffer made clear, "they don't stand a chance." He continued, "The courts usually don't bother much with Negro kids; they send them directly to such places as the State Institution for Mental Defectives. They don't belong there at all: they come out of there bitter and mean and ready for crime." Thus, the clinic's intervention was deemed preventive and, to a certain extent, protective for youths brought to the clinic.[48]

The range of youth treated at the clinic varied, and the *New Republic* writer, Ralph G. Martin, was certain to highlight the differences in the treatments they received while attesting that any treatment was preferable to any punishment issued by the court. To be sure, some youths who were examined did not warrant much treatment. For example, the social worker recalled a "skinny, ragged kid in knickers walking in bashfully, [screaming] I cut my finger. Can you fix it?" Even the ones who were treated, according to the Lafargue Clinic staffer, rarely showed any inclination toward criminal behaviors, especially not violent ones. The unnamed social worker remembered one occasion when a black boy was taken to Bellevue Hospital for a psychiatric examination, and the doctor explained to his parents that the boy "had sexual fantasies because he sang a song that started out, 'Don't you feel my leg because when you feel my leg, you're gonna feel my thigh." In jest, the social worker told Martin, "God Almighty, everybody in Harlem knows that song. It's a popular recording. That psychiatrist just didn't know Harlem, that's all." For the Lafargue Clinic staffer, this validated their work and the work of social psychiatry at large, reiterating that the methods practiced at the Lafargue Clinic were not used by the Bellevue psychiatrist who "diagnosed that kid." Had he known the cultural patterns of the community, the youth's lived experience, and how they affected him— the basic principles of social psychiatry—such a judgment would not have been made.[49]

Before the establishment of the Lafargue Clinic, very few agencies worked with black youths that linked the problem of juvenile delinquency to "the outward manifestation of dangerously unresolved conflicts within." Popular opinion was that since courts and reform schools dealt with offenders of the law, there was no need for any other institution, least of all a psychiatric clinic. But for those who worked primarily with youths at the clinic, this could not be further from the truth. From its inception, the Lafargue Clinic was committed to taking on juvenile cases, and "it was naturally assumed that in Harlem the vast majority of patients would be Negro." Jeanne Smith and Hilde Mosse, two psychiatrists who worked primarily with youths, understood that their role at the clinic was to "take care of frustrated children—and Harlem [was] full of them." In the clinic's brief yet impactful existence, more than a quarter of its patients were under twenty-one years old. Notwithstanding, the Lafargue Clinic's role as a participant in the postwar criminalization of black youths in Harlem remains underexplored.[50]

The Lafargue Clinic, however, was very much an active participant, whether it knew it or not, in the postwar discourse surrounding youth, race, and crime. The psychologist S. I. Hayakawa made it clear in his *Chicago Defender* column on the clinic's efforts at combating juvenile delinquency that "the Lafargue Clinic will be to psychiatry what the front-line ambulance service is to medicine—treatment directly at the scene of action, where the casualties are heaviest and wounds are fresh." Wertham acknowledged this when he actively sought "a group of far-sighted doctors" who would use "medical science in their fight to turn potential delinquents into useful citizens." Smith and Mosse, the latter a pediatrician who worked with Wertham at Queens Hospital prior to the clinic's opening, trusted in Wertham's vision and developed ways to employ social psychiatry as a means to combat crime and delinquency in Harlem. "The principal educational device used in this part of town is punishment," the Lafargue staffers indicated. "Children are hauled into court at the slightest provocation and sent to reform schools in droves." The clinic wanted to change this or at least to disrupt the approach. For Wertham and his staff, social psychiatry did this because it understood "the economic and social lives of patients." This applied to their young patients as well.[51]

For example, Wertham recalled the experience of a sixteen-year-old girl who served a sentence in a reform school for truancy and shoplifting and was referred to the Lafargue Clinic. Following her examination, it was determined that the girl's mother was psychotic and "vented her delusions on the long-suffering daughter and husband." After more than six months of sessions with the family, the clinic arranged for the mother's hospitalization, supported the family through the transition, and "not only persuaded the girl to return to school but also found her a part-time job." The narrative was framed as a success story of a girl whose "self-respect [was] restored" because the prospect of "a normal home environment." The account was concluded with praise of the clinic and a declaration that "when the mother completes her recovery, the clinic will have saved a family." This redemptive rhetoric emphasizes the chief aim of the Lafargue Clinic, and in this particular instance, Wertham and his staff were regarded as a success for instilling "the will to survive in a hostile world."[52]

The Lafargue Clinic ceased its operations in December 1958 as the lack of financial support ultimately proved to be too serious a trouble to overcome. However, Wertham and his staff left an imprint on the broader intellectual debates materializing in Harlem on race and democracy. On the surface, the Lafargue Clinic played an important role in forcing the terms of race and the social implications of race out of sight. Similar to other "antirace" men and women of the time, they realized how such rhetoric was often reversed, so they emphasized "real" democracy by devaluing the distinction of visible racial hierarchies. Wertham and his staff acknowledged the difference between "black" and "white," and because the clinic was a site in which studies of black and white youths took place, the Lafargue Clinic held a particular relevance for civil rights leaders combating segregation throughout the country. For example, in 1951, the NAACP called on Wertham to defend its push to desegregate public schools in Delaware. Wertham cited studies conducted at his clinic to argue that Jim Crow policies affected everyone. Before the Delaware Supreme Court, he declared that both black and white youths suffered an "unsolveable emotional conflict" and that they interpret segregation "in one way and only one way—and that is they interpret it as punishment." Here, Wertham, like the psychologists Kenneth and Mamie Clark, whose Northside Center for Child Development simultaneously emerged in Harlem, understood segregation and racial discrimination as an issue that affected blacks and whites alike.[53]

Speculation surrounding the authenticity of Wertham and his staff's efforts to "treat" their patients, both young and old, emerged; however, evidence of any ulterior motives was difficult to find. The Lafargue Clinic's staff, a conglomeration of peoples from within and from without the community, joined a growing field of social scientists committed to resolving the "crime problem in Harlem." It is important to note, however, that it was spearheaded by white racial liberals who, like their Progressive-era predecessors, sought the rejection of biological determinism and the appeal of "remedial measures" to solve problems magnified by racial barriers. Despite its well-meaning intentions, even some of the clinic's most avid supporters displayed skepticism. For example, Ralph Ellison pointed out that for blacks to experience progress, it must come from within. Ellison believed, "whites impose interpretations upon Negro experience that are not only false but, in effect, a denial of Negro humanity." Thus, the idea of cultural universalism that may or may not have existed among the Lafargue staff, founders, and supporters would not prevail because, as Ellison put it, "Negroes live nevertheless as they have to live, and the concrete conditions of their lives are more real than white men's arguments."[54]

Waiting for a city-bound bus, the well-known nonfiction writer Robert Keith Leavitt noticed a "CRIME WAVE" headline plastered across a New York City newspaper. Leavitt was not able to see the rest of the story because "the words were half hidden under untended money" left for the anonymous news dealer who always left the papers for taking. The irony of untended money left for the trusting news dealer whom, he recalled, "none of us ever saw" covering a story printed to defame a people who were essentially virtuous was "as though some Wise and Humorous Hand had flung those shining discs across the black-faced type to give the lie to a slander upon mankind." Leavitt was not ready to lose faith in people amid such lawless times. "There are crimes, of course," he acknowledged, "and some ugly ones, [but] even all together they are no more than a ripple on the surface of a great, calm sea of human honesty and decency." The Harvard-educated writer was right. "For every man who betrays his kind there are ten thousand doing the honorable thing all day long, as a matter of course, a custom, a way of life," Leavitt reiterated to his readers, and he declared that people "by and large, are square shooters." As the 1940s came to an end, however, such optimism was rare. These postwar societal forces combined to build a public fear around crime that was both raced and aged. It was going to take valiant efforts by those who thought about humanity as Leavitt did to overthrow this cycle of injustice and protect its future.[55]

"Beware of the Cat on the Corner"

Deconstructing a Cycle of Outrage

There seems little doubt that juvenile delinquency is more than just the rise of a few young punks who can be speedily locked up in order to solve the whole problem. It is a social sickness which affects a great many kids in varying degrees and must be recognized and dealt with as such. Yet, unlike some diseases, its virus cannot be isolated. There is no single germ which causes it. It is but one part of a sickness of our whole social body.
—Jackie Robinson, September 9, 1959

"Just one word of warning, kids," Sammy Davis Jr. cautioned the Harlem youths who rallied against juvenile delinquency. "Beware of the cat on the corner." The acclaimed African American singer, dancer, and actor took time away from his Broadway commitment to speak to more than fifteen hundred youngsters about the perils they faced in New York City. Davis, the native Harlemite who rose from childhood stardom to become one of the most famous African American entertainers of his time, was the headliner at an event intended to add momentum to local efforts to reduce youth crime in the city. The program was organized by neighborhood leaders and sponsored by the Police Athletic League (PAL); its goal was to begin to raise funds to build a new PAL recreational center in Harlem. In Davis's address, he reminisced about his childhood days in Harlem and remembered that ten years prior he had been "a 'cat' on a Harlem corner, and [was] much too 'cool' to do with the 'squares' in the P.A.L." He told the crowd on Dewey Square (now A. Philip Randolph Square), "thanks Heaven" that show business had taken him away from the streets before he got into any serious trouble, like his close friend who was shot and killed. Admitting that he thought

PAL in his day put forth "suspiciously dull wholesome efforts," Davis encouraged youth participation because he now knew that PAL was certainly not "square."[1]

Davis, who by the end of the 1950s became mostly known in the entertainment world as a member of the Rat Pack, continued to be a voice in the nationwide efforts to curb juvenile delinquency. In a letter to the editor of the *Pittsburgh Courier*, the star of the Broadway hit *Mr. Wonderful* outlined a six-point plan for the entertainment industry, mainly people involved in the music world, to consider how they can join the fight against delinquency. First, "we would establish an organization called 'The Music Industry Council to Combat Juvenile Delinquency,' or some similar name," Davis wrote, and in addition to well-known personalities, the organization would include heads of recording companies, network representatives, representatives from talent agencies, and members of the local government. Then, Davis called on songwriters and composers "to create 10-second, 20-second, half-minute, minute, and three-minute jingles and songs on the theme, 'Don't Be a Juvenile Delinquent.'" This would encourage artists, Davis gathered, to devote time from their recording sessions to record them. Further, "leading disc jockeys throughout the nation would be solicited to join the music industry's campaign," Davis opined, "utilizing the slogan 'D.J.s Fight JD.'" The expectation was that the DJs could play the anti-juvenile-delinquency commercials and songs they were given "'round the clock." Then, he suggested, jukebox operators could join the efforts by placing "eye-catching decals on all their machines bearing hard-hitting anti-juvenile delinquency slogans." Finally, Davis pressed other top stars of the music industry to "go out into the field and make personal appearances before youth groups, settlement houses, etc." Davis concluded his letter hopeful that the outlined project was "functional, [and] workable," and because the music industry "really cover[ed] the age group concerned with juvenile delinquency, we are hitting at the heart of the situation."[2]

Unfortunately, Davis's plan to organize the Music Industry Council to Combat Juvenile Delinquency was never achieved. After several meetings with major record companies and representatives, Davis learned it was "agonizingly slow work getting a thing like this going." Disappointingly, he did not receive the support he anticipated and, sometimes, met

African American police officers instructing boys at the Police Athletic League, 1944. (Herbert Gehr / The LIFE Images Collection / Getty Images)

immediate rejection: stick to music. Goddard Lieberson, for example, was straightforward in his rejection of the proposal. Lieberson, the president of Columbia Records, did not see value in the music industry joining antidelinquency efforts and conceded to the "very well established agencies treating the problem." He admitted, somewhat cynically, that these agencies "would like nothing better than assistance from various members of the music industry." Further, Lieberson held, "such a procedure would take away the possibility of considering an interest of this sort by the music industry as being a publicity gimmick." In any case, Davis's effort was profound and one of the many attempts made by celebrities to curb juvenile delinquency at both the national and local levels.[3]

By the 1950s, not only did everyone have something to say about crime in Harlem, but there was little doubt that youth crime was a nationwide concern that warranted the attention and resources of all who were willing and able to address the problem. It was in the 1950s, the decade of delinquency, when the United States committed fully to curbing juvenile delinquency in a way comparable to the Progressive-era child-saving efforts, which led to the establishment of the juvenile court system. Of all the dramatic social changes throughout the first half of the twentieth century, it was shifts in youth behaviors and youth culture that dominated popular discourse at midcentury. And as the problem of youth crime came to the forefront, carceral responses in policy and practice attempted to find a one-size-fits-all solution. But this was not a problem that garnered such resolve, because each state, each city, and even each neighborhood faced its own issues and endured its own causes of crime. Thus, each required its own cure. Various agencies and organizations, both formal and informal, put forth efforts to combat youth crime in New York City as they saw fit—some more successfully than others. While programs offered by organizations such as the Harlem YMCA and PAL gave youths an opportunity to occupy their idle time with structured play, the stigma of criminality that attached to shifts in youth behaviors proved to be unescapable, especially for youths who did not participate in such programs. In the end, conflicting strategies on how to reach the "squares" as well as the "cats on the corner" fell short, and they reinforced a good kid / bad kid binary, with race as the focus of youth criminality.

"The Shame of America": Everybody's Problem in the Decade of Delinquency

To close the 1940s, the *Ladies' Home Journal* compiled an exhaustive report on a cross-section of American youths and published its findings in more than twenty articles.[4] The "Profile of Youth" series, produced by fifteen editors, writers, and researchers who traveled to all but three of the forty-eight states, sought to uncover the facts "about our 15,372,000 teen-agers [and] their life—and their future—as they see and live it." Further, the report aimed to disclose their thoughts about "morals, religion, politics" and what "they like to eat, to wear, and to do." These questions, according to the series editors, helped to determine "what America will be like in twenty years." In the end, the reports did not demonstrate any compelling trends or currents among American youths; instead, they showed a more obvious result: while the group demonstrated similar interests, no two young people were the same. And this was a good thing. The absence of automatic conformity was "precisely what lends strength and vigor to American democracy." Maureen Daly, one of the series editors, wrote, "They represent the modern miracle of the melting pot, in which individual energies and individual ideas are enabled to mingle harmoniously with other, contrasting energies and ideas." Further, Daly defended the nation's youths and described them as "the products of a society that trusts its own strength to the point of letting its members think for themselves."[5]

American youths entering the decade of delinquency were the products of a social and economic era that was much different from the previous decade. "Early dating, long educational years and late marriage raise[d] many problems fresh to this generation," Daly explained, "problems that make our American adolescents that most talked-of, puzzled-over and conjectured-about age group in our society." Many of the youths interviewed for the "Profile of Youth" series remembered their brothers and, in some cases, their fathers going away for World War II and assumed that their generation would engage an international fight and be charged to keep peace. They feared their personal plans for college, marriage, or a career would be "partly governed by the plans of the world." And while there were no direct mentions of the looming Cold War, the series editors alluded to the role that American youths would play in "an ideological battle that can be won or lost, without a shot being fired or a bomb being dropped," as all nations were "fighting for the loyalties and minds of their youths."[6]

Additionally, black youths, and youths of color generally, involved in the series provided valuable context on the state of race relations heading into the decade of delinquency. Myrdice Thornton, for example, a "pretty, talented senior from Hyde Park High School and daughter of the first Negro member of the Chicago Park police," discussed "the everyday insults that Negroes sort of get used to" and was adamant that her life would not be like that. Thornton, after all, was a "better-off than average" black youth in Chicago whose early childhood years were spent "in a protected 'little girl' world, with few troubles or worries." Her account included the death of her father, Spencer, who was shot and killed on duty in Chicago when he tried to break up a brawl at a picnic at the Thirty-First Street beach on Labor Day 1946. As survivors of a Chicago policeman, Myrdice Thornton and her mother, Wilda, received a pension for more than two thousand dollars a year "to help Myrdice get ahead." Still, as the teenage Thornton conveyed, neither the pension nor

the personal ties to the police department could shield her from personal experience with and memory of prejudice against her race.[7]

Myrdice Thornton was not alone. Several youths shared their experiences with blatant racism and how it impacted their early lives. One
high-school senior recounted a trip to Texas to bury her father in his
home state: "several white men came to her grandparents' home, tied the
grandfather to the bumper of the car by his feet and dragged him down
to the end of a country lane, bleeding and bruised." The unnamed teenager concluded, "we never did find out what made them mad." Others
expressed their own theories. For example, a black University of Chicago
freshman exclaimed, "I don't know why colored people keep on pretend-
ing. The white people want nothing but race extermination. Americans
still want slaves, but they're scared to say so!" Another black youth was
a bit more hopeful. "It may take a long time, maybe two or three centuries, before we're all treated equal," he described. "But things are getting
different, I can tell." He concluded, "Already people are nicer to me than
they were when I was a little boy," which shows that even the most optimistic black youth experienced racism.[8]

The progress of youth culture heading into the 1950s was more pragmatic than hopeful, according to the series editors. The compilation of
articles closed with a note reminding its readers that no one can predict with certainty what the reactions of American youths would be to
the problems and decisions they would face in their upcoming years.
At best, an educated guess revealed that youth would be "something of
what they are like now." And for those who were involved in the production of the series, this was fine, because they believed the "Profile" series
was breaking new ground journalistically and that so long as youths can
talk for themselves about themselves "on a large-scale, nation-wide,"
then informed decisions can be made about their futures. Each time
the *Ladies' Home Journal* printed a new "Profile of Youth" article, different interest groups emerged as different discussions relating to youth
culture surfaced. These included the faculty at Columbia University requesting twenty-five sets of the material to be used in different states;
a school board in Portland, Oregon, banning high-school sororities
and fraternities after *Time* magazine featured a story on sex education
prompted by a "Profile" article, "Where Do Teen-Agers Get Their Sex
Education?"; a Chicago high school using several articles as text material

for social studies classes; and a theater in San Francisco displaying pictures and texts from various articles. Parents, educators, and teenagers alike regarded the series as "important," as "something to talk about," and "something to talk over." Letters poured into the *Ladies' Home Journal* offices from high-school youths, teachers, and parents that ranged from "It isn't true" to "I can't believe it!" But most agreed, "you're writing about teen-agers as they really are."[9]

The "Profile of Youth" series did not engage much with crime and delinquency debates. This is somewhat surprising since it seemed to be the topic of conversation for mostly everyone invested in youth culture in the 1950s. The series did reaffirm, however, the Progressive-era stance of individualizing youth when it reiterated that no two youngsters were "typical—yet all [were] typical." But social scientists, especially sociologists and criminologists, and politicians were beginning to disassociate themselves from this approach in their research. For example, Paul W. Tappan, a professor of sociology and law at New York University, published a textbook, *Juvenile Delinquency*, in 1949 "to make available to students of sociology and social work, to lawyers and laymen, an up-to-date and comprehensive analysis of the major developments and problems in dealing with the juvenile delinquent and the adolescent offender." Tappan thought it was no longer feasible for legal structures to individualize youth crime and pointed to World War II and its aftermath as having served as a pivotal moment in which the significance of youth crime "matured into chronic adult criminalism." Consequently, Tappan believed, however strong one's sentiment toward youths may be, "the analysis of juvenile delinquency by sociologists, social workers, or lawyers should be clear sighted and unsentimental." He concluded, "For an understanding of delinquency or an effective method of dealing with it through social action, critical detachment will serve far better than the maudlin emotional involvement that is so easy to substitute for thinking where children are concerned." This perspective deviated drastically from earlier methods of policing youth crime.[10]

Tappan recognized the complicated nature of juvenile delinquency. In several instances, in various publications, he inquired rhetorically, "What, then, is delinquency?" Certainly, there was no more important question for Tappan and seemingly none more difficult to answer. Still, seeing as though many people continued to debate delinquency in the

1950s, it was imperative for the "experts" to have, at least, a definition established. It was suggested that the general terms of juvenile-delinquency statutes allowed courts to construct their own definitions under broad circumstances of conduct, attitude, or social situation, and to a large extent these courts did exercise their own discretion in dealing with young criminal offenders. This gray area was problematic for social scientists such as Tappan; however, one emerges from a consideration of the elements relevant to delinquency with an indefinite and unsatisfying conclusion. According to Tappan, "the juvenile delinquent is a person who has been adjudicated as such by a court with proper jurisdiction," even though he or she may be no different up until the time of court contact and adjudication from the masses of youths who were not delinquent. And delinquency, as defined by Tappan, "is any act, course of conduct, or situation which might be brought before a court and adjudicated," whether it comes to be treated in court or some other resources or remains untreated. It is important to note that under these definitions, an action may be defined as delinquent, but it cannot be measured as delinquency until a court has found and established the facts to exist. This mattered, because the numbers of youths entering the justice system steadily increased through the 1950s.[11]

In 1950, roughly 30 percent of the total arrests were persons under twenty-five years old. More specifically, the number of persons under twenty-one years of age arrested and fingerprinted reached 118,426, or 14.9 percent of all arrests. Though this percentage was slightly lower than what the Uniform Crime Reports (UCR) tabulated in the immediate aftermath of World War II, the total number of arrestees under twenty-one was up by almost ten thousand persons. It is also important to note that prior to 1942, the UCR, which was published annually by the Federal Bureau of Investigation and considered to be official data on crime in the United States, did not categorize arrests by age. Still, during the 1950s. the UCR changed how it categorized arrests by age several times. For example, the 1953 document was the last report to highlight arrests of persons under twenty-one. Thereafter, the age distinction highlighted in the "Age of Persons Arrested" section was "17 or under." This does not imply that youths under seventeen were not documented; they were included in the under-twenty-one count. By the end of the 1950s, however, changes to how youths were categorized were made because the under-twenty-one arrests had risen to roughly 20 percent of all arrests—a raw number that was well over half a million.[12]

These arrest statistics revealed not only an increase in the overall rate of youth crime based on arrests but also its spread. In 1958, the UCR first included rural arrests in its numbers. Even so, small cities, suburban towns, and rural areas were considered by that time. Courts serving communities of less than one hundred thousand persons showed an increase greater than 40 percent in juvenile delinquency. Some smaller courts reported increases over 100 percent over the course of a two-year span. A police official in a small city in the state of Washington reported, "Gang warfare reared its ugly head in our community, and already reports have reached our ears of a number of beatings having taken place. Numerous weapons, including zips made from car battery cables and car fan belts, along with a large collection of assorted knives and a homemade .22 pistol, have been seized from juveniles." Thus, the preconceived notion of youth crime as a city problem was beginning to change to an understanding of it as a problem that confronted all parts of the nation, and national politicians reentered the debate to propose solutions.[13]

"I am not an alarmist, nor is my distinguished colleague," Robert C. Hendrickson, a Republican senator from New Jersey, advised the Senate. "We do not subscribe to the gloomy prophecy that American youth is deteriorating beyond redemption, but we are disturbed by the results of our investigation." The New Jersey senator was referring to the Senate Subcommittee on Juvenile Delinquency established in 1953 to investigate the problem of youth crime throughout the nation. "The evidence received conclusively establishes juvenile delinquency as a problem of sharply increasing severity," Hendrickson continued. "Annually since 1948 both its volume and rate have mounted." In addition to an increase in rates, Hendrickson commented on the kinds of crimes that required national attention. "Younger children in larger numbers are becoming involved in serious crime," the New Jersey senator noted, and "although individual communities may be excepted, we find that all sections of our country have experienced aggravated juvenile delinquency problems." Hendrickson's stance on youth crime tracked a fine line between pessimism and truthfulness, and he concluded, "in terms of volume we are waging a losing battle against juvenile delinquency."[14]

What seemed to be overnight, American politicians with national relevance rediscovered youth crime and juvenile delinquency as a significant issue. Of all the studies, analyses, and recommendations to emerge from various authorities, including prominent political leaders, perhaps no testimony was more influential than the Senate Subcommittee on Juvenile Delinquency. In 1953, Senator Estes Kefauver presided over the Senate Judiciary Committee's nationwide investigation into juvenile delinquency. This probe was an extension of earlier hearings that investigated the causes of delinquency and potential remedies. The Democratic senator from Tennessee led the investigation, and the first witnesses to testify included a judge, a welfare worker, and a Catholic priest. The judge, Phillip B. Gilliam, was a juvenile judge from Denver, Colorado, who also served as the president of the National Council of Juvenile Court Judges. Judge Gilliam told the subcommittee that the rising rate of juvenile delinquency "provided a danger signal to the American people that their moral standards were becoming increasingly weakened," and he declared the danger to be "worse even than Communism." Further, Judge Gilliam, who said he talked with over forty or fifty youths a day while presiding over the Denver Juvenile Court, described an attitude of indifference toward the moral consequences of crime as an alarming factor in the current problem of delinquency. "There was too great an inclination not to feel badly about cheating the law," he proclaimed, "both on parts of adults and children." Judge Gilliam concluded his testimony listing the crimes most commonly committed by youths in Denver, which included auto theft and grand larceny; however, he asserted, "all juvenile troubles started with skipping school." The priest, James Moynihan, and the welfare worker, Ray Gordon, generally supported Gilliam's testimony. Father Moynihan, for example, testified that "kids in trouble don't come from religious homes," and Gordon put partial blame on the parents and suggested, "there was a great need for training men and women for the 'tremendously responsible' job of parenthood." Senator Kefauver and his subcommittee concluded their Denver visit and prepared for their next scheduled session in Washington, DC. These hearings occurred in most of the nation's major cities over the course of several months.[15]

For Senator Kefauver, his political career benefited from taking the lead on the hearings. On the one hand, he capitalized on the "panic" surrounding juvenile delinquency. Senator Kefauver described delinquency as "a symptom of the weakness in our whole moral and social fabric," and he believed its causes were "many." Such a broad definition and approach allowed the Tennessee senator to justify separate investigations and, according to some of his critics, gave him a platform that sought publicity to aid a 1956 campaign for the presidency. Acknowledging that Kefauver "would probably be a good President," Senator Thomas Hennings from Missouri believed such aspirations were driving the Tennessee senator's interests in juvenile delinquency. "He never showed any interest in the hearings on juvenile delinquency until the witness was Mrs. Eugene Meyer, wife of the owner of the *Washington Post*," Senator Hennings explained. "He knew he'd get a headline out of her." Senator Kefauver's efforts did not secure him a presidential nomination; however, he did earn the vice presidential nomination over the young Massachusetts senator John F. Kennedy, his fellow Tennessee senator Al Gore Sr., and then New York City mayor Robert F. Wagner. The Democratic pairing of Kefauver and the presidential nominee, Adlai Stevenson, lost in a landslide decision to the popular Republican incumbent, Dwight D. Eisenhower, and vice president, Richard Nixon.[16]

On the other hand, Senator Kefauver's political climb was ingrained in tough-on-crime policies—first, in the 1950 Senate Special Committee to Investigate Crime in Interstate Commerce (more popularly known as the Kefauver Committee), followed by the Senate Subcommittee on Juvenile Delinquency—and it forced President Eisenhower to take a staunch position on the problem of youth crime to stay ahead. After the findings of the Subcommittee on Juvenile Delinquency were disclosed to the Eisenhower administration, the president focused considerable attention on this "American problem." In his 1955 State of the Union Address, President Eisenhower insisted federal legislation would be proposed to assist state handling of juvenile delinquency. "To help the states do a better and more timely job," President Eisenhower affirmed in his seventy-eight-hundred-word message, "we must strengthen their resources for preventing and dealing with juvenile delinquency." Further, the president "propose[d] Federal legislation to assist the states to promote concerted action in dealing with this nation-wide problem."[17]

Less than two weeks after the 1955 State of the Union Address, President Eisenhower called for $3 million in his "Budget Message" to Congress to combat juvenile delinquency. This was by far the largest request by any president of the United States to curb youth crime. Even for President Eisenhower, whose 1954 budget allocated $75,000, this increase was substantial. "About fifty leaders in all aspects dealing with delinquents" met to discuss how the resources ought to be allocated about a month before the announcement. According to these reports, the $3 million budget would be distributed as needed, and "if the advice of these leaders is followed, each state would make its own vigorous plan for dealing with the particular juvenile crime situation in which it finds itself." In theory, it made sense; in practice, such resources were unequally distributed, and black youths were the least to benefit.[18]

"Our Lawless Youth": Curbing Youth Crime in 1950s New York City

Juvenile delinquency was a national problem, but "this one least of all" required a federal solution.[19] Federal acknowledgment of the problem was significant, because, like in the late 1930s, it strengthened individual state claims that the problem existed. It also suggested that "the institutional job of diagnosis and correction belongs mainly to the states," though federal funds were welcome. As most states and cities confronted the unyielding task of addressing youth crime, New York City was often among those considered "doing their best."[20]

Senator Estes Kefauver praised the efforts to combat juvenile delinquency in New York City. Because he believed newspapers can "both instigate and implement self-analysis of a community," the Democratic senator commended the city's efforts in a letter to the editors of the *New York Herald Tribune* and, more specifically, lauded Margaret Parton's ten-article series "Our Lawless Youth" for informing the public about the problems of youth crime in the city. "Only through an aroused community interest," Senator Kefauver wrote, "based on factual reporting, that we can ever finally solve this complex problem." And he believed Parton's articles were a start in the right direction.[21]

In June 1955, the *Tribune* printed Parton's series and declared that it was a sweeping account of youth crime in New York City. For Parton, to study juvenile delinquency, one must be prepared "to study life itself." In the introductory article for the series, Parton wrote, "For the behavior of children and adolescents, one soon discovers cannot be studied in isolation any more than the leaves of the tree can be fully understood without reference to the tree itself." Further, she explained to her readers that "to understand youth one must understand the multitudinous factors acting upon them." Thus, the search for a solution to juvenile delinquency leads down many byways—most of which become a lifetime study. The objective of "Our Lawless Youth" was not to find the "panaceas" for juvenile delinquency in New York City but to call attention to the search process.[22]

The search for solutions, according to Parton, "leads among others into the realms of biology, medicine, sociology, penology, politics and moral philosophy." The search "leads to the offices of psychiatrists, those new priests of the human soul; to pool halls, where boys lounge in desperate boredom; to courtrooms, where judges sit with varying comprehension." The search "forces the student to look with new appalled eyes at the hideous homes, streets and schools in which many of our children spend their youth, at the hypocrisy of a society which preaches moral values to its young and permits the spread, through all the media of communication, of basically immoral values." The search forces questions such as "why will we spend millions on wars, millions on highways, millions on our own entertainment, yet refuse to pay decent salaries to our teachers, our social workers, our probation officers, our young psychiatrists, our police and all the other overworked, underpaid men and women whom we ask to deal with the problems of our children?" Parton held no qualms about calling out the shortcomings of the juvenile justice system and its associated authorities that contributed to the city's problem.[23]

Although juvenile delinquency was one of the nation's most discussed problems in the 1950s, in New York City the problems were doubled because of the massive population. In 1950, 20 percent of the city's population fell within the "delinquency-hazard age bracket," between five and twenty years old; it was estimated that by 1960, roughly one in every four New Yorkers would make up the "hard core" age group of juvenile delinquents. This was on the mind of various city officials. "If juvenile delinquency is a problem now," the deputy mayor of New York City, Henry Epstein, wrote in a report to Mayor Robert Wagner, "we really have something to insure against, with regard to the future." Citing the City Planning Commission statistics, Epstein emphasized, "if the delinquency rate were to stop rising, if we could merely hold our own, *the number*

New York City teenagers with weapons, 1957. (AP Photo)

of delinquents in the larger youth population—at the present delinquency rate (roughly 2½%)—would by 1960 stand 9,000 higher than the present figure." The deputy mayor's report to Mayor Wagner led to a delinquency-prevention program in which the city invested over $3 million.[24]

In what some people considered "the most comprehensive attack on juvenile delinquency presented any community in these United States," *Perspectives on Delinquency Prevention* was the result of an eight-month investigation and suggested "new and improved programs to cope with the problem of juvenile delinquency in our [New York] city." Epstein's sixty-seven-page report was designed to help speed planning and to inform the public about some of the problems New York City faced in regard to youth crime. "I have not endeavored to produce a piece of promotional material," the deputy mayor explained; "attention in this report is focussed upon many areas where our performance is less than perfect, sometimes less than adequate." *Perspectives on Delinquency Prevention* prioritized ten programs ranging from parent education to remedial reading programs, from expanded recreation facilities to expanded police services. And while each program served a purpose, Epstein emphasized that this particular youth crime problem was not new, "nor one we can expect to meet with temporary expedients."[25]

On police services, for example, the deputy mayor reviewed the role of the police in meeting the challenge of youth crime with Police Commissioner Francis W. H. Adams. The two men agreed on the importance of adequate provisions for law enforcement, and according to Epstein, "Our city must dedicate itself to a reign of law and order." Further, this call for a more stringent "law-and-order" police force was directed at the city's youths. Epstein and Adams concluded, "youth who think they are outside limitations which the rest of society accepts have got to learn the facts of life." Thus, the primary task of the police dealing with youths was no different from when they were dealing with adults: to enforce law and order. To discern if this was successful, they turned to police reports. In particular, they cited the numbers from the Twenty-Fifth Precinct, a "high-delinquency" area in East Harlem that was "saturated" with police officers for four months in 1954. The police report disclosed that "incidents of crime dropped by 55 per cent compared with the same period in 1953." Put differently, it was determined that the increased police surveillance deterred criminal acts and improved the conditions that caused higher rates of crime and delinquency.[26]

Epstein and Adams knew that while force may "clamp down the lid for a while," it was not a long-term solution to the problems faced in their city. This was, at least for Epstein, where a police unit such as the Juvenile Aid Bureau (JAB) could come back into the picture. The JAB, though it still officially existed, was not nearly as prevalent in the 1950s as it was in the pre–World War II years. The organization, whose officers served youths under twenty-one years old by visiting their families, referring them to appropriate social agencies, and working in any way they could to eliminate specific conditions contributing to youth crime, was inadequately staffed in the 1950s. Experts recommended that 5 percent of a city's police force should be allocated to JAB work, but New York City, whose JAB staff dwindled to 196 members, had only 1 percent of its officers allocated by 1955, even as their caseloads continued to increase. Still, Police Commissioner Adams and Deputy Mayor Epstein agreed that it was imperative to pick out the areas in which the incidence of juvenile offenses was greatest.[27]

Juvenile-delinquency rates by area in the mid-1950s, according to the data collected by the New York City Youth Board, were sporadic; however, when the rates, which were composed of arrests and police referrals, were examined, Harlem loomed as the most active section of the city. In 1954, according to the precinct of occurrence, there were over nine hundred arrests and police referrals in New York's "Negro City." These statistics were skewed by perception and did not reflect an exceptional crime problem in Harlem but a policing preference. In Flushing, Queens, for example, a neighborhood in the north-central part of the New York City borough that reported a comparable delinquency rate to Harlem, the number of arrests and police referrals was half of what Harlem youths faced the same year. Further, many people interpreted the statistics as a shift toward an overpolicing of youths in general. "Police vigilance has increased since the glare of publicity began to focus on teen-agers," it was reported, and "police [were] now arresting adolescents who formerly would receive only a reprimand for their misdemeanors." Others, while not denying that a problem existed, argued that any statistics at the midpoint of a decade were not important because the figures would be "based on estimates rather than known facts." Still, policy makers needed the numbers to divvy up the resources as they looked to make use of their new monies and federal assistance for new prevention efforts.[28]

But more policing disguised as prevention continued to ramp up the criminalization of black youths in New York City. Various methods of youth crime prevention were applied, and these efforts ranged in tactics, resources, and, most important, effectiveness. Some youth-serving agencies were more traditional in their approach, and they built new community centers that mimicked Progressive-era settlement houses, which preached recreational activities for youths to divert their intrinsic turn to violence. Others were more analogous to the area approach, a model introduced by Clifford R. Shaw in the 1930s and 1940s that met the city's youths in their own spaces. Even so, as the latter became more prominent, both techniques had problems.[29]

For example, the Catholic Charities of the Archdiocese of New York acquired the Harlem Boys Club in 1953 "to spearhead its drive against the onslaught of juvenile crime and lawlessness in Harlem." With a budget of over $100,000 a year donated by Catholic charities, Rev. George L.

Mooney headed the $1 million center on West 134th Street near Fifth Avenue (now the Hansborough Recreation Center) and within the first five months of operation built a membership of over one thousand Harlem youths. The center offered various recreational activities that included activity clubs centered on checkers, softball, basketball, boxing, dancing, photography, and music. The youths were divided into two groups by age, "youngsters" (seven to fourteen years old) and teenagers (fourteen to eighteen years old), to maximize their space and to better manage out-of-town camp trips. For Father Mooney and his staff, grouping the youths in clubs at a young age was important. "Psychologists call the ages from 9 to 14 the 'gang age,'" the Irish, gray-haired, affable Father Mooney explained, "because youngsters of that age group tend to gang up." This, for the Catholic priest, was good. "There's nothing in the world wrong with gangs—or clubs—if they are taken off the streets and placed under adult supervision," Father Mooney continued. "All human beings in every sphere and in every activity form clubs." For him, the center encouraged youngsters and teenagers to "gang up in a good way"; however, the message was being lost because he was, arguably, preaching to the choir.[30]

The Harlem Boys Club's biggest problem, like PAL as discussed by Sammy Davis Jr. and like the settlement houses "in the old days," was its demographic makeup. Most of the youths who participated in the center's activities did not have criminal records or histories, and they were more likely part of the "sound" youths, not the "three to five per cent delinquent." This was presumably the biggest problem that New York City's scores of community centers and community-center approach in general faced. "The so-called bad kid outside," admitted the director of the Riis–Red Hook Community Center in Brooklyn, Walter J. Weinert, "usually needs the community center activities more than the good kids inside." Weinert's sentiment captured a quandary that even the most community-oriented organizations could not figure out. "If you opened the doors to the hostile, destructive teen-agers," he recognized, "you will drive out the cooperative ones already in the fold." This, however, was laden with presumptions about "bad kids," and further, in a city such as New York, the question of racial membership in community centers intensified the already complicated predicament.[31]

Social workers, according to Parton's reports of spot-check visits, took on this problem directly. According to Parton, "some like the thriving

Hudson Guild in Chelsea" (a neighborhood on the West Side of Manhattan) were "meeting the flux of Puerto Ricans into the neighborhood by an all-out integration program which includes Spanish lessons for the white members of the guild." The *Herald Tribune* reporter also mentioned the Educational Alliance on the Lower East Side of Manhattan, which focused on "keeping the 'good' kids in their fold busy with dozens of activities tailored to their individual needs," as an organization succeeding in its handling of this problem. As a result, the center was "a great professionalized beehive of a place, buzzing with happy teen-agers," even though, admittedly, "outside the streets [were] dark and the gangs congregate[d]." Generally, Parton reported, social workers and their respective agencies housed in disparate centers continued to face the problems of youth crime and delinquency with established techniques and blind optimism. One exception, though, was the Manhattanville Center, which "scrapped a great deal of the traditional 'social worker' approach, and who branch[ed] out imaginatively in new directions."[32]

The Manhattanville Center, located on West 126th Street, was different from other community centers that cropped up across the city. Not only did it lack the grandeur of some of the other centers, but when one walked through the battered front door into the scuffed entrance hall of the Manhattanville Center, the boys and girls who turned up were not at all like the youngsters in other agencies. Plainly, these were tough kids, "weedy, belligerent, suspicious, [and] swaggering in the black leather jackets which distinguish so many gang members." And as difficult as this may have made the job for the center's workers, it was a welcome challenge for most. "Sure, they're members of gangs, and real tough gangs too," Roy Kurahara, a social worker at the center expressed. "That's the whole point of our place—to hell with the good kids!" Kurahara, a native Californian of Japanese descent, worked primarily with Puerto Rican and Irish youths in Harlem, most of whom belonged to different neighborhood gangs.[33]

Kurahara was described as "one of those rare persons who is able to subordinate all the techniques learned in schools of social work to his own warm enthusiasm for youngsters." He made use of the youth gang organization to impart democratic methods. He considered learning self-government vital to curbing delinquency rates and conducted House Council meetings with the youths of the Manhattanville Center as a tactic. "The House Council," Kurahara explained, "had been created to try to give the young anarchists a sense of group responsibility, and it seemed to be working." The participating youngsters voluntarily discussed subjects of interest to neighborhood kids, covering topics relevant both inside and outside the center. For example, in a mimeographed magazine put out by the House Council, among the interesting items were a vote on whether smoking was allowed in the pool room, debates on drinking, and also an original poem on "dope addiction." Parton's *Herald Tribune* reported on a House Council meeting led by Kurahara, in her report on the Manhattanville Center. "Mr. Kurahara sat down near the center of the table," Parton wrote, "and grinned around at the group." The group included a dozen boys, ranging from thirteen to sixteen, and one girl, "the leader of a girls' gang called 'The Rubies.'" Almost all the youths who were present had been in trouble with the law, ranging from car theft to assault with a deadly weapon. Parton noted, "Almost all of the boys, even the thirteen-year-olds, smoked incessantly."[34]

Parton's report of these meetings provides valuable insight into not only how they ran but also how these youths viewed their own spaces from their own perspectives. To start the meeting, Kurahara announced that the people at Riverside Church invited the youths of Manhattanville Center to a dance at their hall. He followed, "Can anybody think of a way we might help them?" After a spell of silence, the youths started to toss around ideas. "Maybe we could take in money at the door, and make some dough for them," one boy proposed; however, Kurahara explained that the dance was free. Then a Puerto Rican boy offered to lend his collection of mambo records to the dance committee—everybody agreed that was a fine idea. Then Kurahara reminded the youths that they were to be on their best behavior as guests at the Riverside Church dance. "Now look fellows," Mr. Kurahara said, opening a new subject. "Here at the center you're kind of at home, and you can do some things which outside people might not like very much. Dancing the fish, for instance. Tonight you've gotta decide whether or not you're gonna dance the fish at Riverside Church." The fish, as described by Harry Alpert, a social worker from the Bronx, was "their favorite dance these days." Alpert continued, "You don't move at all when you dance the fish. Just take a step now and then, maybe. Or sway a little bit, or turn your head." While there was a chorus of protest from the youngsters, who believed it was "not a dance unless they could 'go fishin,'" one of the older boys in the group spoke up: "You gotta remember a church is different." In the end, they decided by a democratic vote not to insist on fishing at Riverside Church.[35]

After the House Council meeting adjourned, Kurahara stuck around to follow up with Parton. "Did you see that little kid I had my arm around?" Kurahara asked Parton after the meeting. "Well, last week he got hurt in an accident, and one of our workers went to the hospital with him," Kurahara continued. "You know what he told her, while the doctor was stitching him up?" The young boy, according to Kurahara, told the social worker, "Don't bother letting my Ma know where I am—she don't care." The boy's mother, Kurahara added, "was a mental defective with ten other children." Kurahara believed that most of the parents of the youngsters who populated the Manhattanville Center were this way. "Alcoholism, drugs, over-breeding, broken homes, imbecility—around here they usually have it in their background," he said of the parents. Therefore, Kurahara maintained that it was the primary responsibility of the center and its workers to do the things the parents were supposed to do. "We take 'em to the dentist, because most of their teeth are falling out. We go to court with them. We listen to their problems. We try to get them jobs, and to raise their standards and ideals. We try to get them out of this neighborhood, because there's nothing good about it," Kurahara affirmed; "we're acting as substitute parents."[36]

As innovative as Kurahara and the Manhattanville Center were in regard to promoting integration while curbing youth crime, their substitute-parent attitude toward delinquency was as antiquated as the term itself. The popularization of the concept of juvenile delinquency in Western societies, according to the criminologist Geoff K. Ward, can be traced to the late eighteenth century and early nineteenth, "when the United States and older Western European nations were transitioning from rural, agricultural societies to rising industrial powers." Since the founding of the modern juvenile justice system, regulating a parental state to steer troubled youths into paths of self-discipline and social integration was always employed. In this way, the Manhattanville Center was not exceptional, and there were little qualms about it among the center's staff. "We've given up trying to work with the parents because the parents have already rejected the kids," Kurahara expressed. "It's a big job we have, because it takes maybe three or four years to get one of these kids straightened out. But if the parents have defaulted, who's to do the job?" In theory, the substitute-parent method was less problematic than in practice. In theory, most efforts to combat juvenile delinquency involved some element of establishing a parental state. In practice, on the other hand, such an approach increased the gap between the community and the state because the growing social distance reduced levels of trust and familiarity, limited professional accountability to constituent communities, and diminished the political capital of civic leaders.[37]

This problem was not necessarily alleviated when state institutions carried out more community-based methods. Acting on the advice of civic groups and surveys conducted among citizens, for example, New York City Youth Board members dedicated to reconstructing and guiding youngsters went out to meet the city's youth in their own element. In what resembled the area approach, the "detached worker" program employed by the Youth Board planted its employees in their assigned communities. "Differing distinctively from the give-a-kid-a-ball theory and its antithesis the strap-on-the-end-now-and-then-makes-better-men," the Youth Board members infiltrated street gangs and clubs determined to gain the confidence of its members and alter their direction. "Working on a 'round the clock schedule," Malcolm Nash of the *New York Amsterdam News* reported, "the street worker hangs out in the area, talks to the neighborhood people, tries to learn what gang hangs out there, where and who the leaders are." The problem with this approach was less about the method and more about the people involved. Because most Youth Board workers were from outside the community they served, it often took too much time to gain the trust required for success.[38]

"Understand Us. Help Us.": Youth Efforts to Combat "Our" Delinquency

"The problems of the youth of any community must be counted among the most important problems of the community as a whole," Constance Curtis of the *New York Amsterdam News* wrote, "for in youth lie all the seeds of tomorrow, either for good or for ill."[39] This message resonated across all five boroughs of New York City as members of each made efforts to address the issues pertinent to their youths. George Gregory

Jr., for example, director of the Forest Neighborhood House in the Bronx, like Kurahara and the Manhattanville Center, assigned house council leadership roles to its young members to prime "young people to grow into real leaders." Gregory, a graduate of Columbia University and its first black basketball player to be elected captain, believed that "education for democracy and community improvement" was the "basis for being." Similarly, in Brooklyn, Albert Edwards, the executive director of the Stuyvesant Community Center and former principal of the academic school of the State Training School for Boys at Warrick, maintained a corrective attitude toward juvenile delinquency and made use of it at the community center. "The supervisor of a Community Center should have had experience in a corrective institution before going into work on the preventative level," Edwards disclosed. "In this manner the supervisor will be able to recognize tendencies which may eventually lead to trouble for a boy." Edwards was passionate about his kids at the center and was dedicated to the social problems facing the youths of Brooklyn.[40]

In Harlem, the community-based efforts to combat youth crime were extensive, and not all took the form of a center. For example, the residents of 141st Street printed a newsletter, *Your Block Is Your Concern*, that covered topics from sports to local news and business, as well as announced local events from charities to Sweet Sixteen birthday parties. Edited by Esther Stanley and Ann Langford, this local newsletter built on a long history of community-based initiatives and organizing that reminded Harlemites in the 1950s that long ago, "families realized that teamwork was the only way to build a better community." Implied, in the decade of delinquency, was a call for community members to increase their organized efforts to curb youth crime in their own neighborhood. Ranging from large institutional endeavors to on-the-ground attempts made by the youths themselves, the Harlem community became diligent in its efforts to protect its young people.[41]

The Harlem Branch YMCA, under the leadership of Rudolph J. Thomas, was already a social and cultural center; however, by the 1950s, it became, arguably, the largest community-based institution committed to combat juvenile delinquency in the city. When the branch celebrated its fiftieth anniversary in 1951, the Harlem Renaissance poet Langston Hughes professed, "Almost every young colored man arriving in New

York during the last thirty years has stopped for a period at the Harlem Branch YMCA." And Thomas was present through it all. Thomas started working at the Harlem YMCA in 1920 as an elevator operator and witnessed many of its changes firsthand. He brought that same drive and persistence with him into the executive director position and continued to improve the activities, membership, and the physical spaces of the Harlem branch.[42]

In the Harlem YMCA's more concerted efforts targeting youth crime and delinquency, it sought youth gang members to participate in organized activities. More specifically, in the mid-1950s, the Harlem Tigers, "a gang of 15-year-olds on [their] way to Sing Sing," were regularly arrested after street fights in the city. In one instance, when the involved youths were expected to go to jail for their fracas, the arresting officer "knew that even a bad boy could be good, if given a chance," and required the boys to spend hours at the Harlem YMCA. By agreement, the youths started working out their excess energy at the Harlem branch, and the gang became a team. The Harlem Tigers gang became the Harlem Tigers athletic sports team that represented the Harlem YMCA in interbranch basketball games, baseball games, swim meets, and boxing matches. Many Harlem residents, including professional athletes such as Jackie Robinson and Roy Campanella who were invested in curbing juvenile delinquency, donated their time to aid the many programs sponsored by the branch and "helped to make responsible citizens of today's 'Harlem Tigers.'"[43]

Not all youth gangs refocused their energies to the gym, and there were still many who stayed involved in street activities. From the Imperial Counts to the Dukes, the Viceroys, and the Bladesman, countless youngsters involved in street gangs never crossed paths with the organizational antidelinquency efforts and instead regularly encountered detectives and police officers. Benjamin Olivo, for example, a member of a Harlem gang known as the Seminoles, shared his account of a gang execution in 1955 with a reporter from *Life* magazine. Olivo recalled the "kangaroo court" decision to shoot Carlos Luis Feliciano for stabbing Johnny, an ally to the Seminoles. After conferring with the leader of the Seminoles, "Dillinger" Ramirez, a fellow Seminole took it upon himself to take action. Olivo told the *Life* reporter that after Dillinger shot Feliciano, "we all gave each other some skin." For Olivo, the gang's loyalty to one another provided a sense of belonging, a common trope among youths in the decade of delinquency. For those who were involved in combating youth crime in Harlem, these rare but criminal acts were what worried them most, because they had tremendous repercussions.[44]

These kinds of occurrences did not deter members of the community from continuing to be diligent in their efforts toward curbing juvenile delinquency in Harlem. In fact, because "the multi-million dollar juvenile delinquency program, [was] the same old story—white folks talk about Negro crime, but when they get the cash they hire the whites and keep the projects in the white neighborhoods," most programs in Harlem were effectively grassroots and relied on their own people and resources.[45]

There were few Harlemites who were more committed to organizing on the ground in the 1950s than Samuel Richardson, a black businessman who operated a novelty shop in Harlem. Committed to racial progress on the communal level, Richardson routinely organized groups to contest unfairness and promote justice in several realms. For example, with the assistance of the Reverend Millard A. Stanley and William Spruill, Richardson initiated the model-block program in 1954, which sparked a clean-community campaign in Harlem. The following year, he founded the Harlem Business Council "to bring together small business operators and other self-employed persons; to initiate a general program for them, and to build and perpetuate good will for Harlem locally, nationally and internationally." Richardson's business interests combined with an interest in combating youth crime, and he applied his organizing skills to start a drive against delinquency.[46]

In August 1958, Richardson formed the United Drive Against Juvenile Delinquency with the support of other small-business owners in Harlem. They approached the problem of delinquency with a six-point program that exposed youths to government, chambers of commerce, employment, entertainment, public relations, and a publication. This represented a shift from the approaches that emphasized democratic leadership as a means of prevention, as Richardson used his specialty as a businessman to address the problem. "The chamber of commerce," Richardson said, was "designed to stimulate interest and encourage youngsters to go into business." He continued, the employment exchange "screen[s] teenagers for jobs and teach[es] them to appreciate earning money instead of begging for it." Moreover, the entertainment bureau was established "to seek out talented youngsters and help them develop such talents." As Richardson constructed plans to get other businesspeople involved in his endeavor, perhaps the most significant accomplishment to come out of the initial campaign was setting up a mothers conference as a method of reaching the "junior citizens."[47]

Several weeks after the first meeting, Richardson and United Drive Against Juvenile Delinquency set up "a committee of conscientious and civic minded Harlem mothers" and formulated plans for the Harlem Mothers Conference. Ruth Hill, Orneater Jackson, and Olivia Fisher Cooper met with Richardson to develop a high-reaching purpose for the conference. According to Richardson, the purpose of the conference was to arouse the interest of all mothers of the Harlem community, to acquaint them with the details of the six-point program, to discuss how the community would benefit from actively participating in the campaign, and "to reason together and get a full understanding as to how we can and will work together with our little citizens, junior citizens, senior citizens, landlords, neighborhood business people and public officials harmoniously to root our juvenile delinquency."[48]

The Harlem Mothers Conference Against Juvenile Delinquency held its first official meeting at Richardson's Service Center in September 1958. There, they adopted a program and started to discuss the formation of a Harlem Young Citizen Council, a committee designed by and led by Harlem youths. The enthusiasm surrounding a potential organization spread rapidly. The Reverend Robert Woolbright from the Universal Baptist Church on West 135th Street reached out to the Harlem Mothers Conference and offered his church as a space for the youth council to be headquartered. Even Senator Estes Kefauver sent a letter to Samuel Richardson commending him on the organizational efforts in Harlem and wished him continued success.[49]

Richardson returned the gratitude not only to his supporters but also to the *New York Amsterdam News* for its encouragement. "Words are insufficient to enable me to express my appreciation for the sincere cooperation your paper the *New York Amsterdam News* gave me in this drive," the executive director of the United Drive Against Juvenile Delinquency wrote. Richardson acknowledged how instrumental the *Amsterdam News* coverage of his efforts and the efforts of those involved in the Harlem Mothers Conference was in capturing both the local and national attention needed to extend the drive "to bring a new life to our youth in our community." For the youths in Harlem, this "new" life inspired them to organize their own efforts to combat juvenile delinquency—as they experienced it.[50]

The Harlem Young Citizens Council (HYCC) was an outgrowth of the Harlem Mothers Conference Against Juvenile Delinquency, and it was composed of an enthusiastic group of youths from the neighborhood who wasted little time in pinpointing what they knew to be "the real cause of juvenile delinquency"—adult delinquency. The HYCC joined a longer history of youth-centered organizing against juvenile delinquency. The *New York Amsterdam News* reporter Allan McMillan covered earlier efforts of youth organizing in the 1950s. "The youngsters want to do something about it," McMillan wrote; "they want better living conditions, better food, clothing and education." He continued, "No matter what the grownups say or do, the young folk, the teenagers who make up our coming generation are tired of being cramped up with no place to breathe." Further, McMillan reported on organized efforts by the United Youth Movement for the Prevention and Elimination of Crime. Under the guidance of the Reverend Arcelius Ashburn, the pastor of the little Model Baptist Church in Harlem, Vera Trotter, fourteen, and Joseph Singleton, fifteen, organized a group of youngsters in the neighborhood who "wanted an opportunity to help themselves." Reverend Ashburn, "a man possessed with vision and courage," explained to McMillan that it had been his dream for more than fifteen years to help youths who rebelled against their conditions. The change, according to Reverend Ashburn, was that "the kids themselves have decided to do something about their conditions and it's a great thing." Within a month, the United Youth Movement for the Prevention and Elimination of Crime recorded one hundred members.[51]

But the HYCC stood out for several reasons. First, unlike some of the earlier youth-inspired organizations, it was not founded in the church. Second, and perhaps more importantly, it gave much more agency to its youth in how they organized and what was placed on their agenda. This was important because for the youths involved in the council, they believed it was unfair to brand youths as delinquents and allow adults to shed responsibility without reproach. The HYCC held a community

The Brooklyn Dodgers' Jackie Robinson and Roy Campanella instructing youths at Harlem YMCA, 1948. (Bettmann / Getty Images)

forum and unanimously agreed that in fairness to all concerned, they would "strike out the word 'juvenile' and use the word 'our' instead." The parents in attendance agreed to cooperate and to accept more responsibility for juvenile delinquency. They also committed to stepping up their efforts to relieve the conditions that led young people to delinquent behaviors in their neighborhood. Even Samuel Richardson, who was in attendance, was persuaded by the youths' call and changed the name of his own campaign against youth crime to United Drive Against *Our* Delinquency. There was little question that this was their council, their fight, and their community that they served.[52]

Jackie Robinson was perhaps one of the most unheralded proponents of youth culture and opponents of juvenile delinquency in the 1940s and 1950s. He often reminisced about his own childhood and how he needed the right guidance to dodge trouble as a youth. Admitting that he was "no angel" as a kid, Robinson blamed this on the fact that he had too much free time on his hands to keep out of mischief. For that reason, he committed time and money to combating juvenile delinquency from the earliest days of his professional baseball career forward. Robinson hosted numerous sports camps at the Harlem YMCA; wrote various newspapers columns on the problem of youth crime; regularly called on athletes and celebrities to be more involved with youth organizations seeking to steer youngsters down the right path; and, in 1959, started a program, Athletes for Juvenile Decency, that connected professional athletes with young adults in schools, settlement and youth houses, PAL and Catholic Youth Organization groups, the YMCA, and other youth organizations. Though the various antidelinquency programs and organizations that Robinson worked closely with targeted youths of all races and ethnicities, he made no apologies "for being particularly interested in the youngsters of [his] own race." In February 1962, on the eve of his election to the Baseball Hall of Fame, Robinson wrote, "I just want to say that if this can happen to a guy whose parents were virtually slaves, a guy from a broken home, a guy whose mother worked as a domestic from sun-up to sun-down for a number of years; if this can happen to someone who, in his early years, was a delinquent and who learned he had to change his life—then it can happen to you kids out there who think that life is against you." Such rhetoric, which combined self-help and racial uplift, saturated antidelinquency programs in post–World War II America, and, here, Robinson was no exception.[53]

Unfortunately, even with all the crime and delinquency prevention efforts that emerged in the 1950s, the number of youths, especially black youths, arrested continued to rise, which pointed to a function of policy and practice as opposed to changes in behaviors. By the 1960s, persons under twenty-one years old routinely constituted over 20 percent of all reported arrests in the United States. In 1964, there were as many arrests of persons under twenty-one as the total number of arrests recorded just one decade earlier—in the height of the decade of delinquency. But because arrest statistics continued to be used as the indicator of crime, regardless of the prevention efforts in place, the police controlled the crime and delinquency rates, decided who was presumed criminal, and perpetuated the cycle of outrage.[54]

"In All Our Harlems"

Policing Black Youths through the War on Crime

They are dying there like flies; they are dying in the streets of
all our Harlems far more hideously than flies.
—James Baldwin, "A Report from Occupied Territory," July
11, 1966

"This is the hardest day of our lives," William Craig told reporters at a
crowded news conference outside New York's State Supreme Court on
April 4, 1973. Having spent nearly a decade in jail on a first-degree murder charge, Craig was one of the four Harlem Six youths released after
pleading guilty to a lesser manslaughter charge; the other two continued
to serve sentences. The court's promise of freedom forced the four young
men to make the pragmatic decision rather than face the uncertainty of
another trial for the 1964 murder of Margit Sugar, a white secondhand-
clothes dealer in Harlem. The three previous trials were complicated,
and it became clear that nobody wanted to go through another trial
that promised an uncertain verdict. In recognition of the overwhelming
power of the state, the difficult decision was made to accept guilt for an
offense for which they upheld their innocence.[1]

What started on a sunny April day in 1964, the case of the Harlem Six
confirmed the persistence of race as a decisive factor in American notions of crime and delinquency. A sequence of events that spanned three
decades, the intertwined stories of William Craig, Wallace Baker, Walter Thomas, Ronald Felder, Daniel Hamm, and Robert Rice—the latter
two were released in 1974 and 1991—expand our understanding of youth
encounters with the carceral state in the twentieth century. More specifically, their experience in Harlem was, as James Baldwin poignantly
described it, "true of every Northern city with a large Negro population."
The plight of black youths in postwar American cities demanded that

they learn how to navigate the currents of urban spaces—knowing that at any given moment, they can swell. Such currents, in this instance, involved a justice system and associated authorities that reified black youths' preconceived notions of an unjust system.[2]

The story of the Harlem Six, for all its particularities, points to a critical juncture in the carceral turn in the "City That Never Sleeps." Despite inklings of progress in the first half of the twentieth century, crime was recast as a racial problem that warranted punitive state responses, and efforts to create a fair and impartial justice system gave way to systemic and institutionalized racism. By the 1960s, anticrime laws, most notably "stop-and-frisk" and "no-knock," were disproportionately being enforced in predominantly black communities, the police were reaffirming their position as the "frontline soldiers" for the impending War on Crime, and black youths continued to bear the burden of a justice system that denied their innocence and presumed their criminality.[3]

"Harlem Is a Police State": Creating a Climate for Civil Unrest

"The police in Harlem, their presence is like occupation forces, like an occupying army," Malcolm X told the audience at the Militant Labor Forum of New York on May 29, 1964. "They're not in Harlem to protect us; they're not in Harlem to look out for our welfare," the black Muslim minister continued. "They're in Harlem to protect the interests of the businessmen who don't even live there." Malcolm X had just returned from a trip abroad, and his charges concerning the police state in Harlem reinforced many of the claims made by other Harlem residents and organizations. In 1964, the temper of central Harlem had grown sullen as its residents faced a surge in police presence directly connected to new anticrime laws and a "Hate-Gang scare" in the print media. Combined with the political buzz surrounding Harlem, this created an environment that sparked both major and minor incidents between the police and the community.[4]

The incident that sparked the case of the Harlem Six took place on April 17, 1964, when a fruit stand was overturned by black and Puerto Rican youths around 128th Street and Lenox Avenue. The documented reports of the "Harlem Fruit Riot" changed over time; however, the one constant was that when the police showed up to stop the youngsters from smacking each other with apples and oranges, the youths then "changed their targets, hurling fruit at the policemen." The policemen apprehended several of the youngsters and sent out a call for help, to which roughly twenty-five more police officers responded. Several of the eyewitness accounts that detailed what ensued were disturbing. In a tape-recorded statement with a representative of Harlem Youth Opportunities Unlimited (HARYOU), Wallace Baker, nineteen, recalled seeing "some little boys picking up fruit from the ground," when three policemen "grab[bed] one between his legs and [got] ready to hit him with a stick." Baker continued, "So I ran over and tried to stop him. And two of them jumped on me and beat me for nothing." Baker was then put in the patrol car and handcuffed to Daniel Hamm, eighteen, who also intervened "to keep him [the policeman] from shooting the kids." For Baker and Hamm, this marked the beginning of their long struggle with the justice system.[5]

For many Harlem residents, the "policemen's inept handling of a minor situation" reinforced their skepticism of the heightened police presence in the community. "The black people of Harlem have come to understand the situation quite well," one writer wrote in *Challenge*, a weekly newspaper funded by the Progressive Labor Movement. "When the deal goes down, these cops will murder, maim, and brutalize the Negro people of New York just as fast as their partners in the south." For black youth especially, their trepidation toward law enforcement existed for years; however, in this moment, the newly prepared "stop-and-frisk" and "no-knock" state laws roused a different antipolice sentiment—a feeling fueled by dishonesty and injustice.[6]

These two bills, "stop-and-frisk" and "no-knock," were proposed at a conference with New York's Governor Nelson A. Rockefeller in January 1964. Subsequently, top law enforcement officials from New York City agreed on the terms "to reestablish law and order." The two bills implemented proposals to combat crime, as well as clarified the rights of police to frisk suspects and expand the use of search warrants to be executed without notice to the occupants of a building. The 1964 Uniform Crime Reports tell the tale: New York City was engulfed with street crime, reporting a 23 percent increase since the turn of the decade. "In an era in which crime is increasing four times as fast as the population," said Governor Rockefeller, these new laws were needed "because of the uncertainty in the present law and because the police must be provided now with the sound tools to carry out their sworn duty to protect the public against serious crimes." These anticrime bills were not passed without protest from liberal Republican and Democratic legislators, African American political organizations such as the National Association for the Advancement of Colored People (NAACP) and the Congress of Racial Equality (CORE), and resident New Yorkers from all parts of the city. Nor were they passed without countless victims, mostly black youths, who entered the criminal justice system for the first time.[7]

In the case of "stop-and-frisk," it was argued, the uncertainty around detainments caused tumult between citizens and police because police officers were rarely certain whether a detention was constitutionally valid. Police officials argued that the mandatory exclusionary rule of *Mapp v. Ohio* restricted effective police action. Prior to the 1961 Supreme Court decision, which declared that evidence obtained in direct violation of the Fourth Amendment's prohibition on unreasonable search and seizures could not be used in criminal prosecutions, half of the country's state courts, New York included, permitted incriminating evidence in state and federal courts regardless of how it was seized. Police officials demanded that their state legislature pass a law that "would permit a policeman to detain and frisk a suspect on the grounds of reasonable suspicion, thereby eliminating the necessity of grounds for arrest." Thus, urged by law enforcement agencies including district attorneys, police chiefs, sheriffs, the state police, the State Commission of Investigation, and the State Council of Churches, New York enacted a "stop-and-frisk" statute. The bill was passed by a near-party-line vote of thirty-three to twenty-two—only one Democrat voted for it, and only one Republican voted against it.[8]

There was less opposition to the "no-knock" bill, which was approved by a vote of forty-three to twelve. The "no-knock" law allowed police officers to break open a door or window without prior notice to the occupants of the building to execute a search warrant. The bill's proponents, who included Governor Rockefeller and New York City's Mayor Robert F. Wagner, argued that the necessity for such a law was twofold. First, the element of surprise did not allow the occupants time to destroy convictable evidence. "Such evidence as narcotics or policy slips are often thrown out of windows or flushed down toilets before police can seize it," New York assemblyman Richard J. Bartlett imparted. The other aim of the bill was to protect police officers. According to Bartlett, "A policeman who knocks or announces that he is about to enter often gives the suspect enough warning to get out a gun or a knife." Though the "stop-and-frisk" law dominated the headlines, perhaps rightfully so, the combination of the two anticrime laws drastically transformed the relationship between police authority and the residents of New York City, especially in Harlem.[9]

Opponents of the new anticrime laws in New York questioned their constitutionality and vagueness. Of the "stop-and-frisk" bill, for example, a representative of the State Bar Association who argued for the bills to be vetoed said, "Nowhere, in the history of Anglo-Saxon jurisprudence have we so closely approached a police state as in this proposal to require citizens to identify themselves to police officers and 'explain their actions' on such a meager showing." Even the less-opposed "no-knock" bill, according to the association, "flies in the face of a long-established policy that 'a man's home is his castle,' and for the state to invade it, it must strictly comply with safeguards which have been found to be important over the years." Black members of the Progressive Labor Movement in Harlem, the Marxist-Leninist political organization established after a split with the Communist Party, were more direct in their critique of the laws, describing them "as close to any of Hitler's laws as any other law in this country." But all the concerns were met with a straightforward rebuttal from city authorities: times have changed.[10]

The New York City Police Department, at least according to its commissioner, Michael J. Murphy, had its hands full in 1964. Not only did these two laws impede the perception of police throughout the city, especially among communities of color, but it also added to the visibility of the police state being established. Fully aware that *"police are confronted with serious problems in 1964; problems not encountered a few brief years ago,"* Commissioner Murphy negotiated complicated terrain. On the one hand, with the world's fair set to open in New York City, the police were responsible to preserve the peace and protect the people. "As the threats and boasts of wild and unreasonable actions" loomed, the police commissioner showed an ardent stance on crime because he believed that "the show of strength is the greatest deterrent to unlawful action." And as a result, more than twenty-five thousand men were assigned to twelve-hour shifts throughout the city.[11]

On the other hand, the many police brutality charges that the department confronted, including ones stemming from the "Harlem Fruit Riot," suggest that the department's strength was not just a show. The national director of CORE, James Farmer, declared, "Police brutality in our city is not a problem which began or ended with the World's Fair." Farmer pointed to several instances in which excessive police force was utilized, and he concluded there existed "an ongoing problem of police violence against individual Negroes and Puerto Rican unjustified and unprovoked." But according to Commissioner Murphy, his police force was being "subjected to unfair abuse and undeserved criticism" from those who sought "to destroy their effectiveness and to leave the city open to confusion." Contrary to what the CORE director penned in his statement, which captured the viewpoint of people throughout the streets of New York City, the police commissioner was adamant that there was "*no pattern of brutality in the New York City Police Department. There has not been—there will never be.*"[12]

If the Commissioner Murphy's claims about the brutality allegations were true, there were masses of black New Yorkers who never received the memo. For the youths involved in the fruit-stand scuffle, for example, the course of their lives was significantly altered by their interactions with the police on that day. Once the confrontation ended, several members of the crowd were taken away in patrol cars to the 135th Street station. Unbeknown to the authorities, about thirty youths followed and formed a picket line, chanting, "Stop police brutality!" Outside the police station, the marching and chanting lasted for three hours; inside, according to the youths' recorded testimonies, the police brutality was just starting. "When they got us to the precinct station," Wallace Baker detailed, "they beat us practically all that day, and then at night they took us to Harlem Hospital to get X-rays." Daniel Hamm's experience was similar. "They beat us till I could barely walk and my back was in pain," Hamm described. "They got so tired beating us they just came in and start spitting on us." The police department denied all accusations.[13]

The evidence connected to these beatings proved otherwise. The mothers of both Baker and Hamm affirmed their sons' testimonies and contacted a black lawyer, George Sena, to defend their claims. In a tape-recorded statement with an interviewer from HARYOU, Mrs. Baker remembered going to the hospital "to sign for Wally because they thought they had broke his neck." "His neck was over one-sided," Mrs. Baker described. "He had a patch right across his lip, [and] his face was swollen." Daniel Hamm's mother was unaware of the disturbance that led to her son's arrest. "They didn't call me," Mrs. Hamm stated. But when she was finally permitted to see Daniel, she remembered, "He couldn't pull up his pants. He had a blood clot on each leg." Their attorney used this evidence to plead their case for release.[14]

The next morning, Sena argued to the presiding judge, Maurice W. Grey, that his clients were "beaten by police after they had been arrested" for asking an officer "why he was beating another youth." Baker and Hamm accompanied Sena to court wearing bandages; however, Judge Grey dismissed the police-brutality charge and told attorney Sena "to take his complaint to Police Commissioner Michael J. Murphy." The young men were forced to post $500 bails, except Daniel Hamm, who was paroled in consideration of possible hardship to his widowed mother, and both men were charged with assault and malicious mischief. Unfortunately for Baker and Hamm, they and four of their friends were rearrested within days of the fruit-stand incident. This time they were being charged with the murder of Margit Sugar, a white secondhand-clothes dealer in Harlem. Such allegations leveled at these six black youths incited racial and political disarray throughout New York City.[15]

"They Don't Want Us on the Street": Fear and the Policing of Black Youths

"The police were afraid of everything in Harlem," James Baldwin wrote. "This means that citizens of Harlem, who, as we have seen," Baldwin continued, "can come to grief at any hour in the streets, and who are not safe at their windows, are forbidden the very air." Baldwin's articulation of living in occupied territory poetically described the lived experience of many black New Yorkers, especially young Harlemites, in the 1960s. "The children, having seen the spectacular defeat of their fathers—having seen what happens to any bad nigger and, still more, what happens to the good ones—cannot listen to their fathers," Baldwin avowed, "and certainly will not listen to the society which is responsible for their orphaned condition." Moreover, speaking directly to the case of the Harlem Six and the passing of the "stop-and-frisk" and "no-knock" laws, Baldwin asserted that black people in New York City were no longer safe from the occupying forces of the state, not even in their own homes. "Harlem believes, and I certainly agree," he wrote, "that these laws are directed against Negroes."[16]

People close to the case of the Harlem Six believed, like Baldwin, that the pursuit of the six youths started before even the fruit-stand incident. The new anticrime laws and the heightened police state in New York City caused certain actions and behaviors to attract police attention that otherwise would have not been considered criminal. Some behaviors were tied to the elevated political climate in the city, and they included rent strikes, school boycotts, spontaneous picketing, demonstrations, and the formation of a militant rank and file. For example, when civil rights organizations such as CORE intensified their efforts to achieve complete school integration in the city, encounters with law enforcement officials increased. Such was the case when New York CORE members blocked traffic with signs reading, "Are Crowded Roads Worse than Crowded Schools?" and "In East Harlem, Children Are Integrated with Rats and Garbage." Seven demonstrators were booked on charges of interfering with the police, disorderly conduct, obstructing automobiles, and violating traffic regulations.[17]

Other behaviors included innocent acts of adolescence such as pigeon keeping. Many youths were pigeon fanciers, and they kept and trained pigeons on the roofs of residential buildings. One youth, not connected to the Harlem Six, explained to a *New York Times* reporter that he "hated" the police because "they took our pigeons." The youth told the reporter about a confrontation with a policeman who accused him and his friends of "hiding bricks" on the roof. All the Harlem Six were pigeon fanciers, and though there was no record of them having run-ins with the police because of this hobby, they were all very aware of the youths who did. At an open forum in Harlem after the fruit-stand riot, before the youths' arrest, Hamm pointed to constant harassment that he and his peers faced from police and expressed, "They don't want us on the street." It was a message they all heard loud and clear.[18]

When the *New York Times* printed its first detailed account of the murder of Margit Sugar, it did so under the headline, "3 Youths Seized

Three—Ronald Felder, Walter Thomas, and Willie Craig—of the Harlem Six escorted to the police precinct, 1964. (AP Photo / Anthony Camerano)

in Harlem Killing: A Racial Motive in Recent Assaults Is Investigated." The writer goes into detail about the three "Negro youths" who were arrested in connection with the fatal stabbing of a Harlem shopkeeper and the wounding of her husband, Frank Sugar, who survived and was in fair condition at Physicians' Hospital in Jackson Heights Queens. Mr. Sugar told police that a group of boys entered the store just before 5:00 p.m. and took up position around the shop. He recalled, "When one of the youths asked to see a suit, Mrs. [Margit] Sugar replied that they had none in his size." Another youth then drew a knife and stabbed the woman once in the heart. The commotion in the store caused the operator of the adjacent drugstore to come over and see what was going on. The drugstore operator, Julius Levitt, described seeing a group of youths run out of the clothing store, and he called the police. The following morning, Ronald Felder, Walter Thomas, and William Craig were arrested and arraigned on charges of felonious assault and a violation of the weapons law; the homicide charge was held open until it could be determined which "boy did the killing."[19]

Coverage of the incident continued the next day when the *New York Times* printed a photograph of Robert Rice and Daniel Hamm attached to an article connecting the youths to the death of Margit Sugar. "Altogether, five teen-agers have been arrested in the shopkeeper's murder," the longtime *New York Times* reporter Martin Arnold stated, "and a sixth [was] being sought." The police issued an alarm that spanned a thirteen-state radius in their efforts to capture the sixth, Wallace Baker, who was believed to have "actually stabbed Mrs. Sugar to death." As a result, the hunt for Baker received national attention; however, on May 5, Baker, accompanied by his lawyer, George Sena, turned himself in. With the six officially in police custody, perhaps the most important question yet to be answered was, Why were six black youths all arrested,

Robert Rice and Daniel Hamm of the Harlem Six, 1964.
(AP Photo / Anthony Camerano)

Wallace Baker of the Harlem Six, 1964. (AP Photo / Harry Harris)

indicted, and arraigned for a murder that the police say "was committed by one stroke of a knife in a human heart by one bloody hand." Why so many?[20]

Multiple accusations of such hostility can fix an ugly stain on a whole race or nationality. Otherwise, it would *just* be a random act of violence. For black youths in the twentieth century, these were not uncommon; there were the Scottsboro (Nine) Boys and the Trenton Six. It was believed, according to the novelist Truman Nelson, who published a great deal in support of the Harlem Six, that "whenever a crescendo of racist fear and guilt begins to build in the white community, it seems that it must always be resolved by a frenzied hue and cry, brutal arrests, and hysterical trial of multiple black defendants accused of a crime so monstrous that the whole apparatus of the state backed by a totally terrorized and convinced public opinion can be brought into a direct onslaught against them." This was indeed true in the case of the Harlem Six.[21]

From the onset of the arrest of the Harlem Six through all the events that followed, they experienced harsh treatment by the various authoritative figures—the police, their lawyers, the courts—whom they encountered, reinforcing their notions about the unjust powers of the state. Aside from Wallace Baker, who turned himself in to police custody, the other five youths and their families faced "no-knock" enforcement in their arrests. "On the night of April the twenty-ninth," two months before the "stop-and-frisk" and "no-knock" laws were set to become official, Mrs. Craig, William's mother, recalled hearing a noise coming from the roof. She opened her door to look out and saw roughly twenty men, some coming up the stairs and some down from the roof. "One walked to the door and he asked me if this was where Billy Craig lived," Mrs. Craig recollected. "I said Billy Craig? No, there's no Billy Craig here. There's a Willie Craig live here." But William was out running an errand. This did not prevent the policemen from going into Craig's room, and four of the men stayed in the house to wait for Craig's arrival. "The others left, and I'd say about forty-five minutes later," Mrs. Craig stated, "one come up the stairs and say we got him." Mrs. Craig followed the police officers back to the precinct, where she waited hours for any questions to be answered. Mrs. Craig left the police station, per a detective's request: "go home and get some rest so you can be in court in the morning, 'cause we are keeping these boys." "I didn't know why they were holding them no more than just as assault," Mrs. Craig explained. "I couldn't think of anywhere I could go for help. I felt everything was hopeless." When Mrs. Craig arrived back home, her daughter and neighbor told her they saw the "three boys on television," and unbeknown to them, they were arrested for murder.[22]

Each of the mothers shared similar stories of the day their sons were arrested. Mrs. Rice, Robert's mother, was said to have weighed 152 pounds before her son's arrest and dropped to 125 pounds within a month. "I haven't been able to eat a meal since all this started. All I do is smoke and drink coffee," Mrs. Rice told Selma Sparks, a feature writer for *Challenge* who interviewed the six mothers to reveal "what it feels like to be a black mother in a white world when your child is being framed and tortured." Sparks's interviews were published in a pamphlet titled *A Harlem Mother's Nightmare: The Story of Six Harlem Youths Who Face Possible Death for a Crime They Did Not Commit*. Committed to raise awareness, and money, to help defend the Harlem Six, the Committee to Defend Resistance to Ghetto Life (CERGE), a New York–based defense front organization for the Progressive Labor Movement and its affiliates, promoted the pamphlet, and it launched a national, arguably international, campaign to free the Harlem Six; their mothers led the charge.[23]

It was Truman Nelson's *Torture of Mothers*, a self-published account of the mothers' experiences and the early media coverage of the case of the Harlem Six, that established the national conversation and "create[d] publicity and public indignation." Nelson, a white northerner, held little qualms in calling out what he knew to be "a racial incident." For Nelson, "if six Irishmen kill a Jew, if six Jews kill a Pole, if six Poles kill a Negro, if six Negroes kill a white, the guilt is flung in the face of a whole people." In the case of the Harlem Six, Nelson had no doubt that this was the case. To be sure, the work was not without its skeptics. These included James Baldwin, who questioned Nelson's ability to understand the intricacies of the case as a "white liberal Southerner." Additionally, the general public also held reservations about Nelson's underlying motives. In an unlabeled letter mailed to Beacon Press, which eventually decided to publish the work in late 1965 "with the hope that the book will now attract the concern which it deserves," a writer described Nelson's work as "frank propaganda." The unnamed writer professed that the book only "succeeds in demonstrating to a white reader how far removed he is from the kind of justice, the kind of law, and the police the Negro knows." This was certainly true; however, in his time of writing, Nelson never proclaimed to do more than expose the injustices that the six youths and their families faced. He built his case around the Harlem Six mothers and their "excruciating torture, which comes out of love." "It comes out of uncertainty and fear," Nelson wrote. "Out of wanting to protect, in this case, and not being able to find the object of the compulsion to protect." Such words set the tone for the first trial, which began in March 1965—ten months after the youths' arrests.[24]

"They Are All Your Children": The Case of the Harlem Six

"No one in Harlem will ever believe the Harlem Six are guilty," James Baldwin wrote. "God knows their guilt has certainly not been proved." Baldwin voiced what many black New Yorkers felt about the six youths who faced the death penalty for the felonious murder charge. "Harlem knows, though, that they have been abused and . . . possibly destroyed, and Harlem knows why—we have lived with it since our eyes opened on the world." The case of the Harlem Six was an ordeal for all involved and proved to be a daunting challenge for those who were on the defense, including their mothers, who formed the Mother Defense Committee "in an effort to free their children."[25]

Countless Harlem residents wanted to trust that the six were in fact innocent, but not many were forthcoming in their defense. "Everybody turned their back on us and gave us the run-around," Walter Thomas's mother remembered. Mrs. Hamm supported this claim, testifying that a representative of the NAACP told her "they wouldn't touch the case with a ten-foot pole." Even George Sena, the attorney who represented the youths after the fruit-stand incident, denied the role to defend the six in the Margit Sugar case. It was generally believed that this was in large part due to the media coverage of the case. According to Truman Nelson, "Somehow the press had been able to implant in them a new form of original sin." Reminiscent of the postwar crime-wave coverage, the media's depiction of the Harlem Six convinced the public "that they were killers because they were black."[26]

The racial undercurrent of the media coverage tied to the Harlem Six connected the murder of Margit Sugar to "four other Harlem murders, all of white persons," and tied the six youths to an antiwhite Harlem gang that may have been indoctrinated by rebel black Muslims. The first to report this connection was Junius Griffin, an African American reporter for the *New York Times*. Griffin broke the story on the "Blood Brothers" of Harlem and attested that the gang had upward of four hundred members. He claimed to have received the information on this gang from a HARYOU researcher and implicated the Harlem Six, particularly Wallace Baker and Daniel Hamm, in his front-page story. "The gang last clashed with the police on April 17 on the east side of Lenox Avenue," Griffin wrote, and "two members of the gang were arrested in that clash and were later implicated in the fatal stabbing of a white woman on April 29."[27]

For obvious reasons, the presence of this gang "indoctrinated in hatred of all white persons" was problematic. Griffin's report on the Blood Brothers of Harlem detailed how a radical sect of Muslims who left the Nation of Islam preached a nationalist rhetoric to youths and encouraged them to hold a strong resentment toward police and other state authorities. Beyond ideology, the Blood Brothers of Harlem trained various karate and judo techniques and, according to Griffin, were designated different duties. "Some members of the gang [were] used as drug pushers and numbers runners," Griffin wrote; "others [were] taught to steal." The slightest inkling of this gang's existence was "chilling news."[28]

A day after the *New York Times* printed its first story on the antiwhite Harlem gang, it followed it up with a detailed account of how the police were addressing the problem. To investigate the gang's existence, Griffin reported, "more than 40 Negro police undercover men moved into Harlem yesterday." They fanned out into community centers, restaurants, bars, and "other haunts where members of the gang [were] reported to gather during and after school hours." Griffin reported that there were two leads on adult suspects who were responsible for organizing the gang and "preaching Black Nationalism and hatred for the white man." But when challenged to present evidence, Griffin and the *New York Times* denied all requests.[29]

To be sure, there were some African American leaders who, unsure of the gang's existence, admitted that it would not be surprising if such a group did exist. For example, James Farmer, the national director of CORE, wrote, "I think the Blood Brothers are merely another indication of the sickness of our society. They reflect the growing anger, frustration and sense of hopelessness in the Negro ghetto, especially among our youth, most of whom are unemployed." Perhaps more notably, at the symposium "What's Behind the 'Hate-Gang' Scare?" in May 1964, Malcolm X responded to a personal invitation to address the initial reports of the Blood Brothers of Harlem. "The first time I ever heard about the 'Blood Brothers,' I happened to be in Nigeria," Malcolm X explained to the audience. "And someone, a doctor, . . . was the first one to bring it to my attention and ask me about it." Though the gang's formation was allegedly tied to his break from the Nation of Islam, Malcolm X affirmed he was unaware of the gang's existence; however, he admitted he would not be surprised if it did exist. "I am one person who believes that anything the black man in this country needs to get his freedom right now," Malcolm X declared, "that thing should exist." Rhetorically swinging the question from *do* they exist to *should* they exist, he concluded his address insisting that the different forms of oppression faced by blacks daily eroded any chance for equal democracy. As far as Malcolm X was concerned, it was the conditions these young men faced that "made them brothers," and if the Blood Brothers of Harlem did not exist, maybe they should.[30]

In any case, black media outlets were not as willing to accept the existence of the "Blood Brothers" and warned their audience of the possibilities that may arise if they accept what emerged elsewhere. The New York branches of the NAACP and CORE demanded "the city to produce the facts to justify the hysteria that has been created." Whether the intentions were to better the business opportunities for non-Harlem residents to feel more comfortable moving to Harlem or to permit the establishment of the heightened police presence, Marshall England, chairman of the New York CORE, articulated that the reports were "an indication of how far the white press will go to create hysteria." In the end, the gang's existence eluded all evidence presented; however, the damage was done as it related to the fate of the Harlem Six.[31]

In the initial hearings of the Harlem Six, they faced questions such as, "Are you a follower of Islam?" "How do you get your X?" and "Where do you fellows practice your karate?" The assistant district attorney, Robert J. Lehner, even asked Daniel Hamm directly, "When Rice [Robert] called you brother, what does he mean?" To which Hamm responded, "Just something new that come in the street. Instead of pal it's brother." The implication in these questions was directly tied to the idea that the six youths belonged to the "Blood Brother" gang that was never proved to be more than a myth. The manufactured hysteria, unfortunately, was not.[32]

Because of the hysteria, though, many lawyers believed providing a credible defense would be extremely difficult, even if they knew the "Blood Brother" connection to be untrue. Those who were close to the case of the Harlem Six labored to find an attorney to conduct their defense. As a result, after their arraignment, a public defender signed a notice of appearance for all the youths. This meant that when any other lawyer, whether chosen by their mothers or not, asked for permission to see the boys, he or she would be denied. The mothers believed that the lawyer who signed the notice of appearance did so for the money; the court-appointed lawyer was "paid $2,500 per boy." Like most people in Harlem, the mothers and their sons both had a deep distrust of court-appointed counsel, and they refused to settle.[33]

The Mothers Defense Committee was determined to obtain a defense counsel it was confident in; however, as Mrs. Baker acknowledged, "We didn't know where to go, we didn't know where to turn." The mothers' next option was William Epton, a black communist who at the time was the head of the Harlem Defense Council. An ardent opponent of the "no-knock" and "stop-and-frisk" laws, what he referred to as "the northern version of the Black Codes," Epton was hesitant to take on the case out of fear that "Rockefeller, Wagner, and 'Bull' Murphy" would use his radicalism against him. Even though Epton denounced his affiliation with the Communist Party in 1964, "because it no longer represented the aspirations in general of the working class or the black people in particular," the stigma was still prevalent.[34]

Epton suggested that the Mothers Defense Committee talk the situation over with Conrad Lynn, a civil rights attorney who had recently defended Epton on a charge of illegal assembly. Known for his "oratorical power, . . . openness, compassion, and above all . . . innate sense of righteousness and prophecy that was the hallmark of the great abolitionists of the 1850s," Lynn seemed to be the perfect fit. Truman Nelson, a Lynn supporter and friend, described the attorney as "a small man, and black, and his smallness and blackness gives the effusions of indestructibility and fearlessness." Nelson admitted that it was easy for him "to understand how the mothers must have felt sitting before him for the first time." Lynn agreed to take the case and assembled a group of distinguished attorneys that included Mary Kaufman, William Kunstler, Sam Neuberger, and Gene Condon. He accepted the case because he believed "the so-called Blood Brother murder is one pre-eminently showing the influence of dominant prejudice against a minority which is deprived of defenses." Lynn also informed the six mothers that actual hard proof of the crime by the boys is missing, and "the prosecution is depending on the existing state of prejudice to obtain conviction." Placing his faith in the mothers' testimony, Lynn was convinced that the boys were innocent, and he accepted the task at hand.[35]

The first step for Lynn and his team proved to be the first hurdle. Sought to represent the Harlem Six, Lynn stated, "My colleagues and I have surveyed every scrap of the alleged 'evidence,' and, without a doubt, we believe these six black youths to be innocent." But because there was already a court-appointed attorney, the court invoked a ruling that denied Lynn's group the defense. Not surprised by the judge's decision to keep the assigned attorney, Lynn expressed his dissatisfaction with "the judge [who] would refuse to appoint any lawyer except the particular political hack in the Democratic Club whom they wished to favor at the moment." Lynn's group immediately motioned to the Supreme Court for a writ of habeas corpus to free the Harlem Six on the grounds that they were being denied the right to counsel. He argued, "The practice of the courts in assigning lawyers against the wishes of indigent clients was to practice a difference in defense based on property qualifications." Lynn and his team were confident that the precedent set in the Scottsboro case to use the class status of the defendants would persuade the judge to reconsider, but they were once again denied. Judge Julius Helfand, who adjudicated the habeas corpus hearing, was unwilling to fold on the class distinction. Judge Helfand was more convinced by the attorney general's argument: "If you let these people pick their own lawyer, pretty soon the indigents in the hospitals will be picking their own doctors and surgeons." Judge Helfand dismissed the plea of the six youths and ordered them to go on trial for their lives with the court-appointed attorney.[36]

As Lynn and his team of attorneys regrouped to work out more ideas on how to free the Harlem Six, the mothers returned home to the streets of Harlem, "the only human part of New York," to keep the case relevant in the public's eye. Searching out platforms to explain their sons' situation, they spoke out at meetings every Saturday with the support of the Harlem Defense Council, and "some days they collected as much as forty or fifty dollars" to help fund legal fees and court expenses. The case of the Harlem Six lost some of its national regard, largely because of the "riot" of 1964, which was sparked by the police killing of a fifteen-year-old Harlemite, and the assassination of Malcolm X. These events rightfully directed the media's attention elsewhere; however, the case of the Harlem Six retained the attention of Harlemites both at home and abroad as they awaited the outcome of the first trial. James Baldwin, in particular, continued to use his international platform to advocate for the six youngsters. From his debate with William Buckley Jr. at Cambridge University to his "Report from Occupied Territory" published in the *Nation*, Baldwin remained committed to keeping the Harlem Six in the public eye. "My activities on the part of the Harlem Six are bound to have repercussions, if they have not already," Baldwin wrote in a letter to his brother, David. "I suppose you saw my Report from Occupied Territory in The Nation. I have also drafted a petition—the petition is really a two-page version of my Report—for international attention, and for signatures from people, prominent or otherwise, from all over the world." Additionally, Baldwin delivered a speech demanding an economic boycott in support of the Harlem Six. These youths were "now ending their childhood and may end their lives in jail," Baldwin disclosed in front of a large audience at the Village Theater in lower Manhattan. "If we cannot reach the American conscience, we must find a way of intimidating its self-interest." Baldwin's call was not alone. Funds continued to be raised by organizations throughout Harlem, and Lynn's group was finally able to achieve its first major feat: a retrial of the Harlem Six.[37]

A little more than three years after the conviction of the Harlem Six, the Court of Appeals in New York City "reversed the first-degree murder convictions of [the] six men, known as the Harlem Six." Because the six youths regarded their court-appointed lawyers as "representatives of the enemy court," they refused to talk to them and, on trial, stood mute in protest. This, combined with the fact that statements and confessions were put into evidence through third parties, exposed "the constitutional infirmity" of the case. Though some people found the reversal controversial, this "prime error" resulted in new trials for all of the young men.[38]

A retrial for the Harlem Six was crucial for many reasons. First, and perhaps most importantly, the six young men were no longer subjected to the attorneys appointed by the court. For Lynn and his associates, attaining a fair environment for this case was a fight they refused to drop. In one instance, the lawyers demanded that Supreme Court Justice Gerald P. Culkin "be censured for his racial slurs." When the Harlem Six appeared before Judge Culkin to attempt to change their counsel, Culkin said, "These boys wouldn't know a good attorney from a good watermelon." Fritz Alexander, president of the Harlem Lawyer Association, expressed to Lynn and his team that the association "found no racial offense in the statement Culkin made." On a separate occasion, according to Lynn and William Kunstler, one court-appointed lawyer "died in court from acute alcoholism while the first trial was in progress." These kinds of occurrences marred the first trial throughout, but the retrial allowed Lynn and his associates to take over the case on a more permanent and official basis.[39]

Second, from the time the Harlem Six were convicted in 1964 to the order for a retrial, the death penalty underwent a number of changes in New York. In 1965, the state legislature passed a law limiting the death penalty "to murder in the first degree when the victim was a peace officer performing his or her official duties, when the defendant was serving a life sentence at the time the crime was committed, if the crime was committed when the defendant was serving an indeterminate sentence of at least fifteen years to life, or if the defendant was in immediate flight from penal custody or confinement when the crime was committed." Further, the law prohibited the death penalty for persons under the age of eighteen when the crime was committed and did not impose the death penalty "when substantial mitigating circumstances existed." Some more amendments were added in 1967 and 1968, but what mattered most for the Harlem Six was that they were no longer facing the electric chair—only life in prison. And, third, the order for a retrial meant that the six—Rice, Hamm, Baker, Felder, Craig, and Thomas—were now to be tried separately. The New York Court of Appeals said, "When a defendant confesses to a crime, he must be given his own trial apart from the trials of his co-defendants." In this particular instance, because Rice and Hamm "confessed" to knifing the Sugars, each was set to face a jury of their peers individually; and a joint trial was set for Wallace, Thomas, Felder, and Craig, who "stoutly maintained their innocence."[40]

Robert Rice was the first to be retried. Because Rice previously confessed to stabbing Mrs. Sugar, at the retrial he told the jury that the confession came "after being beaten by the police." The retrial was short. After hearing testimony from Rice, his mother, his grandmother, a grandmother of a codefendant, and "an alleged eyewitness," the jury, which was made up of three women and nine men—three of whom were black—found Rice guilty of first-degree murder, attempted murder, and attempted robbery. The murder conviction alone carried a mandatory life sentence. Hamm, on the other hand, pleaded guilty to lesser charges of manslaughter, attempted murder, and attempted robbery; he was sentenced to fifteen to thirty-five years in prison.[41]

After the Court of Appeals reversal, there was a new emergence of support for the Harlem Six. Because Rice and Hamm were tried and sentenced separately, the public started to follow the "Harlem Four" case. The sentencing of the four proved to be much more difficult. Following three mistrials, which all resulted in hung juries, relatives and supporters demanded the removal of the assistant district attorney, Robert Lehner, who had prosecuted the case for more than seven years. Ossie Davis, a well-known black actor and activist, called the case "an outrage," and he called for the Harlem Four, "who have been denied bail since their arrest seven years ago," to be released immediately and cleared of all charges. Various petitions supported this call, including one signed by countless psychiatrists, psychologists, social workers, and psychoanalysts who believed that another trial "would impose unbearable psychological stress on these young men."[42]

Still, a fourth trial was set for the Harlem Four. This trial, according to Lynn and his group, was "expected to last about a month," and the new jury was going to "hear most of the same witnesses who testified at previous trials." While this remained pretty standard, similar to the first three mistrials, there were some new additions that made this trial seem different. The *New York Times* assigned a new reporter to the case, Lacey Fosburgh, whose first article on the Harlem Six reintroduced the case to a new audience of readers who may have lost track over the years. Perhaps most notably, in Fosburgh's reporting of the Harlem Six, all connections to an "anti-white hate gang" were absent, and the case was presented as "six teen-agers [who were a part of] an unholy plot to kill proprietors." Fosburgh also made an effort to humanize the defendants. There was mention of Walter Thomas's nine-year-old daughter, who spent most of her young life with her father in jail, as well as William Craig's poems that were exhibited in the Countee Cullen Library in Harlem.[43]

In addition to the new reporter, there was also a new audience—one that included young boys and young girls who saw themselves in the defendants. "I can't help thinking that could be me," Vaughan Dweck, thirteen, told a *New York Times* reporter. "I'd be scared if I was up there like that." Dweck continued, "All those years waiting and wondering what was going to happen to you, I'd be scared and I'd be real glad to see someone like me sitting here watching." Dweck was one of over a hundred youths who regularly attended the trial, which was opened to the public at the Criminal Court Building. Richard M. Edelman, an eighth-grade social studies teacher from the Fieldston School, was just one of many teachers who believed that "the unusual elements in this case—its long history, the fact that it focuses on a murder and, particularly, the defendants' youth—combine to intrigue the students." For Edelman, whose students were assigned to write reflection paragraphs after their day in the courtroom, "the essays revealed the realization that the four boys had been held in jail without bail during a crucial period in their life was confusing and troublesome." Other youth interest in the case came from some younger relatives of the Harlem Six who were writing letters and being engaged. Cheryl Samuels, for example, a thirteen-year-old cousin of Ronald Felder, wrote a letter to the Harlem Six disclosing her experience. "When I was ten I'd hear a cousin of mine was in jail but I didn't know what for," Samuels wrote. "Now that I'm 13 I can really do a little something to help. Pass out leaflets in court that a girl in my class made and a lot of other things that really help get the news around." Lynn and William Kunstler, who by this point in the trial had taken a more prominent role in the defense, welcomed the youths who showed up because they believed "interest among the young in the legal system should be encouraged." It also boosted their defense.[44]

After the three-month trial and days of jury deliberations, the jurors found themselves "hopelessly deadlocked," and Supreme Court Justice Joseph A. Martinis issued another mistrial—except for the first time, Thomas, Felder, Craig, and Baker were set to be released on bail. But as Lewis M. Steel, a member of the defense team, put it, "How can poor black people raise $75,000?" The sum to be paid, Steel argued, was so high as to amount to no bail at all. "I expected after eight years they would be released in their own recognizance." But Justice Martinis felt he was doing the boys a favor "in all good conscience"; however, bail was not posted.[45]

Satisfied with the defendants' inability to pay the fee, Assistant District Attorney Lehner characterized the Harlem Four as "much too dangerous to be granted bail." William Craig responded directly to Lehner in the courtroom, "Then indict me for it!" The judge warned Craig to be quiet, and Craig declined. "I've been sitting here quiet for too long," he voiced. "Through damned near four trials, and I'm not going to keep quiet as long as you keep talking about this justice business." Craig's vented frustration vocalized an undercurrent of distrust, which many black youths shared, in the justice system. What Craig vocalized in the courtroom was enhanced in his writings on exhibit at the Countee

Cullen Library. In a poem titled "Power," he wrote, "After seven and a half years of being promised justice and fairness, We, the 'Harlem 6,' as well as any poor black person, have received injustice and partialness." No longer able to believe in the courts, Craig declared, "The residing judge promises justice, but the moment his mouth opens there's a great contradition [*sic*] and all motions are denied under the color of justice without prejudice." Conrad Lynn concurred. "I'm much more bitter about life and what's happened to them than they are," Lynn wrote about having worked on the trial since its inception. "They're angry naturally about what's gone on these eight years, but they've developed a philosophy of life that's much more serene than I'll ever have." In that moment, when Craig confronted the assistant district attorney in court, Justice Martinis was faced with two options: declare a mistrial or dismiss the original indictment altogether.[46]

All signs pointed to a fifth trial for the four defendants until, perhaps the most significant turning point in the case, a key prosecution witness, Robert Barnes Jr., confessed to his probation officer that "his testimony [against the Harlem Six] was a lie." Aside from the testimony of "two small girls who testified that they had seen the defendants near the murder scene," the prosecution's case rested largely with Barnes, whom the prosecution described as an original coconspirator in the murder plan. For the defense, this new information was a goldmine. Lynn's group argued that if Barnes did not participate in the murder case, "it then becomes obvious the police and other public officials involved most certainly engaged in the wilful subornation of perjury." If this were true, then it would be argued that the prosecution changed the character of Barnes's participation in the crimes "to exculpate him and implicate these defendants therein." The defense called for an immediate release of the four defendants and a thorough criminal investigation of the new findings. Whether or not Justice Martinis was influenced by this information, it led to a number of immediate changes, including the reduction of the bail fee, which was posted, and the four defendants were released from the Manhattan House of Detention on March 31, 1972.[47]

Freedom for the Harlem Four was short-lived, and by the summer of 1972, they were summoned for another trial. Lynn and Kunstler worried about another trial because they believed the choice language

Wallace Baker of the Harlem Six, released, 1972. (AP Photo / Anthony Camerano)

of the justice was "deliberately designed to inflame and prejudice the future jurors." They were, however, prepared to report the progress that their defendants made in the few months of freedom: Felder was accepted into City College of New York and was scheduled to attend in September, Craig was enrolled at Harlem Prep, Thomas was working as a legal aide at the Morrisania Legal Services Clinic, and Baker was actively participating in community work. Justice Martinis acknowledged their "commendable" progress but called for another retrial because he believed the defense sympathizers "violated the general principles of decency and 'subjected' both himself and the jurors to 'unfair pressures.'" But the defense was ready and believed that Barnes's admission to lying, which was submitted in a thirty-eight-page affidavit, gave them what was needed to finally end this case. And it did.[48]

Then, on April 4, 1973, almost nine years to the day after the fruit-stand incident and just days before the retrial was scheduled to begin, the Harlem Four were finally freed after pleading guilty to manslaughter charges. The decision was complicated, as the four, now men, proclaimed their innocence. "We've said all along we are not guilty and what we feel the

Walter Thomas of the Harlem Six, released, 1972. (AP Photo / Anthony Camerano)

world should know is that we are still not guilty," Craig told reporters at a news conference. "We hope our friends, our mothers, our fathers, anybody who cares will understand why we had to do this, why we had to make this decision." For the Harlem Four, the certainty of freedom, even at the price of a criminal record, was the better option than facing the uncertainty of another trial. Later, Supreme Court Justice Jacob Grumet, who took the place of Martinis, made "a highly unusual move" to grant the four a certificate of relief from disability. "I want[ed] them to have every chance," Justice Grumet explained, defending his decision to assure the Harlem Four would not lose any rights or privileges commonly stripped of convicted felons. For all intents and purposes, William Craig, Wallace Baker, Walter Thomas, and Ronald Felder were free.[49]

The fates of Daniel Hamm and Robert Rice, however, were yet to be determined, and it would require further work to overturn their convictions. For Lynn and his defense team, their focus shifted to procuring the same freedoms as the Harlem Four. Hamm, who continued to serve his sentence at Auburn prison in upstate New York for his guilty plea, was denied his first parole opportunity "on the basis of new information." The Charter Group for a Pledge of Conscience, a small community organization composed mainly of Harlem residents, printed "An Appeal to the Community" on behalf of Hamm, and they urged, "ANY MEMBER OF THE COMMUNITY WHO KNOWS ANYTHING ABOUT THIS ALLEGED 'CONFIDENTIAL INFORMATION'—PLEASE COME FORWARD SO THAT IT CAN BE PUBLICLY EXAMINED." As a result of a combination of the group's effort and the persistence of Lynn and his associates, Hamm was released in 1974.[50]

Rice, who the defense team figured would be released after a federal judge dismissed his murder conviction in September 1973, experienced the least good fortune. He went on to face five additional trials and seven appeals with no break. His mother continued her advocacy and used the *New York Amsterdam News* as an outlet for support. Mrs. Rice wrote

Willie Craig of the Harlem Six, interviewed in the Manhattan House of Detention, 1972. (AP Photo / Carter)

"An Appeal to the Harlem Community for Help to Free My Son, Robert Rice," which was printed in the black weekly, urging New York's Governor Hugh Carey to grant her son clemency. Having spent twelve years in prison, Rice was "the only one of the Harlem Six still behind bars." Unfortunately, despite Mrs. Rice's plea and the tireless efforts of Lynn and his defense team, clemency was not granted. Rice continued to serve his sentence; he went up for parole in March 1988, and he was finally released in November 1991.[51]

"Your concern for the children brought about a change in your life," Craig wrote in a note to Wallace Baker. "You, Wallace, was caught in the middle of hells front door, while I tried hard to fight my way to your side," he recounted of the fruit-stand melee. "But the ocean of blue uniforms stoped [sic] me in my tracks." Even years after, Craig admittedly remembers every detail: "because the effects of those blows changed both our lives." As black youths growing up in postwar Harlem, the odds were already stacked against them. In a note to Conrad Lynn, Truman Nelson affirmed, "They know the struggle will not end with them, or perhaps even their grandsons, but they have made a contribution with the dignity and strength with which they have fought the good fight." But such an affirmation was combined with pessimism. "I'm well aware that it's not justice. And I'm sure it's not equality," William Craig wrote of the state of the justice system in America. "But through it all the 'Harlem 6' will maintain strength to fight the struggle against racism, fascism, oppression, injustice, and exploitation." With total sincerity, they endured.[52]

The case of the Harlem Six in its time captured national headlines and international audiences; yet its significance continues to escape the memory and record of many people. Ignited by the 1964 death of a white shopkeeper in New York City, the case and its subsequent events were emblematic of black youth experiences with the carceral state as the nation embarked on its War on Crime. The lived experiences of these six youths reveal that by the 1960s, constructions of criminality were reestablished as a racial problem that would continue to face more punitive state responses influenced by broader discourse on youth, race, and crime. The Harlem Six persevered through a justice system that, long before them, decided to attribute race as the determining factor for those who were presumed innocent and those who were presumed criminal.

Afterword

"Without a Wrinkle in Today": An Ode to "Young Forever"

At some point, Americans decided that the best answer
to every social ill lay in the power of the criminal-justice
system.
—Ta-Nehisi Coates, "The Myth of Police Reform"

On July 19, 2013, the hip-hop artist Jay Z and pop singer Justin Tim-
berlake performed in front of a sold-out concert at Yankee Stadium
in the Bronx, New York. They closed out their "Legends of Summer"
show by dedicating the song "Young Forever," the fourth single from
Jay Z's 2009 *Blueprint 3* album, to Trayvon Martin, a seventeen-year-old
black youth whose death sparked international outrage. Martin was shot
and killed by George Zimmerman, a neighborhood-watch patrolman,
in Sanford, Florida, on February 26, 2012. Following a controversial
trial, Zimmerman was acquitted of all charges, claiming that he was
"standing his ground." In Florida, the stand-your-ground law permits
individuals the right to declare self-defense and use force to evade any
"dangerous situation"—a contentious statute continually amended since
being established in 2004. In an interview with *Rap Radar*'s Elliot Wilson before the performance, the hip-hop icon discussed the anger he
felt upon hearing of George Zimmerman's acquittal. Jay Z told Wilson,
"I didn't sleep for two days. . . . We all knew there was still a bit of racism in America but for it to be so blatant. . . . Didn't Trayvon have the
right to stand his ground? He was being chased and he fought back. He
may have won. That doesn't mean he's a criminal!" As history confirms,
however, the decision to determine who is and who is not presumed
criminal is beyond the realm of black youths in the United States.[1]

The Trayvon Martin case of 2012 was both familiar and exceptional as
it relates to black youth encounters with the carceral state. It was familiar

because it is rooted in the experiences of black youths who continually confront state violence and racialized constructions of criminality in the United States. By the end of the Progressive era, as I have argued in this book, youth criminality was reconstructed as a racial problem that called for state-authorized punishments in place of social reforms. Whereas white juvenile delinquency at the turn of the century was often considered youthful responses to societal changes, black youths almost never benefited from their age or social changes as justification for any misbehavior. This line of inquiry sparked the groundwork for the study. A broad newspaper search for "youth and crime" from 1935 to 1965 returned gripping results. Mainstream papers such as the *New York Times*, the *Chicago Tribune*, the *Los Angeles Times*, and the *Washington Post* provided mostly articles on white youths who committed criminal acts, with few exceptions. These "teen-agers" and "youngsters" were often depicted as having strayed off the right path and required proper guidance to correct their missteps. On the other hand, black youths within the same age range rarely received such treatment. They were almost always labeled "Negro" (during the period under investigation), described as "young toughs" or "hoodlums," and proclaimed to need severe punishment or state intervention to make certain they would not become perpetual criminals. More than seventy years later, the case of Trayvon Martin reaffirmed that such characterizations are still relevant.

Perhaps a more daunting familiarity reflected in the Trayvon Martin case is how black youths routinely encounter state violence. The young Trayvon did not commit any transgressions to justify the unlawful pursuit from the twenty-eight-year-old neighborhood watch captain. In fact, Zimmerman was instructed by a 911 dispatcher to stand down as police officers were being routed in response to his call reporting the "real suspicious" youth. Against the dispatcher's command, Zimmerman took matters into his own hands and pursued the seventeen-year-old son of Sybrina Fulton. The result: "Trayvon's lifeless body was taken away, tagged, and held." If Trayvon Martin had lived to tell his version of the story, there is little doubt that it would veer from a familiar tale of innocent adolescence denied by an authoritative figure with preconceived notions of race and criminality. Like the "pigeon fanciers" who were routinely accosted by police officers on the Harlem roofs, Martin's presence provoked suspicion because "they didn't want him on the street."

But Martin's case was also exceptional. The acquittal of Trayvon Martin's murderer, Zimmerman, inspired a movement: #BlackLivesMatter. This is not to suggest that meaningful demonstrations never transpired in consequence to police brutality or abuses of authority. In fact, as described in this book, there have always been connections between criminality and popular forms of protest. Take, for instance, the organized efforts surrounding the case of the Harlem Six in 1964 or the 1943 uprising in Harlem when James Collins shot Robert Bandy for intervening in the arrest attempt of Margie Polite. Unjust law enforcement and extreme police practices have long been connected to social demonstrations and public outcry; however, technological advancements continue to transform drastically how these practices are experienced.

Alicia Garza, who wrote a love note to black people on Facebook urging them to come together to ensure "that black lives matter," coined the hashtag #BlackLivesMatter, which spread quickly on social media "because it distilled the complexities of police brutality, racial inequality and social justice 'into a simple, easy to remember slogan that fits in a Tweet or on a T-shirt.'" Harnessing twenty-first-century technology, the hashtag moved from social media to the streets because "anyone with a Facebook or Twitter account, a smartphone and a basic belief in social justice could and did join the movement." And that holds a strong appeal for today's youth. #BlackLivesMatter is not only a unique contribution that brings to light the abusive relationship between police and the black community but also "a call to action and a response to the virulent anti-Black racism that permeates our society." Like "Black Power," a slogan that Stokely Carmichael introduced to a crowd of civil rights demonstrators more than fifty years ago, #BlackLivesMatter has rejuvenated the "unfinished work" of the late 1960s "for resources and recognition to a fight to exist, free of state-sanctioned violence." Whereas the tactics may have changed since the tumultuous 1960s, the message prevails.[2]

I started writing *Presumed Criminal* in the wake of Trayvon Martin's untimely death in 2012. I was a graduate student at Indiana University, and in that moment, dissociating the past from the present was difficult. Professors and peers both were preaching, "History is about change over time"; however, I struggled to find that moment, that break from the past, because the sources I was referencing from the first half of the twentieth century were just as relevant. Conflicted, I worried that I was reading too much of the present into the past; and I am sure that I was to some degree. I sought an escape, and like many public intellectuals, I participated in many social media conversations and debates using the #BlackLivesMatter hashtag from its inception. To stay balanced with my project and current events, I posted direct quotes from sources that I was handling for *Presumed Criminal* and attached #BlackLivesMatter to the end—a twenty-first-century application of history. For example, when I watched George Zimmerman walk out of the courtroom, shortly followed by the same gun used to shoot and kill Martin, I tweeted, "The certainty of freedom, even at the price of a criminal record, was better than facing the uncertainty of another trial #BlackLivesMatter." Such an approach eventually attained "follows" from several public intellectuals and even news media Twitter accounts including CNN's.[3]

But after Zimmerman walked free, it appeared that mainstream interest in #BlackLivesMatter somewhat faded, and selfishly I thought, *Presumed Criminal* missed an opportunity to provide historical context for broader conversations related to notions of racialized youth criminality in the United States. A little over a year after President Barack Obama took to the White House podium to weigh in on the case of Trayvon Martin and stated, "This could have been my son," it appeared that the national discourse on race was "back to business as usual in Washington." Then, on August 9, 2014, adversity materialized in Ferguson, Missouri. This time, days away from starting college, the eighteen-year-old Michael Brown was shot and killed in broad daylight by a police officer in the St. Louis suburb, prompting nationwide protests, again. At the time, I was writing my chapter on the 1943 Harlem riot, and the parallels were daunting. Discussions surrounding the "Ferguson-style militarization" of local law enforcement agencies echoed popular recollections of Mayor La Guardia's response to quell the uprising in Harlem. And, once again, "cloaked in the niceties of law and order," the nation confronted white rage in its cities' streets.[4]

After Ferguson, after President Obama called attention to the urgent need throughout the country to build trust between the police and the communities, he found himself standing behind a podium once again, addressing the nation in response to the unrest in Baltimore that followed the killing of another African American, Freddie

Gray, a twenty-five-year-old male who died from spinal-cord injuries sustained while in police custody. This, once again, motivated protestors to take to the streets. "We have seen too many instances of what appears to be police officers interacting with individuals, primarily African-American, often poor, in ways that raise troubling questions," President Obama said. "It comes up, it seems like, once a week now." Regrettably, the president's statement was not much of an exaggeration. Since 2012, there were more than forty unarmed persons of color killed by police. In addition to the aforementioned Martin, Brown, and Gray, this list includes Tamir Rice, twelve; Akai Gurley, twenty-eight; Kajieme Powell, twenty-five; Ezell Ford, twenty-five; John Crawford III, twenty-two; Eric Garner, forty-three; Victor White III, twenty-two; McKenzie Cochran, twenty-five; Andy Lopez, thirteen; Jonathan Ferrell, twenty-four; Deion Fludd, seventeen; Kimani Gray, sixteen; Reynaldo Cuevas, twenty; Chavis Carter, twenty-one; Shantel Davis, twenty-three; Ervin Jefferson, eighteen; Kendrec McDade, nineteen; Rekia Boyd, twenty-two; Wendell Allen, twenty; and Ramarley Graham, eighteen. And while President Obama acknowledges the role that technological advancements such as camera phones and social media play in raising the level of awareness surrounding such incidents, he says, "We shouldn't pretend that it's new."[5]

President Obama was right. The unremitting harassment faced by poor communities of color at the hands of police and other state authorities was anything but new. But who pretended it was? The tragedies of Trayvon Martin, Michael Brown, and Freddie Gray joined the long history of countless black youths victimized by wrongful criminalization practices and state violence. And those who protested their deaths never pretended this was new. In fact, their responses reflect a historical understanding of the connection between public demonstration and criminality. The students and youths who participated in "die-ins" on college campuses and at large shopping malls around the country at no time insisted that their behaviors were unique. The various professional athletes who joined public protests in their respective arenas by wearing hoodies in support of Martin, by taking the field with their hands up in support of Brown, by wearing "I Can't Breathe" T-shirts for warm-ups in support of Eric Garner, by marching hand in hand in the streets of Baltimore, by taking a knee during the national anthem, did so paying homage to the many athletes before them who used their platforms in the fight for equal rights and justice for all. Perhaps most notably, even the "criminals and thugs," like their "hoodlum" predecessors, who tore up their cities were historically conscious of their acts, contrary to popular belief. If only we had been listening.[6]

ACKNOWLEDGMENTS

It was early 2000, and I was a freshman in high school when I watched *The Hurricane*, starring Denzel Washington. The next day, I went to the library and checked out *The Sixteenth Round: From Number 1 Contender to Number 45472*, the autobiography of Rubin "Hurricane" Carter that the movie script adapted. Carter, a former middleweight boxer who was wrongly convicted for a triple murder, spent almost twenty years in prison. Carter's tragic story made a profound impression on me. I remember finishing the book within a week, and I was sitting in home room when Dave Battafarano (Mr. Batt), a history teacher at Glasgow High School in Newark, Delaware, asked if I had read any new books. I told him I had just finished Carter's autobiography and was stunned to learn that "this man sat in jail for years when everyone *knew* he was innocent." Mr. Batt asked, "How are you sure he was innocent?" and the teenage me responded, "Well, it's in the book. And this wasn't a fiction book." The conversation continued, and Mr. Batt queried, "An autobiography? Do you think The Hurricane would write a book admitting to the murders that put him in prison? Or is he more likely to write a story to prove his innocence?" In that moment, whether Mr. Batt knew it or not, I was inspired to challenge presumptions of innocence and presumptions of guilt—and it sent me on the journey that sparked the ideas, the questions, and the stories that gave rise to this book.

The journey to completing this book was hardly a straight line; it is almost impossible to find a beginning, a middle, and an end. Even as I finished, James Baldwin's words continued to resonate: "You never get the book you wanted, you settle for the book you get." Like Baldwin, when the book ended, there was still something there that I did not see. And while it is too late for me to do anything about it here, I hope it inspires others to pick up where I left off, to fill in what I missed, and to build good relationships with good people along the way—much as I did.

It was the relationships with the good people in my life that made this book a reality. Some were personal, some were professional, some were both; nevertheless, they all mattered. They begin with my family. My parents, Betsy and Carl Sr., redefined the standard of love with their support, and there are not enough words to express my gratitude. My sister, Charise, has been, and continues to be, my lifeline since I was born; I try to make her proud every day.

I have lived with this project for nearly a decade, and so has LaNita Campbell. For her support, her patience, her encouragement, and her love, I am thankful and grateful. Truly.

To my extended family—aunts, uncles, and cousins (older ones who have been good examples, younger ones whom I hope to inspire) from New York to Delaware, from the South to Puerto Rico and the various places in between—thank you. The love I received, from conversations and support to meals and hospitality, does not go unnoticed. Our connectedness through my grandparents—Concepción Cruz, Miguel García, Charles Suddler, and Dorothy Ragin—all of whom I miss dearly but am grateful to have known, is a bond that I cherish.

I have been blessed to have several lifelong friends—Kevin Guyton, Ryan Cowgill, Brian Burke, David Bowman, Jhmal Haseen, and Chris Killian—whose camaraderie means a great deal to me. I have been blessed to have cousins who are more like brothers—Vance Barnes, Omar Escabi, Enrique Pabon, Ronald Ragin, and Carlton Suddler Jr.—who inspire me to better and to stay humble. I do not thank them enough for it.

And I would be remiss to ignore that I have also been blessed to have had two English bulldogs—London and Baldwin—who forced me to structure my writing time in a way that I needed to complete the manuscript.

I owe numberless thanks to my undergraduate and graduate professors who contributed to my training as a historian and, in various ways, helped shape the book. At the University of Delaware, the Departments of History and Black American Studies (now Africana Studies) taught me how to study and appreciate African American history as a discipline that extends beyond the classroom. This included Anne Boylan, Benjamin Fleury-Steiner, Carol Henderson, Howard Johnson, James Jones, Wunyabari Maloba, John Montaño, and David Wilson. Erica Armstrong-Dunbar and Yasser A. Payne deserve much of the credit for inspiring me to pursue a PhD in history. I cannot thank Erica enough for the continued mentorship and friendship; her faith in my potential since I was an eighteen-year-old freshman instilled the confidence required for a first-generation college student to navigate the academy. Same goes for Yasser. Through his words and his actions, Yasser convinced me not only that it was possible to be real in academia but that genuineness and love were required. Thank you.

I brought this foundation to Indiana University. The Departments of History and African American and African Diaspora Studies (AAADS) built on this base as I continued to develop as a scholar. I owe a sincere thanks to Cara Caddoo, Arlene Diaz, Ben Eklof, Wendy Gamber, Matthew Guterl, Alex Lichtenstein, Michael McGerr, Jason McGraw, Michelle Moyd, Amrita Chakrabarti Myers, Eric Sandweiss, Micol Seigel, Rebecca Spang, Valerie Grim, the late Frederick McElroy, Ghangis Carter, Dionne Danns, Sylvester Johnson, and Akwasi Owusu-Bempah for suggesting readings and offering mentorship and support during my time in Bloomington. The staff at the *Journal of American History*, especially Ed Linenthal and Stephen Andrews, not only provided gainful employment while I was a graduate student but also offered continued encouragement and support for the project through its final stages. I would be remiss not to acknowledge Frank Motley for the countless meals and words of wisdom and consolation. I am indebted to Claude Clegg, Khalil Muhammad, John Nieto-Phillips, Jakobi Williams, Vernon Williams, and Ellen Wu for their guidance on this project since its inception. Khalil and Claude were the perfect balance of tough love and counsel. Khalil set the standard. His drive and his ambition are contagious. And Claude's timely encouragement saved me more times than I can count. I remain inspired by them both.

It is impossible to recount the ways in which my fellow graduate students at Indiana helped shape my thinking. From the classroom to Nick's English Hut, I am thankful for the #IUHistoryMafia: Marc Antone, Jennifer Boles, Kalani Craig, Susan Eckelmann, Justin Ellison, Charlene Fletcher-Brown, Ángel G. Flores-Rodríguez, Aaron Fountain, Natalie Gwishiri, Rafi Hasan, David Jamison, Andrew Kahrl, Betsy Pease, Eric Petenbrink, Sarah Rowley, Tara Saunders, Jim Seaver, Paula Tarankow, Jordan Taylor, Heather Vrana, Jon Warner, and Jeremy Young. Even those outside the history department—Evelyn Carter, Adeyemi Doss,

Bill Gillis, Kourtney Gray, Fredera Hadley, Brian McGowan, Quentin Speight, and Josef Woldense—helped push me over the finish line. I am especially thankful for Siobhan Carter-David, Eddie Cole, Tanisha Ford, and Kim Stanley. Through graduate school, and thereafter, they have pushed me to be better—not just with their words but with their actions. I chase them every day. Thank you.

My community at the James Weldon Johnson Institute (JWJI) for the Study of Race and Difference at Emory University helped develop the project and expand its scope. Special thank-yous to Andra Gillespie, Kali Ahset-Amen, and Anita Spencer Stevens at the JWJI for the opportunity to spend quality time with the manuscript. To my fellow JWJI Fellows, Michelle Y. Gordon and Nikki Brown, thank you for the advice, the feedback, and the friendship. Beyond the JWJI, I am grateful for the generosity of the people at Emory University who offered genuine support during my time there: Carol Anderson, Joseph Crespino, Brett Gadsden, Leslie Harris, Daniel LaChance, Pellom McDaniels III, Judith Miller, Michael Leo Owens, Pamela Scully, Natasha Trethewey, and Kevin Young.

My friends and colleagues at Florida Atlantic University (FAU) have been excellent. Among my FAU colleagues in the Department of History who offered publishing advice and gave timely encouragement, I would like to thank Evan Bennett, Boyd Breslow, Graciella Cruz-Taura, Miriam Dalin, Stephen Engle, Adrian Finucane, Eric Hanne, Ken Holloway, Doug Kanter, Patricia Kollander, Ben Lowe, Doug McGetchin, Sandy Norman, Mark Rose, Kelly Shannon, and Jason Sharples. I came to FAU with a plethora of English scholars—Devin Garofalo, RJ Boutelle, Stacy Lettman, Stacey Balkan, José de la Garza-Valenzuela, and Ashvin Kini—who have been valuable confidants during the final stages of the project as well.

To the students whom I have had the privilege of working with, and teaching, along the way, thank you. Several graduate and undergraduate students provided key insights about my work and my ways of thinking through conversations about their own work and their own ambitions: Chelsea Jackson, Danielle Lee Wiggins, Harrison Graves, Vanessa Hatton, and Eden H. Negusse. Thank you for teaching me how best to reach your generation.

Many colleagues and scholars have contributed to my continued intellectual growth, and I am indeed grateful that you are who you are. Through the various collaborations and conversations in different settings, I am thankful: Simon Balto, Dan Berger, Martha Biondi, Marcia Chatelain, Alex Elkins, Ansley Erickson, Max Felker-Kantor, Anne Gray-Fischer, Frank Guridy, Ramón Gutiérrez, LaShawn Harris, Kelly Lytle Hernández, Elizabeth Hinton, Maurice Hobson, Hasan Kwame Jeffries, Randal Maurice Jelks, Shannon King, Nora Krinitsky, Talitha LeFlouria, Naomi Murakawa, Donna Murch, Jessica Neptune, Jeffrey O. G. Ogbar, Rebecca de Schweinitz, Carla Shedd, Heather Ann Thompson, and Derrick White.

No history book can be written without the work of librarians and archivists, this one included. The staffs at the Schomburg Center for Research in Black Culture, New York City Municipal Archives, the New York Public Library, Manuscript and Archives Division, the Columbia University Rare Book and Manuscript Library, the Columbia University Center for Oral History, the Howard Gotlieb Archival Research Center at Boston University, and the Stuart Rose Manuscript, Archives, and Rare Book Library at Emory University were critical in providing the resources that carried the evidentiary base in this book. The Queens Borough Public Library, the Library of Congress, Getty Images, and AP Images were also crucial in the reproduction of the images throughout the text. I am indebted; I am grateful—not just for the work you did for me but for the work you do daily to keep these stories alive.

I received generous financial support from Indiana University, Florida Atlantic University, the University of Delaware, and the Andrew W. Mellon Foundation / James Weldon Johnson Institute for the Study of Race and Difference at Emory University. These dollars and cents covered the research costs associated with the book—and also lined the pockets of the countless baristas who kept me caffeinated in the process. Likewise, the editors, production staff, and anonymous reviewers led by Clara Platter and Amy Klopfenstein at New York University Press provided generous assistance and directed the manuscript to publication.

Somewhere along the way, I was asked, "If you only had one stamp and one envelope to send your book to someone, who would you send it to?" With little hesitation, I responded, "To my barbershop, back home." Puzzled by my response, they asked, "Why?" For me, the reason was clear. I was writing a history for the black youths who go to those black barbershops every day. I was writing a history for the parents and grandparents who may take them to get their haircuts or even the ones who may be there to get a haircut themselves. For me, the black barbershop was a space where different generations and different walks of life crossed paths daily. And even though I was writing a history that was place and time specific, I was inspired to write it by the myriad of black youths I encounter at those barbershops and elsewhere. I was inspired to write it by the lives of the nameless who have disappeared in the historical records. I was inspired to write it by those who continue to bear the burdens of America's past. *Presumed Criminal* is, like many African American histories, a labor of love written by you, for you.

MANUSCRIPT SOURCES

Columbia Center for Oral History. Columbia University Libraries. New York, NY.
Oral History Interview with James Baldwin, 1964. Baldwin, James, 1924–1987.
Columbia University Rare Book and Manuscript Library. New York, NY.
Society for the Prevention of Crime Records, 1878–1973. Society for the Prevention of
    Crime (New York, NY). Additional contributor: Lukas, Edwin J. (1941–1950).
Howard Gottlieb Archival Research Center. Boston University. Boston, MA.
Lynn, Conrad, Collection, 1908–1995.
New York City Municipal Archives and Records Center. Manuscripts and Archives
    Division. New York Public Library. New York, NY.
La Guardia, Fiorello H., Papers (1918–1945).
Schomburg Center for Research in Black Culture. Manuscripts, Archives, and Rare
    Books Division. New York Public Library. New York, NY.
Baldwin, James, Collection, 1924–1987.
Bishop, Shelton Hale, Collection, 1889–1962.
Bolin, Jane Matilda, Papers, 1908–2007.
Carrington, C. Glenn, Papers, 1904–1975.
Harlem Neighborhoods Association Records.
James Weldon Johnson Community Center, Inc. Records (New York, NY).
Lafargue Clinic (New York, NY) Records. Additional contributors: Wertham, Frederic
    (1895–1981); Mosse, Hilde L.; Bishop, Shelton Hale (1889–1962).
Marshall, George, Papers, 1904–2000.
Marshall, Kenneth, Papers, 1925–1971.
Reid, Ira De Augustine, Papers, 1901–1968.
Thalheimer, Ross, Papers, 1905–.
Stuart A. Rose Manuscript, Archives, and Rare Book Library. Emory University.
    Atlanta, GA.
Killens, John Oliver, Papers, 1937–1987.

INTRODUCTION

Epigraph: Roy Campanella, "The Way I See It," *Jet*, March 12, 1959, 52.

1. Peter D. Franklin, "Campanella's Son Now Booked as a Burglar," *New York Herald Tribune*, February 25, 1959, 1.

2. Peter D. Franklin, "Campanella Son Held in Queens Gang Fight," *New York Herald Tribune*, February 24, 1959, 1, 16; "Campanella Son Is Seized in Fight: Held with 17 Others in Gang Brawl in Queens—Youth Shot Dead in Brooklyn," *New York Times*, February 24, 1959, 23.

3. "Campanella Son Is Seized," 23. For Mike O'Neill's account of the February 23 incident, see "Roy Campanella's Son, 15, Is Booked as Delinquent," *Baltimore Sun*, February 25, 1959, 1 and esp. 15.

4. Franklin, "Campanella Son Held," 1, 16. In the *New York Times* article that first reported the Campanella arrest, his mother is said to have denied comments to reporters, and "a photographer for the *New York Daily Mirror*, Jack Baumohl, 47, was reportedly roughed up and had his camera smashed by one of the two men accompanying Mrs. Campanella." See "Campanella Son Is Seized," 23. For more details on the hearing with Judge Waltemade, see "Campy's 15-Year-Old Son Booked in Drugstore Burglary Case," *Los Angeles Times*, February 25, 1959, C1; "Campanella Boy Is Held in Theft: Police Say He Confesses to Robbery after Release in Gang Fight Charge," *New York Times*, February 25, 1959, 32; Franklin, "Campanella's Son Now Booked," 1, 12; "Campanella's Son Is Convicted in Gangland Fight," *Atlanta Daily World*, February 25, 1959, 1; "Roy Campanella's Son, 15, Is Booked," 1, 15; "Report Son of Ball Star Admits Theft: Charge Burglary by Young Campanella," *Chicago Daily Tribune*, February 25, 1959, A1; and "Roy Campanella's Son, 15, Booked in Connection with Drug Store Theft: Also Involved in Street Gang Fight," *Washington Post*, February 25, 1959, D1.

5. Campanella, "Way I See It," 52. For biographical information about Roy Campanella and his efforts to curb juvenile delinquency, see Roy Campanella with Jules Tygiel, *It's Good to Be Alive* (1959; repr., Lincoln: University of Nebraska Press, 1995); Neil Lanctot, *Campy: The Two Lives of Roy Campanella* (New York: Simon and Schuster, 2011); and William C. Kashatus, *Jackie and Campy: The Untold Story of Their Rocky Relationship and the Breaking of Baseball's Color Line* (Lincoln: University of Nebraska Press, 2014). In 1959, *Life* magazine covered the transition that Campanella was making from player to manager because of an automobile

accident that left him paralyzed from the chest down. In it, his approach to his son's legal issues was briefly discussed. See "That Holler Guy, He's Back: And It's Spring Again," *Life* 46, no. 12 (March 23, 1959): 19–22.

6. Roy Campanella told reporters that when David returned from his first court appearance, he told his son, "Look, I've scrimped and worked hard for you. Now look at all the shame that you've brought to your mother and me and your brothers and your sisters. It's a lucky thing for you that I'm in a wheelchair." See "Campanella Shaken by Charges That Son Broke into Drugstore: 'Why?' Paralyzed Player Asks, 'the Boy Has Everything'—Mother Weeps as Youth, 15, Is Released on Bail," *New York Times*, February 26, 1959, 21. Most of the newspaper coverage on David Campanella's court appearance makes mention of his status in the press. See "Campanella Son Has 2d Day in Court," *Chicago Daily Tribune*, February 26, 1959, A2; Newton H. Fulbright, "Campanella 'Heartsick' over His Son's Plight: May Not Join Dodgers in Camp as Coach; Boy Gets Bail, Burglary Hearing March 11," *New York Herald Tribune*, February 26, 1959, 3; "Sad Campanella Stands behind His Errant Son," *Los Angeles Times*, February 26, 1959, C1, 3; "Son's Arrest Distresses Campanella," *Los Angeles Sentinel*, February 26, 1959, A3; "Campanellas Close Ranks around Son: Mother Minimizes Case and Roy Is Reported 'Absolutely Sick,'" *Baltimore Sun*, February 26, 1959, 3; and "Campanella Posts Bond for His Son," *Washington Post*, February 26, 1959, D2. On February 28, 1959, inspired by the case of David Campanella, twelve editors of eastern newspapers and press services and six judges held a symposium on the uses of publicity in juvenile court cases. A United States district judge, Luther W. Youngdahl, agreed with his colleagues that the names of juvenile delinquents should not be printed. Youngdahl stated, "If it is the rule not to publish the names of juvenile offenders, the name of a rich man or a famous baseball player should not be published. The publication of Campanella's name does not help to deter juvenile crime." It was to this line of reasoning that Turner Catledge was responding. On the symposium, see Ira Henry Freeman, "Publicity Studied in Juvenile Cases: Judges in Symposium Tend to Advocate Privacy, but Editors Oppose Curbs," *New York Times*, March 1, 1959, 74; and "Campanella Story Subject of Parley," *Chicago Defender*, March 2, 1959, 2.

7. "14 in Gang Fight Freed: Magistrate in Queens Warns Youths against Repetition," *New York Times*, March 7, 1959, 12; "Convict Youth in Gang Fights," *Chicago Defender*, March 7, 1959, 3. On Campanella's charges for breaking into the drugstore, see Newton H. Fulbright, "Campanella Youth Guilty of Breaking into Store: Paroled until April 10 Hearing," *New York Herald Tribune*, March 12, 1959, 17; "Campanella Boy Held Delinquent: Youth, Convicted of Breaking into Store, Is Paroled to Mother Pending Study," *New York Times*, March 12, 1959, 22; "Campanella's Son Placed on Probation," *Washington Post*, March 12, 1959, D2; "Campanella Boy Is Held Delinquent: Son of Ex-Dodger Star Freed to Family; Sentencing Set Later," *Baltimore Sun*, March 12, 1959, 3; "Place Campy's Son on Parole: His Mother and Priest Guardians," *Chicago Defender*, March 12, 1959, 1, 3; "Campanella Boy

Convicted, Must Stay at Home," *Daily Boston Globe*, March 12, 1959, 3; "Campanella Boy Judged a Delinquent," *Chicago Daily Tribune*, March 12, 1959, A1.

8. In a conversation with Justice Sylvia Liese and Daniel Stateman, the drugstore owner, David Campanella recounted an encounter with policemen, who were called by Stateman, when he and his friends were singing at a railroad station near the drugstore days before the robbery. See "Place Campy's Son on Parole: His Mothers and Priest Guardians," *Chicago Defender*, March 12, 1959, 1, 3. David Campanella was a member of a rock-and-roll singing group called the Del Chords. See "Roy Campanella's Son Makes First Recording," *Jet*, November 19, 1959, 62; and "Nizzy Rowe's Notebook: The Fantasy of Fall," *Pittsburgh Courier*, November 15, 1958. After young Campanella's photo was printed in numerous articles because of the Mapleways fight, he was ordered to appear in a lineup before three witnesses to the fatal shooting of a customer in a luggage-store holdup on February 9, 1959; he was cleared by all three witnesses. See "Campanella's Son in Slaying-Case Line-Up, Cleared," *New York Herald Tribune*, February 28, 1959, 5. On Justice Liese's quote, see Will Lissner, "Campanella's Son Put on Probation: Justice of Queens Children's Court Says Boy Can Be Rehabilitated 'Easily,'" *New York Times*, April, 11, 1959, 43; "Campanella's Sorrow," *Washington Post*, February 26, 1959, A20.

9. The "associated authorities" refer to what the historian Eric C. Schneider defines as the "web"—interconnected relationships among private and public agencies and organizations influencing the lives of youths considered delinquent. See Schneider, *In the Web of Class: Delinquents and Reformers in Boston, 1810s–1930s* (New York: NYU Press, 1992). The term "criminalization" is also used to refer to being stereotyped as a criminal, as well as to being criminalized; however, it is important to make the distinction between the two. Though the definitions and uses are not mutually exclusive and often overlap, they do have different relationships in the justice systems. Lisa Marie Cacho illustrates these differences effectively by using gang members as an example. According to Cacho, "To be stereotyped as a gang member means that someone, perhaps a law-abiding citizen, was misrecognized as a gang member because of his or her racial background. In contrast, gang members are criminalized because they have a different relationship to criminal law and the U.S. justice system, because they face regulations other people do not have to follow." See Cacho, *Social Death: Racialized Rightlessness and the Criminalization of the Unprotected* (New York: NYU Press, 2012), 5.

10. For a history of the criminalization of black girls in the urban North, see Tera Eva Agyepong, *The Criminalization of Black Children: Race, Gender, and Delinquency in Chicago's Juvenile Justice System, 1899–1945* (Chapel Hill: University of North Carolina Press, 2018), esp. 70–96; Marcia Chatelain, *South Side Girls: Growing Up in the Great Migration* (Durham, NC: Duke University Press, 2015), esp. 19–58. On the continued criminalization of black girls in the contemporary moment, see Monique W. Morris, *Pushout: The Criminalization of Black Girls in School* (New York: New Press, 2016).

11. On black boys as being seen as older and less innocent, see Phillip Atiba Goff, Matthew Christian Jackson, Brooke A. L. Di Leone, and Natalie Ann Ditomasso, "The Essence of Innocence: Consequences of Dehumanizing Black Children," *Journal of Personality and Social Psychology* 106, no. 4 (2014): 526–45. On race, wealth, incarceration, and youth, see Khaing Zaw, Darrick Hamilton, and William Darity Jr., "Race, Wealth and Incarceration: Results from the National Longitudinal Survey of Youth," *Race and Social Problems* 8, no. 1 (2016): 103–15. On black youth experiences with police violence, see Corey Williams and Emily Swanson, "Poll: Police Harassment Familiar to Young Blacks, Hispanics," *AP News*, August 4, 2016, https://apnews.com.

12. The historian Khalil Gibran Muhammad suggests that statistical discourse on black criminality from the 1890s forward was a modern invention that encapsulated northern and southern ideas about race and crime. Referencing many postbellum race-relations writers who pointed out that the country's highest rates of black criminality could be found in the "cosmopolitan, freedom-loving urban North," Muhammad argues that cities such as Chicago, New York, and Philadelphia have been at the heart of modern ideas about race and crime since the nineteenth century. See Muhammad, *The Condemnation of Blackness: Race, Crime, and the Making of Urban America* (Cambridge, MA: Harvard University Press, 2010), 4–5. For a sample of the literature on late-nineteenth- and early-twentieth-century southern criminal justice history, see Edward L. Ayers, *Vengeance and Justice: Crime and Punishment in the Nineteenth-Century American South* (New York: Oxford University Press, 1984); Joel Williamson, *A Rage for Order: Black-White Relations in the American South since Emancipation* (New York: Oxford University Press, 1986); and David Oshinsky, *Worse than Slavery: Parchman Farm and the Ordeal of Jim Crow Justice* (New York: Simon and Schuster, 1996). For a sampling of more recent scholarship that emphasizes how southern criminal justice practices contribute to the modernization of the New South, see Alex Lichtenstein, *Twice the Work of Free Labor: The Political Economy of Convict Labor in the New South* (New York: Verso Books, 1995); Mary Ellen Curtin, *Black Prisoners and Their World: Alabama, 1865–1900* (Charlottesville: University Press of Virginia, 2000); and Talitha L. LeFlouria, *Chained in Silence: Black Women and Convict Labor in the New South* (Chapel Hill: University of North Carolina Press, 2015); Sarah Haley, *No Mercy Here: Gender, Punishment, and the Making of Jim Crow Modernity* (Chapel Hill: University of North Carolina Press, 2016).

13. Much of the pioneering scholarship on youth criminality and juvenile delinquency stemmed from Anthony M. Platt's 1969 foundational study, *The Child-Savers: The Invention of Delinquency*, that led future scholars, not just historians, to question the intents and outcomes of the Progressives' agenda and their race, class, and gender biases. See Platt, *The Child Savers: The Invention of Delinquency* (1969; 40th anniversary ed., New Brunswick, NJ: Rutgers University Press, 2009). On the establishment of the juvenile court as an Americanizing influence over European immigrants, see Gary Gerstle, "The Protean Character of American

Liberalism," *American Historical Review* 99 (1994): 1050–51. For a sample of the literature on the Progressive-era approach that was consulted for this study, see Steven Schlossman, *Transforming Juvenile Justice: Reform Ideals and Institutional Realities, 1825–1920* (1977; repr., DeKalb: Northern Illinois University Press, 2005); David J. Rothman, *Conscience and Convenience: The Asylum and Its Alternatives in Progressive America* (1980; rev. ed., New York: Routledge, 2002), esp. 236–92; Mary E. Odem, *Delinquent Daughters: Protecting and Policing Adolescent Female Sexuality in the United States, 1880–1925* (Chapel Hill: University of North Carolina Press, 1995); Barry C. Feld, *Bad Kids: Race and the Transformation of the Juvenile Court* (New York: Oxford University Press, 1999); Anne Meis Knupfer, *Reform and Resistance: Gender, Delinquency, and America's First Juvenile Court* (New York: Routledge, 2001); David S. Tanenhaus, *Juvenile Justice in the Making* (New York: Oxford University Press, 2004); David B. Wolcott, *Cops and Kids: Policing Juvenile Delinquency in Urban America, 1890–1940* (Columbus: Ohio State University Press, 2005). By the end of the Progressive era, as Americans increasingly classified all whites as belonging to a single race and used "ethnicity" to differentiate among white people, the Americanizing power of the juvenile court transformed to address the overrepresentation of racial minorities. On "white" becoming a singular race divided by ethnicity in America, see Matthew Frye Jacobson, *Whiteness of a Different Color: European Immigrants and the Alchemy of Race* (Cambridge, MA: Harvard University Press, 1998), 92.

14. In 1903, the first year that data on race were available, the social scientist Earl Moses found that there were 56 cases of black delinquency in Chicago—41 boys' cases and 15 girls' cases. In 1930, there were 657 cases; 503 involved boys, and 154 involved girls. During the same time, the overall black population in Chicago increased from 1.8 percent to 6.9 percent; see Moses, *The Negro Delinquent in Chicago* (Washington, DC, 1936), 14. The criminologist Geoff K. Ward examines "the rise and fall of Jim Crow juvenile justice" through a study of its contested cultural and institutional threads from the Progressive era to the 1960s. Whereas Platt recounted the progressive child-saving narrative through a white immigrant lens that is largely class based, Ward's work positions race as the driving force to expose a system that failed to include black youths. See Ward, *The Black-Child Savers: Racial Democracy and Juvenile Justice* (Chicago: University of Chicago Press, 2012), 6, 8. More recent studies that go beyond the Progressive era and focus on black youths and other racial minorities include Andrew Diamond, *Mean Streets: Chicago Youths and the Everyday Struggle for Empowerment in the Multiracial City, 1908–1969* (Berkeley: University of California Press, 2009); William S. Bush, *Who Gets a Childhood? Race and Juvenile Justice in Twentieth-Century Texas* (Athens: University of Georgia Press, 2010); Miroslava Chávez-García, *States of Delinquency: Race and Science in the Making of California's Juvenile Justice System* (Berkeley: University of California Press, 2012); Ellen Wu, *The Color of Success: Asian Americans and the Origins of the Model Minority* (Princeton, NJ: Princeton University Press, 2014), esp. 181–209; and Tera Eva Agyepong, *The Criminalization*

of Black Children: Race, Gender, and Delinquency in Chicago's Juvenile Justice System, 1899–1945 (Chapel Hill: University of North Carolina Press, 2018).

15. On increased surveillance of city spaces through the Progressive era, see Jennifer Fronc, *New York Undercover: Private Surveillance in the Progressive Era* (Chicago: University of Chicago Press, 2009). Several urban historians and scholars of various disciplines have documented the long-standing problem of police brutality and police misconduct in postwar northern cities. The historian Marilynn S. Johnson chronicles police violence in New York City from 1846, the New York Police Department's first year of operation in which twenty-nine individuals claimed to have been assaulted by the police, to the 1990s. See Johnson, *Street Justice: A History of Police Violence in New York City* (Boston: Beacon, 2003). For more on police brutality in New York City in the post–World War II period, see Clarence Taylor, "Race, Class, and Police Brutality in New York City: The Role of the Communist Party in the Early Cold War Years," *Journal of African American History* 98, no. 2 (2013): 205–28; and Taylor, *Fight the Power: African Americans and the Long History of Police Brutality in New York City* (New York: NYU Press, 2018). On police brutality in Detroit, for example, the historian Heather Ann Thompson points to survey data from the 1950s that revealed that the "abominable state of police-community relations is what encouraged Detroiters to participate in the civil rights movement." Thompson, *Whose Detroit? Politics, Labor, and Race in a Modern American City* (Ithaca, NY: Cornell University Press, 2001), 21. The historian Edward Escobar examines how Mexicans in Los Angeles were often lumped with other racial minorities, notably blacks, as "inherently inclined toward criminality," which meant they could not depend on the police for protection and also influenced how the police responded to their misbehaviors, especially during the World War II period. Escobar, *Race, Police, and the Making of a Political Identity: Mexican Americans and the Los Angeles Police Department, 1900–1945* (Berkeley: University of California Press, 1999), 132. See also Escobar, "The Unintended Consequences of the Carceral State," *Journal of American History*, June 2015, 174–84. For a sampling of other historians who have focused on police-community relations outside the South, see also Martha Biondi, *To Stand and Fight: The Struggle for Civil Rights in Postwar New York City* (Cambridge, MA: Harvard University Press, 2003); Thomas J. Sugrue, *The Origins of the Urban Crisis: Race and Inequality in Postwar Detroit* (1996; rev. ed., Princeton, NJ: Princeton University Press, 2005); Robert O. Self, *American Babylon: Race and Struggle for Postwar Oakland* (Princeton, NJ: Princeton University Press, 2003); Matthew J. Countryman, *Up South: Civil Rights and Black Power in Philadelphia* (Philadelphia: University of Pennsylvania Press, 2006); Kevin Mumford, *Newark: A History of Race, Rights, and Riots in America* (New York: NYU Press, 2007); Michael W. Flamm, *Law and Order: Street Crime, Civil Unrest, and the Crisis of Liberalism in the 1960s* (New York: Columbia University Press, 2005); Kelly Lytle Hernández, *Migra! A History of the U.S. Border Patrol* (Berkeley: University of California Press, 2010); Fritz Umbach, *The Last Neighborhood Cops: The Rise and Fall of Community Policing*

in New York Public Housing (New Brunswick, NJ: Rutgers University Press, 2011); and Max Felker-Kantor, *Policing Los Angeles: Race, Resistance, and the Rise of the LAPD* (Chapel Hill: University of North Carolina Press, 2018).

16. I build on Elizabeth Hinton's *From the War on Poverty to the War on Crime: The Making of Mass Incarceration in America* (Cambridge, MA: Harvard University Press, 2016), which explores the roles of juvenile institutions as extensions of the carceral state since the 1960s, and the existing literature that demonstrates how authorities separate from the justice system reinforced the criminalization process from the "top down." This scholarship highlights "the federal government's power in the pursuit of twinned social welfare and social control goals" as well as the criminalization of urban civil disorders. Hinton, *From the War on Poverty to the War on Crime*, 13n22, 14n24. In a review of *From the War on Poverty to the War on Crime*, Simon Balto questions the chronological bracketing, not as a critique per se, but to probe if "supposedly progressive public policies prior to 1960 were bound up in . . . anticrime initiatives," as well as the costs of this "top-down" approach, which "obscures the ways that local politicians and police officials and officers crafted . . . mechanisms of control entirely on their own." Balto, "The Carceral State's Origins, from Above and Below," *Labor: Studies in Working-Class History* 14, no. 4 (2017): 69–74, esp. 71–72. On social scientists and juvenile delinquency in New York City, see Dennis Doyle, *Psychiatry and Racial Liberalism in Harlem, 1936–1968* (Rochester, NY: University of Rochester Press, 2016), esp. 55–75.

17. Scholars have chosen the term "carceral"—"of or belonging to prison"—to invoke a wide range of punitive state action. "It includes aggressive policing; border patrol, military, and immigrant detention; public and private surveillance; imprisonment of adults, juveniles, and undocumented workers; courts, prosecution, and parole; and even restrictive and means-tested welfare and social service policy, with links to broader systems of criminal and juvenile justice." Donna Murch, "The Many Meanings of Watts: Black Power, *Wattstax*, and the Carceral State," *Organization of American Historians Magazine of History* 26, no. 1 (2012): 38–39. The June 2015 special issue of the *Journal of American History* published thirteen essays that take an "expansive approach to the historical drivers of the carceral state." See Kelly Lytle Hernández, Khalil Gibran Muhammad, and Heather Ann Thompson, eds., "Historians and the Carceral State," *Journal of American History*, June 2015. The September 2015 issue of the *Journal of Urban History* published seven essays in a special section that called on urban historians to consider new ways to think about American cities and suburbs through the lens of the carceral state. See Heather Ann Thompson and Donna Murch, eds., "Special Section: Urban America and the Carceral State," *Journal of Urban History*, September 2015. For a sampling of historical articles and monographs on the modern American carceral state, see Heather Ann Thompson, "Why Mass Incarceration Matters: Rethinking Crisis, Decline, and Transformation in Postwar American History," *Journal of American History*, December 2010, 703–34;

Michelle Alexander, *The New Jim Crow: Mass Incarceration in the Age of Color-blindness* (New York: New Press, 2010); Marc Mauer, *Race to Incarcerate* (1999; rev ed., New York: New Press, 2006); David Garland, *The Culture of Control: Crime and Social Order in Contemporary Society* (Chicago: University of Chicago Press, 2001); Donna Jean Murch, *Living for the City: Migration, Education, and the Rise of the Black Panther Party in Oakland, California* (Chapel Hill: University of North Carolina Press, 2010); Christian Parenti, *Lockdown America: Police and Prisons in the Age of Crisis* (1999; 2nd ed., New York: Verso Books, 2008); Kelly Lytle Hernandez, *Migra! A History of the U.S. Border Patrol* (Berkeley: University of California Press, 2010); Muhammad, *Condemnation of Blackness*; Kelly Lytle Hernandez, *City of Inmates: Conquest, Rebellion, and the Rise of Human Caging in Los Angeles, 1771–1965* (Chapel Hill: University of North Carolina Press, 2017); Robert Perkinson, *Texas Tough: The Rise of a Prison Empire* (New York: Metropolitan Books, 2010); Ruth Wilson Gilmore, *Golden Gulag: Prisons, Surplus, Crisis, and Opposition in Globalizing California* (Berkeley: University of California Press, 2007); Dan Berger, *Captive Nation: Black Prison Organizing in the Civil Rights Era* (Chapel Hill: University of North Carolina Press, 2014); Elizabeth Hinton, *From the War on Poverty to the War on Crime: The Making of Mass Incarceration in America* (Cambridge, MA: Harvard University Press, 2016); Naomi Murakawa, *The First Civil Right: How Liberals Built Prison America* (New York: Oxford University Press, 2014); Jordan T. Camp, *Incarcerating the Crisis: Freedom Struggles and the Rise of the Neoliberal State* (Berkeley: University of California Press, 2016); James Forman Jr., *Locking Up Our Own: Crime and Punishment in Black America* (New York: Farrar, Straus and Giroux, 2017); Max Felker-Kantor, *Policing Los Angeles: Race, Resistance, and the Rise of the LAPD* (Chapel Hill: University of North Carolina Press, 2018). I use "racial liberalism" to analyze "racially equal opportunity in social and political life, as well as some state intervention," especially regarding juvenile justice. I borrow this definition of "racial liberalism" from Self, *American Babylon*, 14. For more on racial liberalism, see Charles W. Mills, *Black Rights / White Wrongs: The Critique of Racial Liberalism* (Oxford: Oxford University Press, 2017), esp. 28–48; Dennis A. Doyle, *Psychiatry and Racial Liberalism in Harlem, 1936–1968* (Rochester: University of Rochester Press, 2016), esp. 1–15, 136–55. The historian Andrew Diamond offers in his account of the relationship among youths, street culture, race, and racial violence in Chicago that these young people were more than simply "conduits of community attitudes." This is an important work for understanding how youths from the early part of the twentieth century have shaped the racial landscape of twentieth-century cities, primarily in Chicago. Diamonds writes, "Teens and young adults stood at the vanguard of grassroots mobilizations in White working-class Chicago [by] playing leading roles in articulating community identities, defending neighborhood boundaries, and, ultimately, making the first and second ghettos." See Diamond, *Mean Streets*, 8. By the 1920s, largely because of World War I and federal immigration restrictions, European immigration to

New York City slowed considerably; however, by the end of the decade, these persons of many races and ethnicities who arrived in New York City during the first decade of the twentieth century had their hopes of progress and prosperity tampered by the Great Depression. The historian Cheryl Lynn Greenberg's examination of Harlem during the Great Depression, which complements other works of public policy and African Americans in the urban North, not only shows the impact of the Depression on "ordinary people" but also demonstrates how they attained greater cohesion in a time of crisis. Greenberg points to the Harlem uprisings in 1935 and in 1943 as examples of effective "extensions of political activity" caused by the "failure of the external community to address black grievances adequately." However, the lasting images of "so-called rioters" reinforced the association between blacks, especially youths, and criminality. Greenberg, "Or Does It Explode?": Black Harlem in the Great Depression (New York: Oxford University Press, 1991), 10–11, 214. On the "so-called rioters" and how their images intensified the association between black Americans and criminality "that had permeated the popular imagination since slavery," see Elizabeth Hinton, "Creating Crime: The Rise and Impact of National Juvenile Delinquency Programs in Black Urban Neighborhoods," Journal of Urban History 41, no. 5 (2015): 808–24, esp. 810. For complements of earlier works on public policy and African Americans in the same period, see Harvard Sitkoff, A New Deal for Blacks: The Emergence of Civil Rights as a National Issue; The Depression Decade (1978; 25th anniversary ed., New York: Oxford University Press, 2008). Greenberg's work also fills a historiographical void on black Harlem prior to World War II; unlike other important studies of prewar Harlem, which include Osofsky's Harlem, Huggins's Harlem Renaissance, Lewis's When Harlem Was in Vogue, and Naison's Communists in Harlem during the Depression, Greenberg's work is not constrained by topic and presents a fuller picture of Harlem in the 1930s. See Gilbert Osofsky, Harlem: The Making of a Ghetto; Negro New York, 1890–1930 (1966; 2nd ed., New York: Ivan R. Dee, 1996); Nathan Irvin Huggins, Harlem Renaissance (1971; updated ed., New York: Oxford University Press, 2007); David Levering Lewis, When Harlem Was in Vogue (1979; repr., New York: Penguin Books, 1997); and Mark Naison, Communists in Harlem during the Depression (1983; repr., Urbana: University of Illinois, 2005). For a sampling of key texts on immigration to northern cities in the US, see Oscar Handlin, The Uprooted: The Epic Story of the Great Migrations That Made the American People (1951; repr., New York: Little, Brown, 1979); Olivier Zunz, The Changing Face of Inequality: Urbanization, Industrial Development, and Immigrants in Detroit, 1880–1920 (1982; repr., Chicago: University of Chicago Press, 2000); John Bodnar, The Transplanted: A History of Immigrants in Urban America (Bloomington: Indiana University Press, 1987); George J. Sánchez, Becoming Mexican American: Ethnicity, Culture, and Identity in Chicano Los Angeles (New York: Oxford University Press, 1993); Donna Gabaccia, From the Other Side: Women, Gender, and Immigrant Life in the U.S., 1820–1990 (Bloomington: Indiana University Press,

1995); Nayan Shah, *Contagious Divides: Epidemics and Race in San Francisco's Chinatown* (Berkeley: University of California Press, 2001); Mae M. Ngai, *Impossible Subjects: Illegal Aliens and the Making of Modern America* (Princeton, NJ: Princeton University Press, 2004); Eli Lederhendler, *Jewish Immigrants and American Capitalism, 1880–1920: From Caste to Class* (Cambridge, MA: Harvard University Press, 2009); and Tobias Brinkmann, *Sundays at Sinai: A Jewish Congregation in Chicago* (Chicago: University of Chicago Press, 2012). For a sampling of the key works that emphasize black progress and protest in other northern cities during the same period preceding World War II, see Joe William Trotter, *Black Milwaukee: The Making of an Industrial Proletariat, 1915–1945* (Urbana: University of Illinois Press, 1985); Peter Gottlieb, *Making Their Own Way: Southern Blacks' Migration to Pittsburgh, 1916–1930* (Urbana: University of Illinois Press, 1987); Elizabeth Clark-Lewis, *Living In, Living Out: African American Domestics in Washington, D.C., 1910–1940* (Washington, DC: Smithsonian Books, 1994); Kimberley L. Phillips, *Alabama North: African-American Migrants, Community, and Working-Class Activism in Cleveland, 1915–1945* (Urbana: University of Illinois Press, 1999); Andrew Wiese, *Places of Their Own: African American Suburbanization in the Twentieth Century* (Chicago: University of Chicago Press, 2004), esp. 11–33; Davarian L. Baldwin, *Chicago's New Negroes: Modernity, the Great Migration, and Black Urban Life* (Chapel Hill: University of North Carolina Press, 2007); and Shannon King, *Whose Harlem Is This, Anyway? Community Politics and Grassroots Activism during the New Negro Era* (New York: NYU Press, 2015).

18. The historian Martha Biondi posits that "the struggle for equality in New York invites a reevaluation of the narrative of the civil rights movement as a whole." Biondi, *To Stand and Fight*, 33, 273. For a sample of literature on civil rights and postwar New York City, see Joshua B. Freeman, *Working-Class New York: Life and Labor since World War II* (New York: New Press, 2000); Craig Steven Wilder, *A Covenant with Color: Race and Social Power in Brooklyn* (New York: Columbia University Press, 2000); Wilder, *In the Company of Black Men: The African Influence on African American Culture in New York City* (New York: NYU Press, 2001) Clarence Taylor, ed., *Civil Rights in New York City: From World War II to the Giuliani Era* (New York: Fordham University Press, 2010); Suleiman Osman, *The Invention of Brownstone Brooklyn: Gentrification and the Search for Authenticity in Postwar New York* (New York: Oxford University Press, 2011); Brian Purnell, *Fighting Jim Crow in the County of Kings: The Congress of Racial Equality in Brooklyn* (Lexington: University Press of Kentucky, 2013); Brian L. Tochterman, *The Dying City: Postwar New York and the Ideology of Fear* (Chapel Hill: University of North Carolina Press, 2017); and Kim Phillips-Fein, *Fear City: New York's Fiscal Crisis and the Rise of Austerity Politics* (New York: Metropolitan Books, 2017). More recently, the historians Brian Purnell and Jeanne Theoharis have referred to New York City as the "capital of the Jim Crow North." Purnell and Theoharis, "How New York City became the Capital of the Jim Crow North," *Washington Post,*

August 23, 2017, www.washingtonpost.com. For a sample of the postwar historiography that emphasizes the limits of racial liberalism in the urban North to demystify the narrative of the North as a utopian melting pot, see Jeanne Theoharis and Komozi Woodard, eds., *Freedom North: Black Freedom Struggles outside the South, 1940 to 1980* (New York: Palgrave Macmillan, 2003). For a sample of postwar northern urban historiography and its race relations, see Sugrue, *Origins of the Urban Crisis*; Thomas J. Sugrue, *Sweet Land of Liberty: The Forgotten Struggle for Civil Rights in the North* (New York: Random House, 2008); Thompson, *Whose Detroit?*; Self, *American Babylon*; Countryman, *Up South*; Mumford, *Newark*.

19. The historian Rebecca de Schweinitz, whose research connects black youths and social constructions of childhood to the United States' struggle for racial equality during the long civil rights movement, argues that youth roles in the movement not only were meant to bring sympathy but also were critical in changing its course. See Schweinitz, *If We Could Change the World: Young People and America's Long Struggle for Racial Equality* (Chapel Hill: University of North Carolina Press, 2011). Also, the historian Andrew Diamond's *Mean Streets* is an important work for understanding how youths from the early part of the twentieth century have shaped the racial landscape of twentieth-century cities through Chicago as a case study. On teens and young adults "at the vanguard of grassroots mobilization," see Diamond, *Mean Streets*, 4. On the lack of youth experiences in the historical records, the historian George Lipsitz writes, "public records most often reflect the concerns of those in power and only rarely contain evidence of the thoughts, action, or aspirations of teenagers and young adults unless those groups are seen as some kind of threat to people with power." Lipsitz, "Who'll Stop the Rain? Youth Culture, Rock 'n' Roll, and Social Crisis," in *The Sixties: From Memory to History*, ed. David Farber (Chapel Hill: University of North Carolina Press, 1994), esp. 206–34. In 1999, the historians Joe Austin and Michael Nevin Willard edited a collection of essays by many established scholars in the field of youth culture. For many youth studies scholars, the Austin and Willard collection was a break from the literature published before the 1990s, in which youth culture was "more passive than active, more often male than female, white, and approached via adult concerns." Miriam Formanek-Brunell, review of *Generations of Youth: Youth Cultures and History in Twentieth-Century America*, ed. Austin and Willard (New York: NYU Press, 1998), *Journal of American History*, September 1999, 855–56. For a more recent take on the methodological difficulties facing historians of youth, see Joseph M. Hawes and N. Ray Hiner, "Hidden in Plain View: The History of Children (and Childhood) in the Twenty-First Century," *Journal of the History of Childhood and Youth*, Winter 2008, 43–49. For a sampling of the literature on twentieth-century youth culture, see Paula S. Fass, *The Damned and the Beautiful: American Youth in the 1920s* (New York: Oxford University Press, 1977); Beth L. Bailey, *From Front Porch to Back Seat: Courtship in Twentieth-Century America* (Baltimore: Johns Hopkins University Press, 1988); John Modell, *Into One's Own: From Youth to Adulthood in the United States, 1920–1975* (Berkeley: University

of California Press, 1989); Joseph M. Hawes, *Children between the Wars: American Childhood, 1920–1940* (New York: Twayne, 1997); Steven Mintz, *Huck's Raft: A History of American Childhood* (Cambridge, MA: Harvard University Press, 2004); William Graebner, *Coming of Age in Buffalo: Youth and Authority in the Postwar Era* (Philadelphia: Temple University Press, 1990); Mary Louise Adams, *The Trouble with Normal: Postwar Youth and the Making of Heterosexuality* (Toronto: University of Toronto Press, 1997); Thomas Hine, *The Rise and Fall of American Teenager: A New History of the American Adolescent Experience* (New York: HarperCollins, 1999). More recent literature includes Kelly Schrum, *Some Wore Bobby Sox: The Emergence of Teenage Girls' Culture, 1920–1945* (New York: Palgrave Macmillan, 2004); and Jon Savage, *Teenage: The Prehistory of Youth Culture* (New York: Penguin Books, 2007). More recently, historians of African American girlhood have paved the way to better incorporate youth experiences from the margins to the centers of historical studies. See the roundtable by Corinne T. Field, Tammy-Charelle Owens, Marcia Chatelain, Lakisha Simmons, Abosede George, and Rhian Keyse, "The History of Black Girlhood: Recent Innovations and Future Directions," *Journal of the History of Childhood and Youth* 9, no. 3 (2016): 383–401. For a history of New York City's youth gangs from the 1940s to the 1980s, see Eric C. Schneider, *Vampires, Dragons, and Egyptian Kings: Youth Gangs in Postwar New York* (Princeton, NJ: Princeton University Press, 1999).

20. James Weldon Johnson, "The Future Harlem," in *The Selected Writings of James Weldon Johnson*, vol. 1, *The "New York Age" Editorials, 1914–1923*, ed. Sondra Kathryn Wilson (Oxford: Oxford University Press, 1995) 100.

CHAPTER 1. "THE CHILD IS NEVER BASICALLY BAD"

1. "Crime in Harlem," *New York Amsterdam News*, January 28, 1939, 6.
2. "Commission Starts Inquiry Friday: Schwartzwald Will Preside at Meet Hoping to Curb Evils," *New York Amsterdam News*, January 21, 1939, 5.
3. "Harlem Detective Disputes Charges: Pritchard Tells State Hearing There Were Only 71 Homicides in Section Last Year," *New York Amsterdam News*, January 22, 1939, 3.
4. According to Captain Pritchard's testimony, in 1934 there were 114 homicides, in 1935 and 1936 there were 109 and 119, respectively. "Harlem Detective Disputes Charges," 3. On the 71 homicides in Harlem in 1938, see also "Crime in Harlem," 6.
5. "Harlem Detective Disputes Charges," 3.
6. Alain Locke, quoted in *The Old Settler*, directed by Debbie Allen, PBS Pictures, aired April 25, 2001. For a discussion of early-twentieth-century black Harlem through the Great Depression, see James Weldon Johnson, *Black Manhattan* (New York: Knopf, 1930); E. Franklin Frazier, "Negro Harlem: An Ecological Study," *American Journal of Sociology* 43 (July 1937): 72–88; Claude McKay, *Harlem: Negro Metropolis* (New York: Dutton, 1940); Robert C. Weaver, *Negro Ghetto* (New York: Russell and Russell, 1948); Gilbert Osofsky, *Harlem: The Making of a Ghetto* (1966; 2nd ed., New York: Ivan R. Dee, 1996); John Henrik Clarke, ed.,

Harlem: A Community in Transition (New York: Citadel, 1965); Nathan Huggins, *Harlem Renaissance* (1971; updated ed., New York: Oxford University Press, 2007); David Levering Lewis, *When Harlem Was in Vogue* (1979; repr., New York: Penguin Books, 1997); Cheryl Lynn Greenberg, *"Or Does It Explode?": Black Harlem in the Great Depression* (New York: Oxford University Press, 1991); Marcy S. Sacks, *Before Harlem: The Black Experience in New York City before World War I* (Philadelphia: University of Pennsylvania Press, 2006); Shannon King, *Whose Harlem Is This, Anyway? Community Politics and Grassroots Activism during the New Negro Era* (New York: NYU Press, 2015).

7. James Weldon Johnson, "The Future of Harlem," *New York Age*, January 10, 1920, in *The Selected Writings of James Weldon Johnson*, vol. 1, *The "New York Age" Editorials, 1914–1923*, ed. Sondra Kathryn Wilson (New York: Oxford University Press, 1995), 100–101. The historian Gilbert Osofsky defines an "open city" as a city in which its black residents can live "wherever they chose." Osofsky, *Harlem*, 127–28.

8. The "Negro" population in Harlem in 1920 was 15,467; in 1930, it was reported to be 327,706. US Census Bureau, "United States Fact Sheet," 1920; US Census Bureau, "United States Fact Sheet," 1930. William Church Osborne, president of Children's Aid Society, quoted in Owen R. Lovejoy, *The Negro Children of New York* (New York: Children's Aid Society, 1932), 3, 7. Frazier, "Negro Harlem," 73. King, *Whose Harlem Is This, Anyway?*, 1.

9. President's Conference on Home Building and Home Ownership, *Report of the Committee on Negro Housing* (Washington, DC: President's Conference on Home Building and Home Ownership, 1931), 5. Of the 328,000 "Negroes" in New York City in 1930, more than 50 percent (168,537) were born in states *other than* New York. Roughly 17 percent (54,754) were foreign-born blacks. Bureau of the Census, *Fifteenth Census, 1930: Population*, vol. 2 (Washington, DC: US Bureau of the Census, 1933), 216–18; Channing H. Tobias, "Barriers to Negro Progress: Many of the Stumbling Blocks in Our Path in New York Were Put There by Ourselves," *New York Amsterdam News*, September 7, 1935, 6A.

10. Osofsky, *Harlem*, 127–28.

11. Greenberg, *"Or Does It Explode?,"* 42. "Harlem Needy Get First Soup Depot: Salvation Army Station Feeding 250 as Civic Group Plans to Fight Want," *New York Amsterdam News*, October 29, 1930, 3. For a broader discussion of New York during the Great Depression, see Beth S. Wenger, *New York Jews and the Great Depression* (Syracuse, NY: Syracuse University Press, 1999); and Dorothy Laager Miller, *New York City in the Great Depression: Sheltering the Homeless* (Charleston, SC: Arcadia, 2009). For a more specialized discussion of Harlem during the Depression, see Greenberg, *"Or Does It Explode?"*; Lewis, *When Harlem Was in Vogue*; Jervis Anderson, *This Was Harlem: A Cultural Portrait, 1900–1950* (New York: Farrar, Straus and Giroux, 1982); Raymond Wolters, *Negroes and the Great Depression: The Problem of Economic Recovery* (Westport, CT: ABC Clio, 1970); and Mark Naison, *Communists in Harlem during the Depression* (Urbana: University of Illinois Press, 1983).

12. "Sister Minnie, Benefactress of Harlem's Poor, Waited for No Depression to Begin Relief Work," *New York Amsterdam News*, December 10, 1930, 11. For more on Sister Minnie Bedell's efforts in Harlem, see "Sister Minnie Bedell Thanks Liberal Public," *New York Age*, January 21, 1928, 3; "Social Service Worker Declares Harlem Has More Homeless People Than at Any Time since the War: 'Sister Minnie' Cites Number of Cases Which Have Come under Her Observation while Ministering to Harlem's Poor," *New York Age*, March 10, 1928, 3; and "Sister Minnie Asks Public Support for Work for Unfortunates," *New York Age*, April 7, 1928, 10.

13. "Blames Low Pay for Immorality: Rev. A. C. Powell Sees Moral Status Impossible for Man Earing $15 Week," *New York Amsterdam News*, February 12, 1930, 3.

14. "Blames Low Pay," 3. At the same community forum that Allen and Powell presented their recommendations for Depression relief, Arturo Schomburg urged Harlem residents to challenge residential segregation, which he saw as the primary culprit of the economic hardship, by moving to outlying suburbs where rents were cheaper. Property crimes are often defined as crimes to obtain money, property, or some other benefit.

15. Greenberg highlights that the percentage of families on relief in Harlem varied from block to block. See Greenberg, *"Or Does It Explode?,"* 178–79. For example, between 137th and 138th Streets, Seventh and Lenox Avenues, 16 percent of families received government relief, and the average annual family income was $1,059. Between 133rd and 134th Streets, Seventh and Lenox Avenues, 42 percent of families received government relief, and the average family income totaled $842.52. It is important to note, however, that those who were arrested for possession of policy slips "ranged in skin color from white through brown to black; they were often men and women whose first tongue was Spanish." Shane White, Stephen Garton, Stephen Robertson, and Graham White, *Playing the Numbers: Gambling in Harlem between the Wars* (Cambridge, MA: Harvard University Press, 2010), 29. Irma Watkins-Owens emphasizes the role of immigrants from the Caribbean in the game of numbers. See Watkins-Owens, *Blood Relations: Caribbean Immigrants and the Harlem Community, 1900–1930* (Bloomington: Indiana University Press, 1996), esp. 136–48. J. Richard Dixie, "Thing I Couldn't Tell Till Now," *Collier's Weekly*, August 5 1939, 12–13; Mayor's Commission on Conditions in Harlem, "Negro in Harlem," report, 1935, 59, Box 2550, Fiorello H. La Guardia Papers, Municipal Archives and Records Center, New York, NY, cited in Greenberg, *Or Does It Explode?*, 295n1; "Blames Low Pay," 3; Mayor's Commission on Conditions in Harlem, "Negro Arrests in Police Precincts nos. 23, 24, 26, 30, 32, 34 in Harlem Area, 1930–June 1935," statistics, 1935, Box 755, La Guardia Papers. For a chart examining the data on numbers arrests, see Stephen Robertson, "Numbers on Harlem's Streets," *Digital Harlem Blog*, December 1, 2011, http://digitalharlemblog.wordpress.com. "Officers Round Up Men and Women for Collection of Policy Slips in Harlem: Detective Charges Prisoner Assaulted Him When Arrested as Collector—High Bail Set by Mag-

istrates for Agents," *New York Amsterdam News*, February 12, 1930, 3; *Interstate Tattler*, August 3, 1928, 1. For a more detailed analysis of numbers running in Harlem, see J. Saunders Redding, "Playing the Numbers," *North American Review*, December 1934, 533–42; Ivan Light, "Numbers Gambling among Blacks: A Financial Institution," *American Sociological Review*, December 1977, 892–904; White et al., *Playing the Numbers*; and LaShawn Harris, *Sex Workers, Psychics, and Numbers Runners: Black Women in New York City's Underground Economy* (Urbana: University of Illinois Press, 2016).

16. For a detailed primary account of crime in Harlem during the first half of the 1930s, see "Crime and the Police," *New York Amsterdam News*, July 18, 1936, 20, 24.

17. Lovejoy, *Negro Children of New York*, 8, 14.

18. "Harlem's Block of 3,871 City's Most Crowded," *New York Herald Tribune*, September 16, 1935, 13. Some parents in parts of New York City felt that their children received adequate education, "since many of the children themselves received a part of their education in the schools of the South"; however, in Harlem specifically, most made serious complaints against the schools in the community "on the grounds that they are old, poorly equipped and overcrowded and constitute fire hazards, in addition to the fact that in the administration of these schools, the welfare of the children is neglected and racial discrimination is practiced." "The Problem of Education and Recreation," *New York Amsterdam News*, July 18, 1936, 9. For more analysis on the congested class sizes in Harlem, see Osofsky, *Harlem*, 148. Lovejoy reported in 1932 that 88 percent of married mothers in Harlem were "working away from home or looking for work during the day." Lovejoy, *Negro Children of New York*, 18.

19. Lovejoy, *Negro Children of New York*, 18, 45. "Crime and the Police," 20. The historian Marcia Chatelain, in her work on black girlhood in twentieth-century Chicago, discusses how children's organizations such as the Boy Scouts, Girl Scouts, and Camp Fire Girls promoted nature as a potential solution to anxieties about urbanization and their effects on youths. See Chatelain, *South Side Girls: Growing Up in the Great Migration* (Durham, NC: Duke University Press, 2015), esp. 130–42. "The Problem of Education and Recreation," *New York Amsterdam News*, July 18, 1936, 9. For a sample of early-twentieth-century juvenile delinquency and youth culture, see Chavéz-García, *States of Juvenile Delinquency*; William S. Bush, *Who Gets a Childhood? Race and Juvenile Justice in Twentieth-Century Texas* (Athens: University of Georgia Press, 2010); Joseph M. Hawes, *Children between the Wars: American Childhood, 1920–1940* (New York: Twayne, 1997); John Modell, *Into One's Own: From Youth to Adulthood in the United States, 1920–1975* (Berkeley: University of California, 1989); Beth L. Bailey, *From Front Porch to Back Seat: Courtship in Twentieth-Century America* (Baltimore: Johns Hopkins University Press, 1988); Kathy Peiss, *Cheap Amusements: Working Women and Leisure in New York City, 1880–1920* (Philadelphia: Temple University Press, 1986); and Paula S. Fass, *The Damned and the Beautiful: American Youth in the 1920s* (New York: Oxford University Press, 1977). For

other postwar delinquency references, see Steven Mintz, *Huck's Raft: A History of American Childhood* (Cambridge, MA: Harvard University Press, 2004); William Graebner, *Coming of Age in Buffalo: Youth and Authority in the Postwar Era* (Philadelphia: Temple University Press, 1990); Mary Louise Adams, *The Trouble with Normal: Postwar Youth and the Making of Heterosexuality* (Toronto: University of Toronto Press, 1997); Eric Schneider, *Vampires, Dragons, and Egyptian Kings: Youth Gangs in New York* (Princeton, NJ: Princeton University Press, 1999); Luis Alvarez, *The Power of the Zoot: Youth Culture and Resistance during World War II* (Berkeley: University of California Press, 2008); Andrew Diamond, *Mean Streets: Chicago Youths and the Everyday Struggle for Empowerment in the Multiracial City, 1908–1969* (Berkeley: University of California Press, 2009); and Donna Jean Murch, *Living for the City: Migration, Education, and the Rise of the Black Panther Party in Oakland, California* (Chapel Hill: University of North Carolina Press, 2010).

20. Ollie Stewart, "It's Not All Swing in Harlem: That's Only the Glittering Side of This Large Negro Community, Which Has Its Own Life and Its Own Problems," *New York Times Magazine*, October 1, 1939, 119. Lovejoy, *Negro Children of New York*, 34.

21. "Table VIII: Number of Negro Boys and Girls Arrested for Juvenile Delinquency and Neglect in Seven Police Precincts in the Harlem Area—From 1930 to 1934," and "Table IX: Offenses Charged against Boys and Girls Arrested in the Harlem Area—From 1930 to 1934," in "Crime and the Police," 20. For raw numbers, see Mayor's Commission on Conditions in Harlem, "Juvenile Arrests," cited in Greenberg, *Or Does It Explode?*, 300n36; Lovejoy, *Negro Children of New York*, 25.

22. "Juvenile Crime Bureau Created to Aid Parents: New York Acts to Place Responsibility on Police Inspectors," *Washington Post*, December 18, 1934, 17. "New Set-Up Given for Crime Bureau: Valentine Tells Women It Will Be Known Hereafter as the Juvenile Aid Office," *New York Times*, December 14, 1934, 8; "Anti-crime Bureau Renamed by Mayor," *New York Times*, October 17, 1934, 11. The police commissioner's and Mayor La Guardia's criticism of the Bureau of Crime Prevention was refuted by some city council members who worked closely with the bureau. A telegram from the New York City League of Women Voters was sent to Mayor La Guardia, signed by Mrs. Donald Hutchinson, chair of municipal affairs for the league; it said in part, "Your statement concerning personnel, methods and policy seems to disregard the bureau's many accomplishments and seem to be unwarranted. Your suggestion seems to call for enlarged personnel and appropriations and increased cooperation from other city departments rather than for public criticism demoralizing a hard-working and highly trained force." See, "Model Play Class to Aid Crime Study: O'Ryan Aids Plan Designed to End Gangs—Work of Bureau Is Defended," *New York Times*, March 1, 1934, 21. It is the responsibility of a police inspector to serve as a middle manager, or supervisor, between the constable and the sergeant. For more on the Juvenile Aid Bureau, see Alfred J. Kahn, *Police and Children: A Study of the Juvenile Aid Bureau of the New York City Police Department* (New York, 1951).

23. Dudley Gilbert, "What Causes Delinquency," *New York Times*, April 29, 1934, E5. "Medical experts" were not the only ones advocating for sterilization as a means to curb delinquency. For example, Justice Samuel D. Levy told three hundred schoolteachers, "I am a firm believer in sterilization. There are 20,000 persons sterilized in this country so far, and if this process were carried out for the people who need it the number would run into millions." "Juvenile Crime Laid to Home Negligence: Sterilization of Unfit Parents Favored by Justice Levy to Stop Delinquency," *New York Times*, November 11, 1934, N2. Less drastic ways were presented by Dr. Leo J. Palmer, warden of the Wallkill State Farm, who advocated a drive to fight juvenile delinquency similar to one to combat disease, and Dr. Sheldon Glueck, professor of criminology at Harvard Law School, who advised the establishment of family guidance clinics, more effective control of marriage, professional advice on marriage problems, and sterilization of the extremely unfit. "Wants Guidance Clinics: Harvard Crime Expert Proposes Program to Fight Delinquency," *New York Times*, April 15, 1934, 30; Frederic M. Thrasher, "City Slums Are Shown as Breeders of Crime: Wide Study Finds High Ratio of Juvenile Delinquency and Adult Offenses in the Less Desirable Areas," *New York Times*, August 5, 1934, XX12.

24. Kahn, *Police and Children*, 12, 13. For an example of studies of criminality in the 1920s, see Thorsten Sellin, "The Negro Criminal: A Statistical Note," *Annals of the American Academy of Political and Social Science* 140 (November 1928): 52–64; Carl Murchison, *Criminal Intelligence* (Cambridge, MA: Forgotten Books, 1926), esp. 201–19; Clifford R. Shaw, *Delinquency Areas* (Chicago: University of Chicago Press, 1929), esp. 17; Edward E. Wilson, "The Responsibility for Crime," *Opportunity* 7 (March 1929): 95–97; and Earl R. Moses, "Community Factors in Delinquency," *Journal of Negro Education* 5 (April 1936): 220–27.

25. The amendment authorizing the Crime Prevention Bureau stated, "There shall be a bureau in the Police Department to be known as the Crime Prevention Bureau, to be organized and maintained for the prevention of crime and delinquency among minors and for the performance of such other duties as the Commissioner of Police may assign thereto. . . . Any member of the police force assigned to the said Crime Prevention Bureau shall retain his or her rank and pay in the police force and shall be eligible for promotion as if serving in the uniformed force, and the time served in the said bureau shall count for all purposes as if served in his or her own rank or grade in the uniformed force of the Police Department. . . . The Police Commissioner may also appoint such other person as may be necessary for the conduct of this bureau." Quoted in Kahn, *Police and Children*, 13–14. For background on and the appointment of Henrietta Additon as head of the Crime Prevention Bureau, see "Miss Additon to Be Sixth Deputy," *New York Times*, June 20, 1931, 10; "Miss Additon Takes New Police Office: Crime Prevention Bureau Head Assumes Deputy Commissionership Created for Her," *New York Times*, June 23, 1931, 26.

26. "Crime Prevention," *New York Times*, March 29, 1933, 14.

27. "Crime Prevention," 14.
28. In JAB's first year, there were 17,195 cases reported; in 1940, there were 66,640 cases reported. It is important to note, however, that almost half the cases were carryovers from previous years. James J. Brennan, "The Juvenile Aid Bureau of the Police Department of the City of New York," master's thesis, New York University, 1947. Kahn, *Police and Children*, 14.
29. In 1933, the Crime Prevention Bureau's budget was $346,000; in 1934, the new committees called for a budget of $500,000. See "Model Play Class to Aid Crime Study: O'Ryan Aids Plan Designed to End Gangs—Work of Bureau Is Defended," *New York Times*, March 1, 1934, 21.
30. Kahn, *Police and Children*, 15.
31. For a sample of organized crime prevention efforts in other major cities, see Nathaniel Cantor, "Organized Efforts in Crime Prevention," *Annals of the American Academy of Police and Social Science* 217 (September 1941): 155–63, esp. 159–61.
32. A short case study of the Police Athletic League's first-year efforts was printed in the *Journal of Educational Sociology*. See "Research Projects and Methods in Educational Sociology," *Journal of Educational Sociology* 8, no. 3 (November 1934): 189, esp. 191–92. For an organizational history of the Police Athletic League in New York City, see Police Athletic League, "History," accessed June 18, 2018, www.palnyc.org.
33. Police Athletic League, "History."
34. PAL had over seventy thousand members in 1937 and operated sixty-nine recreational centers. See Police Athletic League, "History." On Additon referring to them as "PALs," see Kahn, *Police and Children*, 14–15.
35. "Harlem Cop Is Charged with Smacking Boy: Juvenile Aid Bureau of 32nd Precinct Gets Alleged Victim," *New York Amsterdam News*, September 3, 1938, 1.
36. Kahn, *Police and Children*, 15. Brennan, "Juvenile Aid Bureau," 8.
37. Federal Juvenile Delinquency Act (FJDA) of 1938, 18 U.S.C. §§ 921–29. "Criminal Law—Federal Juvenile Delinquency Act—Constitutionality of Waiver of Indictment and Jury Trial," *Columbia Law Review* 38 (November 1938): 1318–23.
38. FJDA, 18 U.S.C. §§ 921–29. The previous act that addressed juvenile delinquency was the Act of June 11, 1932, 47 Stat. 301, 18 U.S.C. § 662a. The period of probation "not exceeding his minority" often covered until the young offender turned twenty-one. See S. C. F. Farmer, "Probation and Juvenile Delinquency in the U.S.A.," *Probation: The Journal of the National Association of Probation Officers and the Clarke Hall Fellowship* 4 (April 1945): 119–21, esp. 121; Wendell Berge, "Application of the Federal Juvenile Delinquency Act: The Role of the United States Attorney and Law-Enforcement Officers," *Federal Probation* 57 (1942): 4–7.
39. For discussions on the establishment of juvenile courts, see Anthony M. Platt, *The Child-Savers: The Invention of Delinquency* (1969; 40th anniversary ed., New Brunswick, NJ: Rutgers University Press, 2009); Steven L. Schlossman, *Transforming Juvenile Justice: Reform Ideals and Institutional Realities, 1825–1920* (1977; repr., DeKalb: Northern Illinois University Press, 2005); David J. Rothman, *Conscience*

and Convenience: The Asylum and Its Alternatives in Progressive America (1980; rev. ed., New York: Routledge, 2002); Robert M. Mennel, *Thorns and Thistles: Juvenile Delinquents in the United States, 1825–1940* (Hanover, NH: University Press of New England, 1973); Mary E. Odem, *Delinquent Daughters: Protecting and Policing Adolescent Female Sexuality in the United States, 1880–1925* (Chapel Hill: University of North Carolina Press, 1995); Barry C. Feld, *Bad Kids: Race and the Transformation of the Juvenile Court* (New York: Oxford University Press, 1999); David S. Tanenhaus, *Juvenile Justice in the Making* (Cambridge, MA: Harvard University Press, 2005); Anne Meis Knupfer, *Reform and Resistance: Gender, Delinquency, and America's First Juvenile Court* (New York: Routledge, 2001); and Bradley T. Smith, "Interpreting 'Prior Record' under the Federal Juvenile Delinquency Act," *University of Chicago Law Review* 67 (Autumn 2000): 1431–60, esp. 1433. The concept of the parental state originates in the concept of *parens patriae* (parent of the nation). The Latin term was first applied in sixteenth-century England to define the role of the state in the lives of children whose deceased parents passed on an estate. It was first applied in the United States in the case of *Ex Parte Crouse* (1839), in which the Pennsylvania Supreme Court defended the constitutionality of detaining a youth in the Philadelphia House of Refuge who had not been convicted of any crime. For a further discussion of *parens patriae*, see Geoff K. Ward, *The Black Child-Savers: Racial Democracy and Juvenile Justice* (Chicago: University of Chicago Press, 2012), esp. 25–26; Barry C. Feld, "Criminalizing Juvenile Justice: Rules of Procedure for the Juvenile Court," *Minnesota Law Review* 69 (1984): 141–276.

40. Jeffrey A. Butts and Adele V. Harrell, *Delinquents or Criminals: Policy Options for Young Offenders; Crime Policy Report* (Urban Institute1998), 3. Because juvenile proceedings are civil and not criminal, a youth could not technically be "sentenced." If a youth is found to have committed an illegal act, they are "adjudicated" a delinquent, see Howard N. Snyder and Melissa Sickmund, *Juvenile Offenders and Victims: 1999 National Report* 88, 97–100 cited in Smith, "Interpreting 'Prior Record' under the Federal Juvenile Delinquency Act," 1435n22. Berge, "Application of the Federal Juvenile Delinquency Act," 4. "The model juvenile court judge was seen as a sort of 'doctor-counselor rather than [a] lawyer," Platt, *The Child-Savers*, 142.

41. In 1938, according to US Children's Bureau statistics, 50,451 juveniles appeared before a judge; 35,804 were arrested. The disparity speaks to the broad authority given to the juvenile court. Often the court intervened at the first sign of potential trouble from a youth, even if the behavior was not "criminal." Edward E. Schwartz, "Statistics of Juvenile Delinquency in the United States," *Annals of the American Academy of Police and Social Science* 261 (January 1949): 9–20, esp. 11. Anthony Platt writes, "Juvenile courts could intervene where no offense had actually been committed but where, for example, a child was posing problems for some person in authority, such as a parent or teacher or social worker." Platt, *Child-Savers*, 142. Berge, "Application of the Federal Juvenile Delinquency Act," 4.

42. Marvel Cooke, "Children's Court—Last Outpost against the Ills and Misfortunes of Immaturity," *New York Amsterdam Star-News*, April 12, 1941, 8.
43. "Mayor Swears In Negro Woman as Judge: Summons Her to Office, Then Breaks News," *New York Times*, July 23, 1939, 7; "La Guardia Gives N.Y. First Negro Woman Justice," *Chicago Daily Tribune*, July 23, 1939, 8. Adam Powell Jr. described Bolin's appointment as "probably the finest appointment that La Guardia has given Negroes" in his column in the *New York Amsterdam News*. See Powell, "Soap Box," *New York Amsterdam News*, August 5, 1939, 11. For a discussion of Judge Bolin's appointment and its impact on the Progressive-era child-saving movement, see Ward, *Black Child-Savers*, esp. 188–95.
44. For a complete biographical account of Justice Jane Matilda Bolin, see Jacqueline A. McLeod, *Daughter of the Empire State: The Life of Judge Jane Bolin* (Urbana: University of Illinois Press, 2011).
45. "Judge Jane Bolin," *The Times* (London), February 7, 2007, 59; David Margolick, "At the Bar: In Retrospect, Father Didn't Know Best in the Case of a Daughter with a Habit of Making History," *New York Times*, May 14, 1993, B8; Judy Klemesrud, "For a Remarkable Judge, a Reluctant Retirement," *New York Times*, December 8, 1978, A22.
46. "Editorial: Challenge to Negro Leadership," *Pittsburgh Courier*, July 29, 1939, 3; "Mayor Swears in Negro Woman," 7; Harry Webber, "Woman Made Judge: Jane Bolin Takes Oath; Will Handle Domestic Relations Cases in N.Y.," *Baltimore Afro-American*, July 21, 1939, 1; transcript of Justice Panken's induction of Jane Bolin, July 24, 1939, Box 3, Jane Matilda Bolin Papers, Schomburg Center for Research in Black Culture, Manuscripts, Archives, and Rare Books Division, New York Public Library, New York, NY.
47. Jane M. Bolin, "The Experience of Domestic Relations Court of the City of New York in Relation to the Proposed Unified Family Court," speech to Bar Association of the City of New York, transcript, Box 3, Bolin Papers. For Albert Deutsch's description of the juvenile court, see Deutsch, *Our Rejected Children* (New York: Little, Brown, 1950), esp. 223.
48. McLeod, *Daughter of the Empire State*, 46; Klemesrud, "For a Remarkable Judge," A22; transcript of speech honoring Jane Bolin with Myles Paige Award, December 1983, Awards Folder, Box 3, Bolin Papers; Douglas Martin, "Jane Bolin, the Country's First Black Woman to Become a Judge, Is Dead at 98," *New York Times*, January 10, 2007, A21.
49. Transcript of Justice Panken's induction of Jane Bolin; transcript of Justice Jane Bolin's comments on the occasion of her retirement, December 7, 1978, Box 3, Bolin Papers; Klemesrud, "For a Remarkable Judge," A22.
50. Emma Bugbee, "Justice Jane M. Bolin Shuns Glib Diagnosis of Child Crime," *New York Herald Tribune*, April 18, 1943.
51. Patricia McFall Torbet, "Juvenile Probation: The Workhorse of the Juvenile System," *Juvenile Justice Bulletin*, March 1996, 1–5; Richard A. Chappell, "The Role of the Probation Officer," *Federal Probation* 3 (July–September 1942): 10–15, esp. 10, 15.

52. Jane Bolin, interview with Jean Rudd, 1990, 10, 31, Box 1, Bolin Papers; Klemesrud, "For a Remarkable Judge," A22; "Race Bias Seen Key to Harlem Crime: Citizen Group Holds Opening of Better Jobs to Negroes Is First Consideration," *New York Times*, August 2, 1942, 28; McLeod, *Daughter of the Empire State*, 62.

53. Geoff K. Ward uses the term "Jim Crow juvenile justice" in reference to the period in which "black civic leaders first declared war on these systems of separate and unequal juvenile social control." Ward, *Black Child-Savers*, 4–5, 191. Katherine Hildreth, "The Negro Problem as Reflected in the Functioning of the Domestic Relations Court of the City of New York" (report of the special examiner, New York City Children's Court, June 1934), cited in Greenberg, *Or Does It Explode?*, 171; Klemesrud, "For a Remarkable Judge," A22; Jane Bolin to John A. Wallace, director of New York City Office of Probation, July 31, 1963, Box 3, Bolin Papers; McLeod, *Daughter of the Empire State*, 61–78, esp. 65.

54. Judge Jane Bolin to Maceo Thomas, Chairman of the Colored Orphan Asylum, February 18, 1943, Box 1, Bolin Papers. For a comprehensive history of the Colored Orphan Asylum, see William Seraile, *Angels of Mercy: White Women and the History of New York's Colored Orphan Asylum* (New York: Fordham University Press, 2011). "Negroes' School Faced by Closing: Wiltwyck, Near Kingston, Makes Plan to Continue Treatment of Delinquents; $50,000 Must Be Raised," *New York Times*, May 13, 1942, 17; "Race Bias Seen Key to Harlem Crime," 28; "Wiltwyck School for Boys," Teaching Eleanor Roosevelt, Eleanor Roosevelt National Historic Site, www.nps.gov, cited in McLeod, *Daughter of the Empire State*, 128n12. See also "Wiltwyck School for Boys," in *The Eleanor Roosevelt Encyclopedia*, ed. Maurine H. Beasley, Holly C. Shulman, and Henry R. Beasley (Westport, CT: Greenwood, 2001), 567–69. On Baldwin's praise of the Wiltwyck School, see James Baldwin, "Wiltwyck," n.d., Folder 26, Box 6, James Baldwin Papers, Sc MG 936, Schomburg Center for Research in Black Culture, Manuscripts, Archives, and Rare Books Division, New York Public Library, New York, NY. On similar institutions following suit, "It was through the efforts of Justice Bolin that the Brooklyn Training School for Girls, a private school for Protestant girls, changed its policy of discriminating against races, and adopted one that enabled Negro girls to be admitted." Julius J. Adams, "Meet Justice Jane M. Bolin! The Only Negro Woman Judge in the World's Largest City," *New York Amsterdam News*, January 29, 1944, 7A.

55. The Brown-Isaacs amendment, sponsored by Earl Brown and Stanley Isaacs, was enacted after Bolin had repeated talks about the "disgrace of using public funds to prop up private agencies that refused to accept the city's African American and Puerto Rican children." Earl Brown was the first African American councilman for New York City, and Stanley Isaacs, borough president of Manhattan, was a civil rights advocate. See Martha Biondi, *To Stand and Fight: The Struggle for Civil Rights in Postwar New York City* (Cambridge, MA: Harvard University Press, 2003), esp. 112–36. Madelyn E. Turner to Mrs. James Nicely, December 23, 1950, Box 3, Bolin Papers; Bolin to Wallace, July 31, 1963.

56. "Race Bias Seen Key to Harlem Crime," 28.

57. Klemesrud, "For a Remarkable Judge," A22. For details of the reports, see "Race Bias Seen Key to Harlem Crime," 28. "Harlem: 'Renaissance' to 1942; Harlem Gained Strength after Era of Depression," *New York Amsterdam Star-News*, January 31, 1942, 7.

CHAPTER 2. "MARGIE'S DAY"

Epigraph: Langston Hughes, "Beaumont to Detroit: 1943," *People's Voice*, July 3, 1943.

1. "Harlem Hoodlums Must Go," *New York Amsterdam News*, July 22, 1944, A10. Two days after the Harlem uprising, the *New York Times* printed a short column that referred to the "agitators" as "hoodlums." "Harlem's Tragedy," *New York Times*, August 3, 1943, 18. Even Frank R. Crosswaith, a black socialist politician in New York City, wrote a letter to the *New York Amsterdam News* condemning the protestors in the Harlem uprising and referred to them as "hoodlums." Crosswaith, "Wasn't Race Riot, but Could Have Been," *New York Amsterdam News*, August 14, 1943, 10. The *Chicago Defender* printed a critique of the black newspapers that were referring to the Harlem protestors as hoodlums and reminded them, "Our battle is not against the results, but the cause—not against the Bigger Thomases, but the Bilbos and Rankins." "Why Hoodlums?," *Chicago Defender*, September 4, 1943, 14.

2. Kenneth B. Clark, "Morale among Negroes," in *Civilian Morale: Second Yearbook of the Society for the Psychological Study of Social Issues*, ed. Goodwin Watson (Boston: Houghton Mifflin, 1942), 244–45. For more comprehensive studies of the 1943 race riot in Detroit, see Robert Shogan and Tom Craig, *The Detroit Race Riot: A Study in Violence* (Southborough, MA: Chilton Books, 1964); Dominic J. Capeci and Martha Wilkerson, *Layered Violence: The Detroit Rioters of 1943* (Jackson: University Press of Mississippi, 1991); Dan Georgakas and Marvin Surkin, *Detroit: I Do Mind Dying; A Study in Urban Revolution* (Cambridge, MA: South End, 1998); A. J. Baime, *The Arsenal of Democracy: FDR, Detroit, and an Epic Quest to Arm an America at War* (Boston: Houghton Mifflin Harcourt, 2014). For more comprehensive studies of the 1943 race riot in Los Angeles, see Eduardo Obregón Pagán, *Murder at the Sleepy Lagoon: Zoot Suits, Race, and Riot in Wartime L.A.* (Chapel Hill: University of North Carolina Press, 2006); Luis Alvarez, *The Power of the Zoot: Youth Culture and Resistance during World War II* (Berkeley: University of California Press, 2009); and Catherine S. Ramírez, *The Woman in the Zoot Suit: Gender, Nationalism, and the Cultural Politics of Memory* (Durham, NC: Duke University Press, 2009).

3. The title of this section is from Willard S. Townsend, "Full Employment and the Negro Worker," *Journal of Negro Education* 14 (Winter 1945): 7.

4. On the familiar circumstances detected, Willard S. Townsend, the vice president of the labor organization the International Brotherhood of Red Caps, described that "the Negro remembers World War I, when he was introduced into industrial

employment only to be dismissed in the depression of the thirties." Townsend, "Full Employment," 7. The United States Employment Service examined selected defense industries throughout the country and revealed, "Out of 282,245 prospective job openings, 144,583 or 51 percent were absolutely barred." Lester B. Granger, "Barriers to Negro War Employment," *Annals of the American Academy of Political and Social Science* 23 (September 1942): 72–80, esp. 72. See also Nat Brandt, *Harlem at War: The Black Experience in WWII* (Syracuse, NY: Syracuse University Press, 1996), 73n2.

5. By 1944, the average white worker was making nearly $50 a week, or $2,600 a year. Richard Lingeman, *Don't You Know There's a War On? The American Home Front, 1941–1945* (New York: Public Affairs, 1970), 164–65. Also see Brandt, *Harlem at War*, 126n5; Granger, "Barriers to Negro War Employment," 72–73.

6. For examples of how the black press applied pressure on and exposed racial discrimination in the war industry, see Edgar G. Brown, "Edgar Brown Raps Walter White for Attitude: Committee Called Defense Leaders for Bias Probe," *Pittsburgh Courier*, July 12, 1941, 24; "Group List Names for OPM Board Banning Discrimination," *New York Amsterdam News*, July 19, 1941, 10; and Emmett J. Scott, "FDR Should End Government Discrimination: Federal Departments Worst Offenders—Untouched by Order," *Pittsburgh Courier*, August 2, 1941, 24. Granger, "Barriers to Negro War Employment," 74; John Davis, *How Management Can Integrate Negroes in War Industries* pamphlet (Albany: New York State War Council on Discrimination in Employment, 1942), 4.

7. Granger, "Barriers to Negro War Employment," 78; Executive Order 8802, dated June 25, 1941, General Records of the United States Government, RG 11, National Archives, Washington, DC.

8. Townsend, "Full Employment and the Negro Worker," 6–7; "Negro Betterment Seen: Head of Tuskegee Cites Moves for Utilizing Manpower," *New York Times*, April 11, 1943, 52.

9. Julius A. Thomas, director of the Department of Industrial Relations, made the National Urban League estimate to Harold Orlansky in an interview on August 1943. See Harold Orlansky, *The Harlem Riot: A Study in Mass Frustration*, pamphlet (New York: Social Analysis, 1943), 17; City-Wide Citizens' Committee on Harlem, "The Story of the City-Wide Citizens' Committee on Harlem," May 1943, 23, Box 8, Stanley Isaacs Papers, Schomburg Center for Research in Black Culture, Manuscripts, Archives, and Rare Books Division, New York Public Library, New York, NY; Brandt, *Harlem at War*, 127n9. Illinois was the other state that passed laws forbidding racial discrimination on war contracts. In New York, a special committee was appointed by the governor as part of the State War Council to make this policy effective. See Granger, "Barriers to Negro War Employment," esp. 78–79.

10. E. Franklin Frazier, *Negro Youth at the Crossways* (Washington, DC: American Council on Education, 1940), 166; Townsend, "Full Employment and the Negro Worker," 7; Granger, "Barriers to Negro War Employment," 73, 75–76.

11. Steven Ross Gross, "Harlem during the Second World War: An Analysis of the 1943 Riot and Its Causes," master's thesis, Columbia University, 1969, 55. In Harlem between September 1941 and February 1944, it was reported that 7,601 students dropped out of school. New York Foundation, *Report of the Harlem Project* (New York: New York Board of Education, 1947), 30. The overcrowded conditions forced most Harlem schools to operate in three shifts, which meant that youths were not required to be in school all day and which "put the children in the street for most of the day with nothing to do." Citywide Citizens' Committee on Harlem, "Report of the Subcommittee on Education and Recreation," 1942, 2, Municipal Archives and Records Center, New York, NY. On the dated textbooks, see National Association for the Advancement of Colored People, "School Textbooks," 1943, cited in Gross, "Harlem during the Second World War," 55n56.

12. Though a large number of black families relied on government relief, a significant percentage of the population was denied. According to Cheryl Greenberg, "The Federation of Protestant Welfare Agencies found 40 percent of the black elderly it studied living 'in the very poorest of circumstances,' with only 20 percent receiving any sort of public aid." Further, "In 1943, the average New York City family spent $2,740, slightly more in Manhattan. In Harlem, families spent $2,395." Greenberg, "The Politics of Disorder: Reexamining Harlem's Riots of 1935 and 1943," *Journal of Urban History* 18 (August 1992): 421–22.

13. Greenberg, "Politics of Disorder," 422–23; Dominic J. Capeci, "From Different Liberal Perspectives: Fiorello H. LaGuardia, Adam Clayton Powell, Jr., and Civil Rights in New York City, 1941–1943," *Journal of Negro History* 62 (April 1977): 162, 161n7. For more on Adam Clayton Powell Jr. and his efforts to becoming New York's first black congressional representative, see Michael W. Flamm, *In the Heat of the Summer: The New York Riots of 1964 and the War on Crime* (Philadelphia: University of Pennsylvania Press, 2017), esp. 33–34. *New York Amsterdam News*, January 6, 1940, 8.

14. For a more thorough analysis of La Guardia's relations with black New Yorkers, see Dominic J. Capeci Jr., *The Harlem Riot of 1943* (Philadelphia: Temple University Press, 1977), esp. 4–21, 8. Adam Clayton Powell Jr., editorial, *People's Voice*, May 23, 1942, 20.

15. For a detailed description on the 1935 Harlem riot, see Greenberg, "Politics of Disorder," esp. 395–419, 406, 407.

16. On the details of Frazier's study, see Mayor's Commission on the Conditions in Harlem, "The Negro in Harlem: A Report on Social and Economic Conditions Responsible for the Outbreak of March 19, 1935," 13–15, 18, Box 2550, Fiorello H. La Guardia Papers, Municipal Archives and Records Center, New York, NY.

17. For a sample of comprehensive studies of La Guardia and twentieth-century New York, see Mason B. Williams, *City of Ambition: FDR, La Guardia, and the Making of Modern New York* (New York: Norton, 2013); H. Paul Jeffers, *The Napoleon of New York: Mayor Fiorello La Guardia* (New York: Wiley, 2002); Thomas Kessner, *Fiorello H. La Guardia and the Making of Modern New York* (New York: Penguin

Books, 1989); Kessner, "Fiorello H. La Guardia," *History Teacher* 26 (February 1993): 151–59. Kessner, "Fiorello H. La Guardia," 158; La Guardia to Carrie Brown Shaskan, December 14, 1943, Box 2546, La Guardia Papers. La Guardia to August B. Rechholtz, October 17, 1941, Box 2546, La Guardia Papers; Capeci, "From Different Liberal Perspectives," 161.

18. Lawrence Ervin to La Guardia, January 19, 1943, Box 2564, La Guardia Papers; La Guardia to William Wilson, January 6, 1943, Box 2564, La Guardia Papers; La Guardia to Leathe Hemachandra, January 26, 1943, Box 2546, La Guardia Papers. See also Capeci, "From Different Liberal Perspectives," 165; Capeci, *Harlem Riot of 1943*, 137–38; Greenberg, "Politics of Disorder," 423.

19. Roy Wilkins, *Amsterdam News*, May 8, 1943, 7; Andy Razaf, "'Guilty' Savoy," *People's Voice*, May 22, 1943, 26; *People's Voice*, May 8, 1943, 16, 1, 3. See also Capeci, "From Different Liberal Perspectives," 165; Capeci, *Harlem Riot of 1943*, 138–40; Greenberg, "Politics of Disorder," 423. For more on the Savoy Ballroom and its significance in twentieth-century Harlem and beyond, see Gena Caponi-Tabery, *Jump for Joy: Jazz, Basketball, and Black Culture in 1930s America* (Amherst: University of Massachusetts Press, 2008), esp. 56–59.

20. Warren Brown, *Saturday Review of Literature* 25 (December 19, 1942): 5–6; Memorandum to the Mayor (from Lester B. Stone), December 29, 1942, Box 810, La Guardia Papers; Capeci, "From Different Liberal Perspectives," 165; Greenberg, "Politics of Disorder," 423.

21. "Housing Plan Opposed: 'Walled City for Privileged' Is Seen by Union Council," *New York Times*, May 27, 1943, 27; "Stuyvesant Town Plan Given City for Approval: Ecker Submits Contract for Post-war Housing Project," *New York Herald Tribune*, May 14, 1943, 11; "City Approves Metropolitan's Housing Plan: Stuyvesant Town Contract Voted by Estimate Board after Negro-Ban Debate," *New York Herald Tribune*, June 4, 1943, 1.

22. "Negro 'Freedom Rally' in Garden Draws 20,000: Overflow Crowd of 10,000 Joins in Protest against Racial Discrimination," *New York Herald Tribune*, June 8, 1943, 21A; John Anderson to La Guardia, June 2, 1943, Box 762, La Guardia Papers. For a more thorough examination of the Double V campaign, see Rawn James Jr., *The Double V: How Wars, Protest, and Harry Truman Desegregated America's Military* (New York: Bloomsbury, 2013).

23. Charles R. Lawrence Jr., "Race Riots in the United States, 1942–1946," in *Negro Year Book, 1941–1946*, ed. Jessie Guzman (Atlanta: Foote and Davis, 1947), esp. 232–57. Beaumont, Mobile, Los Angeles, and Detroit all experienced uprisings in 1943. For an analysis of the Beaumont Riot of 1943, see Pamela Lippold, "Recollections: Revisiting the Beaumont Race Riot of 1943," *Touchstone* 25 (March 2006). Leonard E. Golditch to La Guardia, July 24, 1943, Box 762, La Guardia Papers; Robert Moses, "What's the Matter with New York?," *New York Times*, August 1, 1943, 9.

24. The title of this section comes from a black newspaper's account of what happened in Harlem on August 1, 1943: "Hoodlums' Holiday," *Pittsburgh Courier*, August 14, 1943, 6.

25. For the information in this paragraph, see *New York Times*, August 1, 1943, 1; *New York Herald Tribune*, August 1, 1943, 1; Don Cook, "Pay as You Go Aids Budget by 5 Billions: Revised Figures Show Increased Yield, May Limit Rise in Taxes," *New York Herald Tribune*, August 1, 1943, 1; John H. Crider, "Roosevelt Asks More War Taxes, Savings, or Both: Army Outlay Cut," *New York Times*, August 1, 1943, 1. The New York Yankees lost to the Detroit Tigers, 7–6, the Brooklyn Dodgers lost to the St. Louis Cardinals, 2–1, and the New York Giants (baseball) lost to the Cincinnati Reds, 4–2. See "Major Sports Results: Baseball," *New York Times*, August 1, 1943, 1. Evelyn Seely, *PM Magazine*, August 3, 1943, 5; Walter White, *A Man Called White: The Autobiography of Walter White* (1948; repr., Athens: University of Georgia Press, 1975), 223.

26. Orlansky, *Harlem Riot*, 4; Capeci, *Harlem Riot of 1943*, 99–114, esp. 100; Harding to the Police Commissioner; "Harlem Disorders Bring Quick Action by City and Army: Police and Soldiers Patrol the Area—Traffic Is Diverted from Wide Section," *New York Times*, August 2, 1943, 1.

27. Orlansky, *Harlem Riot*, 5; Harding to the Police Commissioner; Seely, *PM Magazine*, August 3, 1943, 6; Capeci, *Harlem Riot of 1943*, 100–101.

28. Orlansky, *Harlem Riot*, 18–19, esp. 19.

29. More than five thousand patrol officers were assigned to Harlem. See "Harlem Disorders Bring Quick Action," 1; *PM Magazine*, August 3, 1943, 6. Claude Brown, *Manchild in the Promised Land* (1965; repr., New York: Scribner, 2012), 13. On the youths who offered goods, see Dan Burley, "Dan Burley's Back Door Stuff: . . . And They Went Wild as They Plundered Harlem," *New York Amsterdam News*, August 14, 1943, 16. Although the Fire Department refused to provide information on the number of fires in the area, one newspaper reported that thirty-two fires had broken out and fifty alarms had been turned in. Two firefighters were eventually stationed to guard each box in Harlem. See Orlansky, *Harlem Riot*, 5–6, esp. 6. "Dewey Mobilizes Guard to Prevent New Harlem Riots: Disorders Subside after Five Are Killed, 543 Hurt and 484 Arrests Made," *New York Herald Tribune*, August 3, 1943, 1.

30. History Channel, "Fiorello La Guardia Imposes Curfew to Halt Harlem Rioting," accessed September 20, 2017, www.history.com.

31. "Harlem Disorders Bring Quick Action," 1; Orlansky, *Harlem Riot*, 5–6; Burley, "Dan Burley's Back Door Stuff," 16; "Report from Commanding Officer Sixth Division of NYPD and Assistant Chief Inspector on Uptown Chamber of Commerce Meeting of September 1, 1943," Folder 191, Box 2550, La Guardia Papers.

32. Powell to La Guardia, telegram, June 22, 1943, Box 2574, La Guardia Papers; transcript of Adam Clayton Powell's Remarks to the City Council, June 24, 1943, Box 2574, La Guardia Papers; White, *Man Called White*, 230; Powell to La Guardia, telegram, August 2, 1943, Box 752, La Guardia Papers. Rather than a "riot," the Citizens' Committee on Better Race Relations, appointed by Mayor La Guardia, preferred to call the disturbance a "social explosion," brought on by "the ever-present problems of isolation, segregation and discrimination to which the Negro

in almost every section of the country, is subjected." "Harlem Riot Probe Asks 10-Point Remedial Plan," *Chicago Defender*, September 25, 1943, 7.

33. "Harlem Disorders Bring Quick Action," 1, 16; "Dewey Mobilizes Guard," 1; Harding to the Police Commissioner.

34. For the complete text of La Guardia's first broadcast, see "Harlem Disorders Bring Quick Action," 16.

35. For next-day, national coverage of the Harlem Riot of 1943, see "Seven Shot, One Dead in Harlem Riot," *Los Angeles Times*, August 2, 1943, 6; "Shooting of Negro Soldier Stirs Trouble in Harlem: Thirty Hurt in Disorders—La Guardia Appeals to Crowds to Go Home—Bars Traffic from Area," *Baltimore Sun*, August 2, 1943, 9. On August 12, 1943, the *London Times* published an articled titled "Harlem Riot Censored," in which the paper claimed that the United States had censored the release of the news to other countries. According to the *London Times*, "Two newspapers featured the line, 'Riot Kept Secret Three Days.'" "Harlem Riot Censored," *London Times*, August 12, 1943. The *Pittsburgh Courier* referred to the Harlem Riot as "Black Sunday." See "Peace Settles over Harlem as Leaders Seek Solution to Rioting," *Pittsburgh Courier*, August 14, 1943, 1. Press Release: Transcript of La Guardia's Broadcast from City Hall, August 2, 1943, 1–2, Box 2550, La Guardia Papers; "Dewey Mobilizes Guard," 1, 6, 12; "Harlem Is Orderly with Heavy Guard Ready for Trouble: Rioting Sunday Night Tapers Off—8,000 State Troops Are Held in Their Armories," *New York Times*, August 3, 1943, 1, 10.

36. "Harlem Is Orderly," 1, 10; "Curfew in Harlem Relaxed to 11:30: But Ban on Liquor Sales Will Stay Until Further Notice—Normal Traffic Due Today," *New York Times*, August 4, 1943, 8; "Police Ease Curbs with Harlem Quiet: But the 11:30 P.M. Curfew Is Continued—Traffic Now Is Back to Normal," *New York Times*, August 5, 1943, 17; "Policing of Harlem Returning to Normal: Force of 1,800 on Duty since Riot to Be Cut Tomorrow," *New York Times*, August 13, 1943, 11.

37. The title of this section is derived from Earl Brown's column on juvenile delinquency in the *New York Amsterdam News*. See Brown, "Timely Topics: Juvenile Delinquency," *New York Amsterdam News*, June 10, 1944, 6A. A "social explosion" is defined by the Citizens' Committee on Better Race Relations. See "Harlem Riot Probe Asks 10-Point Remedial Plan," 7.

38. "Riot Starter Sentenced: Woman Put on Years' Probation for Causing Harlem Trouble," *New York Times*, September 11, 1943, 15; "500 Are Arraigned in Harlem Looting: 100 Women among Prisoners Crowding Courts after Night of Disorders," *New York Times*, August 3, 1943, 11; "11 Tried in Harlem Riot: Suspended Sentences Given in Final Batch of Cases," *New York Times*, August 26, 1943, 11; Wilfred H. Kerr, "Hoodlums Didn't Start Riots; 'Twas Jim Crow," *New York Amsterdam News*, August 14, 1943, 13. For an extensive analysis of Margie Polite as the "riot starter," see Laurie F. Leach, "Margie Polite, the Riot Starter: Harlem, 1943," *Studies in the Literary Imagination* 40 (September 2007): 25–48.

39. Arresting officer Joseph Grady reported, "Logwood encouraged a group of Negroes to break windows in stores at 121st Street and Manhattan Avenue. The

policeman said he ordered the soldier to leave and he did, but returned later with another group and continued to harangue the crowd." Logwood was one of the eleven soldiers arrested that night (not including Private Bandy). See "500 Are Arraigned in Harlem Looting," 11; "Peace Settles over Harlem as Leaders Seek Solution to Rioting," *Pittsburgh Courier*, August 14, 1943, 1. On the young women arrested during the uprising, see Carl Dunbar Lawrence, "Jail 75 Women in Loot Round-Up: 75 Women Nabbed for Taking Goods; Stolen Property Appears on Street as Police Comb Neighborhoods," *New York Amsterdam News*, August 14, 1943, 1, 15. The six men killed, all black, were Sterling Stokes, Neil Lucas, Michael Young, Frank Stoner, Randolph Zinic, and Benjamin Muddy. One policeman accounted for two of the six fatalities. For further descriptors of the six men killed, see Gross, "Harlem during the Second World War," 18; "Report on Harlem Disturbance," 28th Precinct, and "Report on Harlem Disturbance," 32nd Precinct, Folder 193, Box 2550, La Guardia Papers. For a printed list of those who were injured and killed during the uprising, see "The Injured: Riot List of Injured and Dead," *New York Amsterdam News*, August 7, 1943, 7.

40. In Detroit, the riot lasted for more than thirty hours, with a reported thirty-four deaths and roughly seven hundred injuries. Max Yergan to La Guardia, August 5, 1943, Box 752, La Guardia Papers; "Dewey Mobilizes Guard to Prevent New Harlem Riots," *New York Times*, August 3, 1943, 1; Kerr, "Hoodlums Didn't Start Riots," 13.

41. For a historical analysis of race riots in the United States, see Arthur I. Waskow, *From Race Riot to Sit-In: 1919 and the 1960s* (New York, 1966); Allan A. Silver, "Official Interpretations of Racial Riots," *Urban Riots: Violence and Social Change, Proceedings of the Academy of Political Science* 29 (1968): 146–58. For an analysis of the Harlem riot of 1943 as a race riot, see Capeci, *Harlem Riot of 1943*, esp. 115–33. La Guardia to John T. McManus, telegram, August 2, 1943, Box 2550, La Guardia Papers; Elmer A. Carter, "Elmer Carter Hits Harlem Outbreaks," *New York Amsterdam News*, August 7, 1943, 3.

42. "Hoodlums' Holiday," *Pittsburgh Courier*, August 14, 1943, 6; Elmer Carter, "Hits Harlem Outbreaks," *New York Amsterdam News*, August 7, 1943, 3.

43. "Hoodlums' Holiday," 6. Elmer Carter's column in the *New York Amsterdam News* was "Plain Talk," in which he tackled various issues in the community. On Carter's take on the Harlem "outbreaks," in which he took an ardent stance against the rioters and their role in marring relations with white America, see Carter, "Elmer Carter Hits Harlem Outbreaks," 3; and Carter, "Plain Talk: The Reign of the Hoodlum," *Atlanta Daily World*, August 8, 1943, 4. "Hoodlums Wreck Community," *New York Age*, August 7, 1943, 1.

44. Adam Clayton Powell Sr., *Riots and Ruins* (New York: Richard R. Smith, 1945), 50.

45. W. E. B. DuBois, "As the Crow Flies: DuBois on the Riots," *New York Amsterdam News*, August 21, 1943, 10; Carter, "Reign of the Hoodlum," 4; "Harlem Is Orderly," 1, 10.

46. Kerr, "Hoodlums Didn't Start Riots," 13; "Harlem Disorders Bring Quick Action," 1, 16.

47. In a talk at the Museum of Fine Arts in Massachusetts, Lester Granger discussed "problems of minority groups" in their current setting and from the historical perspective. Granger said, "Negroes after the war will be reluctant to give up their economic and political gains and violent explosions must be expected unless the problem is attacked intelligently." Eugene C. Zack, "Race Riots Better than Quitting Fight for Equal Rights, Says Lester Granger," *Chicago Defender*, November 25, 1944, 9.

48. G.W. of Jamaica, Long Island, "The People Speak: Religious Leaders Urged to Get to Work," *New York Amsterdam News*, August 28, 1943, 10; Martin J. Kennedy, "Readers Comment on Recent Rioting: 'Causes,' Suggested Solutions Listed; Here Are Samples of Many Responses," *New York Amsterdam News*, August 14, 1943, 13. One writer, Frank J. Smalls, submitted a "short short story" published by the *Pittsburgh Courier* that captured a snapshot of the 1943 Harlem riot and offered rhetorical solutions to the issues at hand. See Smalls, "Lights on in Harlem," *Pittsburgh Courier*, December 4, 1943, 18. "Still Divided, Still Ineffective," *New York Amsterdam News*, October 16, 1943, 12A.

49. The committee preferred to call the disturbance a "social explosion," rather than a "riot." See "Harlem Riot Probe Asks 10-Point Remedial Plan," 7; also see "10-Point Proposals Follow Harlem Riot," *Atlanta Daily World*, September 23, 1943, 1, 6.

50. The Harlem Field Office of the OPA opened on August 11, 1943, and within its first month had "accomplished a great deal in furtherance of price control and the direct result is the development of better relations between retailers and consumers." See "OPA Sees Gains in Harlem: Field Office in First Month Has Been 'Very Effective,'" *New York Times*, September 12, 1943, 27. For the establishment of the OPA office in Harlem, see "OPA Establishes Office in Harlem: Acts as Sequel to Riot and the Charges that Food Prices were Partly to Blame," *New York Times*, August 7, 1943, 13. On the Board of Education's investment in the Harlem project, see "A Good School Program," *New York Times*, October 3, 1943, E8. Algernon Black encouraged local committees to keep pressure on the mayor and city administration to address the inequalities exposed by the Harlem riot. See "Mayor Receives Brooklyn Report: Valentine Submits Crime Data Gathered by Police and They Confer for 45 Minutes," *New York Times*, November 21, 1943, 3; "End to Prejudice Urged by Mayor: Less Bias Shown Here than in Any Other Big City in U.S., He Tells Conference," *New York Times*, September 26, 1943, 13. On the reopening of the Savoy Ballroom, see Don Seymour, "At Ease, Harlem Savoy Is Open Again," *Chicago Defender*, October 30, 1943, 10.

51. The title of this section is derived from a short piece on the Harlem uprising by Langston Hughes: "Here to Yonder: Simple Looks for Justice," *Chicago Defender*, August 28, 1943, 14.

52. For a sampling of secondary literature on African Americans and police brutality in the United States, especially New York City, see "African Americans, Police

Brutality, and the U.S. Criminal Justice System," special issue, *Journal of African American History* 98, no. 2 (2013), esp. Clarence Taylor, "Race, Class, and Police Brutality in New York City: The Role of the Communist Party in the Early Cold War Years," 205–28. Walter White, "What Caused the Detroit Riots?," n.d., 14, 13, 16, Box 2574, La Guardia Papers.

53. "Methods Used in Handling Disorder amongst Colored and Whites in the City of Detroit," n.d., Box 2574, La Guardia Papers; Roy Wilkins to La Guardia, telegram, June 23, 1943, Box 2574, La Guardia Papers.

54. "Valentine Issues Riot Duty Orders: Specific Points as Well as General Instructions Sent to All Command Heads," *New York Times*, May 28, 1944, 35; Walter White, "Behind the Harlem Riot of 1943," *New Republic*, August 1943, 220–22.

55. Elijah Crump to La Guardia, August 2, 1943, Box 2550, La Guardia Papers; Leonard Johnson to La Guardia, August 10, 1943, Box 2550, La Guardia Papers.

56. Pauli Murray, *The Call*, August 13, 1943; Orlansky, *Harlem Riot*, 23.

57. John T. Baissici (Commanding Officer, 5th Division) to the Police Commissioner, Memorandum: Harlem Disturbances, August 25, 1943, 6, Box 2550, La Guardia Papers; Young Citizens' Committee of New York City on Race Relations, "Digest: Racial Gang Warfare," 1943, 3, Box 2574, La Guardia Papers.

58. For the arrest statistics cited in this paragraph, see *Uniform Crime Reports for the United States and Its Possessions*, vol. 14 (Washington, DC: Federal Bureau of Investigation, 1943), 52, 87; "Delinquency Rise in City Put at 10.8%: 11.6% Increase in Cases of Neglected Children Also Noted in Court Data," *New York Times*, January 9, 1943, 15. According to the NYPD's police report for 1943, the rise in crimes was largely attributed to the uprising, in particular burglary, which increased by 70 percent in 1943. See "Recall Riot in N.Y. Police Report," *Chicago Defender*, May 27, 1944, 3. For a broad, comprehensive study of juvenile delinquency in both world wars, see Walter A. Lunden, *War and Delinquency: An Analysis of Juvenile Delinquency in Thirteen Nations in World War I and World War II* (Ames, IA: Art Press, 1963).

59. "Harlem Riot Probe Asks 10-Point Remedial Plan," 7; "Peace Settles over Harlem," 1, 8.

60. Maybelle Carey, "Predicts More Riots Unless U.S. 'Gets Together,'" *New York Amsterdam News*, August 28, 1943, 10; Walter White, "People and Places: Trouble in 'Little Harlem,'" *Chicago Defender*, December 4, 1943, 15; "Still Divided, Still Ineffective," *New York Amsterdam News*, October 16, 1943, 12A.

CHAPTER 3. "EVERY GENERATION HAS HAD THE HABIT OF GOING TO THE DEVIL"

Epigraph: James Baldwin, "The Harlem Ghetto," *Commentary*, February 1948.

1. "Kid Gang Shoots Lad Five Times: Three Bullets into Back, 2 Fired in Legs," *New York Amsterdam News*, September 15, 1945, A1, A2.

2. "Bye Mommie, I'll See You after School," *New York Amsterdam News*, September 15, 1945, A1; "Tragedy of a Broken Home in Harlem Told through Eyes of a News

Camera," *New York Amsterdam News*, September 15, 1945, A1. There was also a short report on the front page about an eighteen-year-old girl who was arrested for fatally stabbing "her sweetheart." See "Arrest Girl, 18, in Killing Sweetie," *New York Amsterdam News*, September 15, 1945, A1, 12-B. On the *New York Amsterdam News'* position on Harlem's social ills, see "Crime and the Community," *New York Amsterdam News*, September 22, 1945, 10.

3. Different city judges disputed the validity of the predicted postwar crime wave. Henry Chandler, the director of the Administrative Office of the United States Courts, submitted a statement to the annual Judicial Conference of Senior Circuit Court Judges declaring that the prospect of crime after the war may be taken seriously but that there was no need for alarm. Chandler highlighted that "nervous and emotional disturbances resulting from experiences in the war are inevitable"; however, "many returning veterans have a heightened sense of the value of order and security; they will be a stabilizing force." He concluded, "in all there is ground for serious thought but for alarm in the prospect in reference to crime after the war." Comparatively, Justice Samuel S. Leibowitz, famously known for his role in defending the Scottsboro Boys in the 1930s, emphasized the duties confronting the new judges and stressed the expectation of a "major crime wave" in the city. "The crimes won't be committed by doughboys who are going through hell but by those who earned $15 and $18 week before the war and remained here and got easy money at $100 to $150 a week," Judge Leibowitz forewarned. "It will not be easy for this class to return to $15 to $18 a week. We will be confronted with a wave of major crimes." Eventually, most judges aligned with the Leibowitz. On Chandler's perspective, see "Predict Small Rise in Post-war Crime: Senior Circuit Judges See No Cause for Alarm When Service Men Return," *New York Times*, September 27, 1944, 21. On Leibowitz's postwar crime wave predictions that indicated youths to be the cause for concern, see "Judge Predicts Postwar Crime Wave: Says Crime Will Be Committed by Wartime Workers," *New York Amsterdam News*, January 20, 1945, 17; "Crime Wave Is Prediction for Postwar Days," *New York Amsterdam News*, April 7, 1945, 3B. On Leibowitz and his representation of the Scottsboro Boys, see Quentin Reynolds, *Courtroom: The Story of Samuel S. Leibowitz* (New York: Farrar, Straus and Giroux, 1950), esp. 288–314. District attorney Burton Turkus cited wartime crime statistics that categorized juveniles as under thirty years old and emphasized that "of the 15,000 murders, 50,000 holdups and 40,000 burglaries last year [1944], more than half were committed by persons under 30 and more than 20 per cent by persons under 20." "Crime Wave Is Prediction for Postwar Days," 3B.

4. In the work of the historian Khalil Muhammad on the impact of black criminality in the making of modern urban America, he points to Frances Kellor's article "The Criminal Negro" as "the first scholarly attempt by a white northern liberal to highlight southern conditions in relation to the national discourse on black criminality." In doing so, Muhammad highlights Kellor's new line of inquiry as signifying two important changes in the black crime discourse that gradually

emerged among northern white racial liberals during the first two decades of the twentieth century: "the appeal for 'remedial measures' in solving the Negro Problem and the rejection of biological determinism." See Muhammad, *The Condemnation of Blackness: Race, Crime, and the Making of Urban America* (Cambridge, MA: Harvard University Press, 2010), esp. 88–145; Frances Kellor, "The Criminal Negro: A Sociological Study," *Arena*, January–May 1901, 512–20. For examples of New York City police officers' overpolicing tactics and strategies, see "Police Told by Wallander to Tighten Up: Commissioner Gives His High Officers a Lengthy Directive on 30 Topics," *New York Herald Tribune*, November 23, 1946, 1.

5. The title of this section is derived from when Mayor La Guardia told 217 police rookies, 203 of them war veterans, to "go in shooting" in their war on crime. "New Police Told to 'Go In Shooting': Also Shun Gambling, Drinking, Mayor Cautions 217 Who Are Sworn In as Rookies," *New York Times*, December 2, 1945, 20. Two days after this article was published, the *New York Times* attempted to make light of the quote in its "Topic of the Times" editorial section, stating, "For the good of the city we trust the Mayor said it with a smile." "Topics of the Time: Unhappy New Year?," *New York Times*, December 4, 1945, 25.

6. "Police Marksmen Join War on Crime: Pistol Team Experts on Patrol in Cars Equipped with Machine Guns and Rifles," *New York Times*, November 21, 1945, 1.

7. "Police Marksmen Join War on Crime," 1, 36. For biographical information on Arthur W. Wallander and his appointment, see Peter Kihss, "Wallander Named Police Head in Another Choice from Ranks: Mayor Picks Deputy Chief Inspector, War-Time Chief of City's Civilian Defense Forces, for Post, Then Keeps Him in Dark 4 Hours," *New York Herald Tribune*, September 23, 1945, 1.

8. "Police Marksmen Join War on Crime," 1. Several newspaper accounts from outside New York reported on New York's police shortage as being directly related to the war. See "Crime Ridden N.Y. Sends Out 'Arsenal' Cars: Citizens Are Aroused by Lawlessness," *Chicago Daily Tribune*, November 20, 1945, 17; "New York Crime Wave Rolls On Despite 'Rolling Arsenals,'" *Baltimore Sun*, November 20, 1945, 1; "N.Y. Police Use Mobile Units to Stem Crime," *Washington Post*, November 20, 1945, 13; "Repair Squads Put on Beats in N.Y. Crime Wave," *Chicago Daily Tribune*, November 25, 1945, 1. On Mayor La Guardia's prewar policing tactics as the reason police officers were hesitant to rejoin the force upon arrival, see "2 More Slain; N.Y. May Turn to Vigilantes: Blame for Crime Wave Put on La Guardia," *Chicago Daily Defender*, November 22, 1945, 17.

9. "Crime Ridden N.Y. Sends Out 'Arsenal' Cars," 17.

10. "New Police Told to 'Go In Shooting,'" 20. For criticisms of Mayor La Guardia's address to new police officers, see "Mayor Is Criticized: Surpless Assails Order to Police to 'Go In Shooting,'" *New York Times*, December 6, 1945, 28.

11. Meyer Berger, "La Guardia Calls on Armed Forces to Free Policemen: Criminals' Hangouts Face Loss of Licenses—Suspect in $20,000 Robbery Slain," *New York Times*, November 24, 1945, 1; "Mayor to Seek Release of 759 Police in Army: May

Go to Capital Today for Aid in Crime Wave; City Broadens Dragnet," *New York Herald Tribune*, November 24, 1945, 1.

12. "Boy Held in Mobile Clears Up Slaying of Brooklyn Girl: 15-Year-Old Tells Police the Shooting Was an Accident—He'll Be Brought Back," *New York Times*, November 27, 1945, 1; "Serious Crimes in State Increase 12% since June: Lyons Predicts Further Rise in Prison Population," *New York Herald Tribune*, November 24, 1945, 24. It was reported, "Of 214 murders last year [1945], they said, 22 were committed by children under 16, and 29 by persons in the 16-to-20-year-old group." "N.Y. Police Use Mobile Units," 13; and "New York Crime Wave Rolls On," 1; "Crime Ridden N.Y. Sends Out 'Arsenal' Cars," 17.

13. The national averages cited in this paragraph are from the Uniform Crime Reports (UCR) published in 1945 and 1946. It is important to note that the numbers reflect "offenses known to the police" and are designed to include crimes "occurring within the police jurisdiction, whether they become known to the police through reports of police officers, of citizens, of prosecuting or court officials, or otherwise." Federal Bureau of Investigation, *Uniform Crime Reports 1946* (Washington, DC: Government Printing Office, January 1947), 78; Federal Bureau of Investigation, *Uniform Crime Reports 1945* (Washington, DC: Government Printing Office, January 1946).

14. The *New York Times* published most of the letter from Patterson to La Guardia on its front page under the headline, "Army Turns Down Mayor on Release of Policemen: Can't Comply with Request Impossible to Grant to All Others, Says Patterson—Crime Wave Arrests Decrease," *New York Times*, December 4, 1945, 1.

15. "Gang Slaying Deepens Tide of Crime in N.Y.: Dump Ex-Convict's Body at Policeman's Home," *Chicago Daily Tribune*, November 26, 1945, 19; Bill Glover, "Crimes of Violence Spiral over Nation: 'Small Fry' Out of Hand," *Washington Post*, December 16, 1945, B2; "Police Marksmen Join War on Crime," 1; "1,500 Rebuffed as They Apply for Police Jobs: No Test until Next Year, Civil Service Tells Them; Wallander Affirms Need," *New York Herald Tribune*, November 21, 1945, 1A; "Crime Wave Expected as Mobs Buy Souvenir Guns," *New York Amsterdam News*, October 27, 1945, 17; "Call In Firearms, Wallander Urges: At FBI Conference He Asks a Nation-Wide Policy on Citizen-Owned Weapons," *New York Times*, November 24, 1945, 32. Chief Magistrate Edgar Bromberger remarked from the bench, "returning service men do not intend the guns for crime use [but] we must recognize the thoughtlessness and carelessness they show in regard to them." "Mailbox Loot Put at $60,000: Secret Service Takes Hand as New York Crime Wave Rises," *Baltimore Sun*, November 25, 1945, 7. Other cities also implied that military weapons were playing a role in the "rise" of street crimes. For example, Harry A. Ash, state superintendent of crime prevention in Chicago, quoted official police statements that there would be "5,000,000 privately owned guns of foreign make in the area when demobilization was completed." Louther S. Horne, "Central States: Illinois and Chicago Prepare for Expected Crime Wave," *New York Times*, September 16, 1945, E7.

16. "Call In Firearms, Wallander Urges," 32. In November 1945, the police property clerk reported, "more than 900 guns, knives, bayonets and other war souvenirs had been turned in to police voluntarily, nearly half of them in the last two weeks." See "Mailbox Loot Put at $60,000," 7.

17. "Wallander on Crime: Ascribes Rise in Wrong-Doing to Variety of Causes," *New York Times*, August 23, 1946, 20. Excerpts from J. Edgar Hoover's interview on the rise in postwar crime were published by the Associated Press in various newspapers nationwide. These included "Head of FBI Warns of Mounting Crime: He Says Army of Criminals Is Growing Fast and Heads toward 6,000,000," *New York Times*, July 7, 1946, 21; "J. Edgar Hoover Says U.S. Faces Crime Increase: He Sees 'Potential Army of 6 Million Criminals,' 'Puts Accent on Youths' Homes,'" *New York Herald Tribune*, July 7, 1946, 40; and "6 Million Potential Criminals in U.S., Says FBI Director," *Daily Boston Globe*, July 7, 1946, C8. On the state as a "surrogate parent," see Geoff K. Ward, *The Black Child-Savers: Racial Democracy and Juvenile Justice* (Chicago: University of Chicago Press, 2012), esp. 163–98.

18. The order sent through the police department calling on patrol officers to arrest the parents who were guilty of contributing to the delinquency of juveniles was under Section 494 of the Penal Code. Section 494 states, in part, "A parent or guardian having custody of a child under sixteen who omits to exercise reasonable diligence in the control of such child to prevent such child from becoming guilty of juvenile delinquency . . . or permits the child to associate with vicious, immoral or criminal persons, or to grow up in idleness . . . or to enter any place where the morals of such child may be endangered or depraved or impaired . . . shall be guilty of a misdemeanor." See "Police to Act against Parents of Delinquents: Those Who Knowingly Allow Children to Go Astray to Be Dealt with by Courts," *New York Herald Tribune*, November 27, 1946, 40. On the policies further implemented by Wallander "to prevent crime," see "Police Told by Wallander to Tighten Up: Commissioner Gives His High Officers a Lengthy Directive on 30 Topics," *New York Herald Tribune*, November 23, 1946, 1; "Mayor to Seek Release of 759 Police in Army," 1.

19. "Urge Vets to Give Up War Guns to Cops: Souvenir Guns Might Create Crime Wave, States McDonald," *New York Amsterdam News*, June 22, 1946, 15; "Widow, 62, Is Held for Having Pistol: Ohioan Talks of Protection in 'Wild' New York but Court Hears of Old Suitor," *New York Times*, September 22, 1946, 43.

20. "Brass Knuckles 'For Protection' Land 2 in Court: Honor Students, Fearing 'Crime Wave,' Discover Police Are on the Job," *New York Herald Tribune*, November 24, 1945, 24. The outcome of the hearing for Thomas was covered in a front-page article in the *New York Times*, as it included the tale of the two youths in passing in a larger article on the War Department's denial of La Guardia's request for a mass release of police officers in the service. See "Army Turns Down Mayor," 1, 46. For further coverage of the Vejvoda and Thomas incident, see Meyer Berger, "La Guardia Calls on Armed Forces to Free Policemen," 1, 32; "One of 2 Students Freed in Brass Knuckles Case: Youths 'Sought Protection against N.Y. Crime,'"

New York Herald Tribune, December 4, 1945, 38. Young Charles Vejvoda is described in a later article as having served in the Navy and ushering in his sister's wedding. See "Miss Vejvoda Wed to T. K. Murdock: Graduates of Bryn Mawr and Yale Marry in Church of St. Vincent Ferrer," *New York Times*, September 23, 1951, 98.

21. "One of 2 Students Freed in Brass Knuckles Case," 38. "Brass Knuckles 'For Protection' Land 2 in Court," 24. According to one report, there were twenty-four arrests made on Thanksgiving night 1945; "five were teen-agers." Included in the total were six burglary arrests, five for grand larceny, and four for violation of the Sullivan law. "Army Turns Down Mayor on Release of Policemen," 46.

22. The updates on the state of the juvenile justice system in this article do not apply to Morgan's case, a thirty-six-year-old who was being sentenced for a second-time offense. "Ex-Convict Gets 40 to 60 Years as a Lesson for Brooklyn Thugs," *New York Times*, November 20, 1943, 1, 7.

23. "Ex-Convict Gets 40 to 60 Years," 7.

24. "'Mugging' Held Term to Slander Negroes: Young Communists Here Told Harlem Has No Crime Wave," *New York Times*, March 28, 1943, 27.

25. Duane Robinson, "'Mugging' and the New York Press," *Phylon* 6, no. 2 (1945): 169–79, esp. 169, 170, 171.

26. The study did not provide specific names of newspapers or the representatives interviewed. Robinson, "'Mugging' and the New York Press," 172.

27. Robinson, "'Mugging' and the New York Press," 173, 179.

28. Earl Conrad, "N.Y. Dailies Use Crime Wave to Smear Negro Communities," *Chicago Defender*, December 1, 1945, 3. George S. Schuyler, an African American author and journalist, agreed that this practice existed but argued, "no New York daily newspaper is anti-Negro." During a lecture on the New York City press and human relations at the Schomburg Collection of Negro Literature of the New York Public Library, Schuyler's main criticism of the New York City press was that "it tagged Negro criminals as such while they did not do the same for Jewish, Italian, Irish or any other ethnic group's criminals." For Schuyler, he felt that marked improvements had been made and that "aside from slip-ups here and there and sensational 'crime-wave' stories, Negroes receive just about as much space as they deserve by virtue of achievement and accomplishment." "Daily Press Described as Being Not Anti-Negro," *New York Amsterdam News*, May 11, 1946, 7.

29. "The New York 'Crime Wave,'" *Chicago Defender* (national edition), January 12, 1946, 12. For print media coverage on the eighteen waiters, see "18 Waiters Freed in U.S. Trial for Dining Car Fraud," *Chicago Daily Tribune*, November 30, 1945, 31; "U.S. Swindle Case Flops: Charges against 18 Drop; Government Finds Insufficient Evidence Submitted," *Atlanta Daily World*, December 5, 1945, 1; "Cleared of Dining-Car Fraud," *New York Herald Tribune*, November 30, 1945, 30A; "U.S. Trial Opens for 17 Waiters in $90,000 Fraud," *Chicago Daily Tribune*, November 27, 1945, 2.

30. Carl Lawrence, "Cops Say No Crime Wave Here: Gang Wars, Crimes Are at New Low," *New York Amsterdam News*, December 1, 1945, 1. A quick sampling of a

number of New York dailies shows that they were printing headlines on their front pages in bold print that read, "5 Killed in Murder Wave," "Woman Thrown from Window: Grandma Slain," "Bedford-Stuyvesant Area Called 'Hot Bed' of Youthful Crimes."

31. Excerpts from the release were printed in a *New York Times* article. See "Violence Declines in City Crime War: Only 2 Teen-Agers among 59 Persons Arrested during a Period of 24 Hours," *New York Times*, December 3, 1945, 19. For the full press release, a transcript can be found in the Society for the Prevention of Crime Records: Edwin J. Lukas, "Release," Box 35, Folder: Children's Court, 1938–1949, Series X, Society for the Prevention of Crime Records, Rare Book and Manuscript Library, Columbia University, New York, NY.

32. Edwin J. Lukas, "Can Crime Preventive Efforts by Police Be Helpful?," *Proceedings of the National Conference of Juvenile Agencies* 41, no. 4 (1945): 107–11, esp. 107, 109. This report is in Box 53, Folder: Police, 1945–1951, Series X, Society for the Prevention of Crime Records.

33. "Moran Calls Predictions of Crime Wave Just Talk: Tells Social-Work Conference Forecasts Repeat Old Story," *New York Herald Tribune*, November 14, 1946, 22A.

34. The transcript of Frederic A. Moran's speech was printed and published as part of a broader series on delinquents and correction. See Moran, "New Light on the Juvenile Court and Probation," delivered at a Joint Session with the National Conference of Social Work, Division II—Delinquents and Correction, *Proceeding of the National Probation Association*, 1930, 66–75.

35. In response to the proposals of the National Probation and Parole Association to revise juvenile court standards, see Edwin J. Lukas to Hon. Justine W. Polier, July 1, 1948, 1–2, Folder: Children's Court, 1938–1949, Box 35, Series X, Society for the Prevention of Crime Records.

36. "Pupils Give View on Delinquency: They Include Parents, Police and Schools as Sharing Part of the Blame," *New York Times*, February 10, 1946, 17. For a brief discussion on science in the juvenile court, see Moran, "New Light on the Juvenile Court and Probation," 69–70.

37. Julius J. Adams, "Why Not Try New Approach to Solving Juvenile Crime? Urges Police Quiz of Juvenile Crime," *New York Amsterdam News*, January 26, 1946, 11.

38. The Lafargue Clinic was named in honor of Paul Lafargue, the Afro-Cuban physician and social reformer who "spent his entire life opposing bigotry and fighting for the right of the underdog to enjoy the benefits of science." Sidney M. Katz, "Jim Crow Is Barred from Wertham's Clinic," *Magazine Digest*, September 1946, 1–5. For a comprehensive history of the Lafargue Clinic and antiracist psychiatry, see Gabriel N. Mendes, *Under the Strain of Color: Harlem's Lafargue Clinic and the Promise of Antiracist Psychiatry* (Ithaca, NY: Cornell University Press, 2015). For a sampling of the secondary literature on Frederic Wertham and the Lafargue Clinic, see Gabriel Mendes, "An Underground Extension of Democracy," *Transition* 115 (2014): 4–22; Dennis Doyle, "'Where the Need Is Greatest': Social Psychiatry and Race-Blind Universalism in Harlem's Lafargue Clinic,

1946–1958," *Bulletin of the History of Medicine* 83 (Winter 2009): 746–74; Bart Beaty, *Frederic Wertham and the Critique of Mass Culture* (Jackson: University Press of Mississippi 2005), esp. 85–95; Shelly Eversley, "The Lunatic's Fancy and the Work of Art," *American Literary History* 13 (Autumn 2001): 445–68; and Jay Garcia, *Psychology Comes to Harlem: Rethinking the Race Question in Twentieth-Century America* (Baltimore: Johns Hopkins University Press, 2012), esp. 49–74. Adolf Meyer is known as "the most authoritative and influential psychiatrist in the United States." S. D. Lamb, *Pathologist of the Mind: Adolf Meyer and the Origins of American Psychiatry* (Baltimore: Johns Hopkins University Press, 2014), 99. Frederic Wertham is quoted in Richard Wright's "Phychiatry [*sic*] Comes to Harlem," *Free World*, September 1946, 51.

39. Most of the newspaper clippings and primary journal articles cited in this section of the chapter are from the Lafargue Clinic Records, which are housed in the Schomburg Center for Research in Black Culture, in the Manuscripts, Archives, and Rare Books Division of the New York Public Library, New York, NY. Wright, "Phychiatry [*sic*] Comes to Harlem," 49–51, esp. 51. In the article, Wright also refers to the alarming juvenile-delinquency statistics relating to Harlem. He cites, "Harlem's 400,000 black people produced 53% of all the juvenile delinquents of Manhattan, which has a white population of 1,600,000." James Tuck, "Here's Hope for Harlem," *New York Herald Tribune*, January 26, 1947, SM9.

40. Wright, "Phychiatry [*sic*] Comes to Harlem," 51; Tuck, "Here's Hope for Harlem," 9, 13, 20; Ralph Ellison, "Harlem Is Nowhere," *Harper's Magazine*, August 1964, 53–57.

41. Mendes, "Underground Extension of Democracy," 4–22, esp. 22. The historian Dennis Doyle defines social psychiatry as it applies to the Lafargue Clinic as "the practice of assessing a patient's emotional problems and needs within the context of his or her everyday life." Doyle, "Where the Need Is Greatest," 750. For an overview of the history of social psychiatry in postwar America, see Kathleen Haack and Ekkehardt Kumbier, "History of Social Psychiatry," *Current Opinion in Psychiatry* 25 (November 2012): 492–96. The historians Ellen Dwyer and Daryl Michael Scott demonstrated that in the World War II era, a growing number of psychiatrists and mental-health professionals started to abandon the archaic assumptions that the African American psyche was innately different and biologically inferior. See Ellen Dwyer, "Psychiatry and Race during World War II," *Journal of the History of Medicine and Allied Sciences* 61 (April 2006): 117–42; and Daryl Michael Scott, *Contempt and Pity: Social Policy and the Image of the Damaged Black Psyche, 1880–1996* (Chapel Hill: University of North Carolina Press, 1997). Ellison, "Harlem Is Nowhere," 53. On New York as the Jim Crow North, see Brian Purnell and Jeanne Theoharis, "How New York City became the capital of Jim Crow North," *Washington Post*, August 23, 2017, www.washingtonpost.com.

42. Wertham often stated, "all white psychiatrists reject Negro patients ostensibly on the theory that their other patients will object." Robert Bendiner, "Psychiatry for the Needy," *Tomorrow*, April 1948, 22–26, esp. 24.

43. Therese Pol, "Psychiatry in Harlem," *Protestant*, June–July 1947, 28–30; Ralph G. Martin, "Doctor's Dream in Harlem," *New Republic*, June 3, 1946, 798–800.

44. Bendiner, "Psychiatry for the Needy," 22.

45. Bendiner, "Psychiatry for the Needy," 22. The first two patients were described as "a frightened young woman with big-pleading eyes and a man whose eyes were filled with emptiness." Martin, "Doctor's Dream in Harlem," 798, 799.

46. According to one internal document, because demand was so high, the clinic encouraged appointments, and the waiting list was still full in the clinic's final years. For example, in 1947, the staff saw an average of twenty-two cases in its two hours of nightly operation (although the staff usually kept the door open until 9:00 p.m.). Between 1947 and 1956, the clinic saw an average of 69.4 percent adults and 30.6 percent children. See Lafargue Clinic, Letter to Patient's Mother, February 20, 1958, Folder: "Patient Records," Box 3, Lafargue Clinic Records; Donald Blomquist, Betty Moore, and Hilde Mosse, "Statistics Lafargue Clinic: 1947/1956," March 6, 1956 (unpublished internal office document compiled on February 2, 1956), 2, Folder: "Memoranda, 1953–54," Box 1, Lafargue Clinic Records. There are inconsistencies as to which days of the week the clinic was open, but the consensus remains that the clinic was only open roughly four to six hours per week. "With no financial resources of its own, Lafargue Clinic has depended on contributions from well-wishers. At Christmas, greeting cards containing cash and checks flood the mailbox. Other persons and groups have given toys for play therapy, vitamins, and books to establish a circulating library." Norman M. Lobsenz, "Human Salvage in Harlem," *Coronet*, March 1948, 133–36, esp. 136. For more information on the general statistics of the patients treated at the Lafargue Clinic, see Doyle, "Where the Need Is Greatest," 751–53.

47. Lobsenz, "Human Salvage in Harlem," 135; Bendiner, "Psychiatry for the Needy," 29. On psychotherapy as a cure for war neuroses, see Nathan G. Hale Jr., *The Rise and Crisis of Psychoanalysis in the United States: Freud and the Americans, 1917–1985* (New York: Oxford University Press, 1995), 277. Hale explains how discussions generated by psychoanalysts "created a strong impression of the efficacy of psychotherapy and the scientific status of psychoanalytic theory and practice." Garcia, *Psychology Comes to Harlem*, 186n42.

48. Martin, "Doctor's Dream in Harlem," 800.

49. Martin, "Doctor's Dream in Harlem," 800.

50. S. I. Hayakawa, "Second Thoughts: Combating Juvenile Delinquency," *Chicago Defender*, January 11, 1947, 15; Pol, "Psychiatry in Harlem," 30. The Lafargue Clinic did not publish many statistics or its methods of diagnosis. "Freud never gave out figures on cures," they said. "It's too dubious." A small sampling of cases from 1948 found in its records reported nineteen child cases in which ten youths showed "marked improvement," eight were "completely cured," and only one "failed to respond to treatment." The remaining twenty-six cases "were hardly in the psychiatric field at all." Eleven of them were "simply problems in family relations, of which seven were reported solved and the other four mitigated." The

other fifteen youths still unaccounted for "were people who came to Lafargue for mental treatment only to find out that they were in fact suffering from severe, if unsuspected, physical illness." These statistics are cited in Bendiner, "Psychiatry for the Needy," 22. Most of the secondary analysis of the Lafargue Clinic focuses on its role more so as it fits within the expansion of psychiatry and the broader social sciences in postwar America. Even the Lafargue Clinic records housed at the Schomburg Center for Research in Black Culture are categorized by the names of doctors who worked at the clinic (e.g., Hilde L. Mosse, Frederic Wertham) and relevant places (e.g., Lafargue Clinic, St. Philip's Church). Access to the records can also be obtained through the Reverend Shelton Hale Bishop's papers. The key terms associated with the records include African Americans; health and hygiene; community mental health services; mental health; mental health counseling; mental health facilities; and psychiatric clinics. Perhaps the closest examination of the Lafargue Clinic and its role in youth criminalization can be found in James Gilbert's chapter "Crusade against Mass Culture" in his monograph *A Cycle of Outrage: America's Reaction to the Juvenile Delinquent in the 1950s* (New York: Oxford University Press, 1986), 91–108. Gilbert's discussion, however, is centered on Frederic Wertham and his crusade against crime comics in the mid-1950s.

51. Hayakawa, "Second Thoughts: Combating Juvenile Delinquency," 15. Hayakawa, too, trusted the Lafargue Clinic's efforts to provide psychiatric services for the vast masses that could not afford it. He wrote, "Faced on every hand with impossible living conditions, with uncertainty of status, with an environment full of contradictions of democratic precept and undemocratic practice, it is inevitable that the Negro should experience anxieties and frustrations that are sometimes more than he can bear. This is true of every level of Negro society; but at the lowest levels, where the problems of being a Negro are added to the problems of poverty and social disintegration, the burdens are the heaviest—as is manifest in the high crime rate." S.I. Hayakawa, "Second Thoughts: Mental Illness of Negroes," *Chicago Defender*, January 4, 1947, 15. Pol, "Psychiatry in Harlem," 30.

52. Lobsenz, "Human Salvage in Harlem," 135–36.

53. The lack of financial support combined with "Father Bishop's retirement from St. Philip's in 1957 and 'an unforeseen accumulation of deaths and sever illnesses' among staff members in the subsequent years" led to the closing of the Lafargue Clinic. Mendes, "Underground Extension of Democracy," 13. Perhaps the most influential cultural critic to emerge at the beginning of the postwar era who identified the problem of segregation as one that affected both blacks and whites was Gunnar Myrdal and his study on race relations, *An American Dilemma*, published in 1944. Myrdal, like Wertham, was thought to have offered a more unbiased opinion on the topic because he was not American. See Gunnar Myrdal, *An American Dilemma: The Negro Problem and Modern Democracy* (1944; repr., New York: Taylor and Francis, 2017). In addition to Myrdal, for a sampling of anti-race publications from the postwar era, see also "Prejudice: Our Postwar Battle," *Look*, May 1, 1945; and Gunnar Myrdal, "Social Trends in America and Strategic

Approaches to the Negro Problem," *Phylon* 9, no. 3 (1948): 196–214. The Delaware court cases *Gebhart v. Belton* and *Bulah v. Gebhart* derived out of two separate examples in which black students were excluded from the local white public schools. For Wertham's testimony in *Gebhart v. Belton*, see Richard Kluger, *Simple Justice: The History of* Brown v. Board of Education *and Black America's Struggle for Equality* (New York: Vintage, 1977), esp. 426–52, 444. On the history of the Northside Center for Child Development in Harlem, see Gerald Markowitz and David Rosner, *Children, Race, and Power: Kenneth and Mamie Clark's Northside Center* (New York: Routledge, 2000).

54. Ellison, "Harlem Is Nowhere," 57.

55. Robert Keith Leavitt, "It Pays to Believe in People," *New York Herald Tribune*, March 3, 1946, SM2. James Gilbert's 1986 historical study of juvenile delinquency, *A Cycle of Outrage: America's Reaction to the Juvenile Delinquent in the 1950s* (New York: Oxford University Press, 1986), chronicles public response to the issue in the 1950s, especially as it pertains to the rise of mass culture and shifts in youth culture.

CHAPTER 4. "BEWARE OF THE CAT ON THE CORNER"

Epigraph: Jackie Robinson, *Chicago Daily Defender*, September 9, 1959, 11.

1. At the time of the address in Dewey Square, Sammy Davis Jr. was starring in the Broadway production of *Mr. Wonderful*, which started in March 1956. "Anti-Crime Rally Is Held in Harlem: 1,500 Youngsters March to Spur Area Drive against Juvenile Delinquency," *New York Times*, August 12, 1956, 88.

2. Sammy Davis Jr., "Sammy Davis Jr.'s Plan to Fight Delinquency," *Pittsburgh Courier*, September 22, 1956, A20, A22.

3. Davis, "Sammy Davis Jr.'s Plan to Fight Delinquency," A22. On Goddard Lieberson's rejection of Davis's proposal, see "NCDJ to Quit Fund $$ Solicitations: Jocks Air Pro and Con Opinions on National Council Methods," *Billboard Magazine*, February 9, 1957, 18, 20.

4. The title of this section is derived from a five-part series of articles written by Richard Clendenen and Herbert W. Beasers based on the United States Senate Judiciary Subcommittee to Investigate Juvenile Delinquency printed in the *Saturday Evening Post* in 1955.

5. In 1949, the publishing company J. B. Lippincott compiled all the articles published by the *Ladies' Home Journal's* series "Profile of Youth" under the same name with an introduction and conclusion written by one of the contributing editors, Maureen Daly. The information cited is from this compilation: "Teen-Agers Give the Answers," in *Profile of Youth*, ed. Maureen Daly (Philadelphia: Lippincott, 1949), 9–15, esp. 9; "American Youth—Full View," in Daly, *Profile of Youth*, 253–56, esp. 254.

6. "Teen-Agers Give the Answers," 11; "American Youth—Full View," 255.

7. "City Girl: Myrdice Thornton; Chicago, Illinois," in Daly, *Profile of Youth*, 177–93, esp. 177–79.

8. "City Girl: Myrdice Thornton," 177–79, 190–93.

9. "Teen-Agers Give the Answers," 10, 15. On the article that inspired the *Time* magazine article, see "Where Do Teen-Agers Get Their Sex Education?," in Daly, *Profile of Youth*, 64–74.

10. "Teen-Agers Give the Answers," 15; Paul W. Tappan, *Juvenile Delinquency* (New York: McGraw-Hill, 1949), vii. Tappan acknowledges and draws heavily from Kimball Young and Samuel J. Brandenburg for the development of his understanding of human behavior and society; John L. Gillin and Thorsten Sellin for their role in his criminological training and enthusiasm; and Karl N. Llewellyn for bringing some measure of realism about the relation between law and society. See Tappan, *Juvenile Delinquency*, viii. Tappan's accomplishments include chairman of the Board of Parole of the Department of Justice, director of the American Correctional Association, and the professional council of the National Probation and Parole Association. See "Paul W. Tappan, Educator, Dead," *New York Times*, July 10, 1964, 30.

11. Tappan, *Juvenile Delinquency*, 3, 30. For a sample of publications in which Tappan grapples with defining delinquency, see Paul W. Tappan, "Who Is the Criminal?," *American Sociological Review* 12 (February 1947): 96–102, esp. 99; Paul W. Tappan, "Children and Youth in the Criminal Court," *Annals of the American Academy of Political and Social Science* 261 (January 1949): 128–36, esp. 132; Paul W. Tappan and Ivan Nicolle, "Juvenile Delinquents and Their Treatment," *Annals of the American Academy of Political and Social Science* 339 (January 1962): 157–70, esp. 157.

12. Federal Bureau of Investigation, *Crime in the United States, 1950*, Uniform Crime Reports Online (Washington, DC: Government Printing Office, 1951). The years cited in this section (1946–59) are available at http://archive.org (accessed October 28, 2017). The Uniform Crime Reports document arrests of persons who are taken into custody and fingerprinted. It is important to note that police count a young person as arrested when he or she has committed a crime and the circumstances are such that if the individual were an adult, an arrest would be tallied.

13. Benjamin Fine, *1,000,000 Delinquents* (New York: World, 1955), 27.

14. On Senator Robert C. Hendrickson's efforts to combat juvenile delinquency, see "Hendrickson 'Task Forces' to Combat Juvenile Delinquency," *New York Herald Tribune*, October 2, 1953, 17; Eve Edstrom, "Delinquency Probers Ask for Extension for a Year: Sen. Hendrickson Sees U.S. Waging 'a Losing Battle' against Teen Crime," *Washington Post*, January 16, 1954, 1. Fine, *1,000,000 Delinquents*, 27.

15. "Judge Tells Senate Probe Truancy Is Path to Crime," *New York Herald Tribune*, December 15, 1953, 29. On Senator Estes Kefauver and his role on the Senate subcommittee, see Joseph Bruce Gorman, *Kefauver: A Political Biography* (New York: Oxford University Press, 1971), esp. 197–98; Harvey Swados, *Standing Up for the People: The Life and Work of Estes Kefauver* (New York: E. P. Dutton, 1972); Charles L. Fontenay, *Estes Kefauver: A Biography* (Knoxville: University of Tennessee Press, 1980), esp. 317–20.

16. "Youth Crime Deplored: Kefauver Brands Delinquency Threat to U.S. Welfare," *New York Times*, March 27, 1955, 35; Gorman, *Kefauver*, 197. The Missouri senator Thomas Hennings spoke highly of Senator Kefauver's traits that would make him a good president. On Senator Kefauver's presidential traits, Hennings wrote, "He knows how to put together a good staff. He has some very striking abilities. He has a good mind and a phlegmatic nature which would help him bear the White House burdens." Senator Hennings's critique of Kefauver was derived from personal communication highlighted in Riggs, "The Man from Tennessee," Washington, DC, December 22, 1970, cited in Fontenay, *Estes Kefauver*, 305n1, 318n37.

17. On the United States Senate Special Committee to Investigate Crime in Interstate Commerce, the Kefauver Committee, see William Howard Moore, *The Kefauver Committee and the Politics of Crime, 1950–1952* (Columbia: University of Missouri Press, 1974). Both the *New York Times* and the *New York Herald Tribune* printed the full transcript of President Dwight D. Eisenhower's State of the Union Address. See "Text of President Eisenhower's Annual Message to Congress on the State of the Union," *New York Times*, January 7, 1955, 10–11; "Eisenhower's Message," *New York Herald Tribune*, January 7, 1955, 6–7. For an outline of President Eisenhower's 1955 State of the Union Address, see Walter Trohan, "President Outlines Program for 1955: 'Peace Insecure,' State of Union Message Says," *Chicago Daily Tribune*, January 7, 1955, 1, 16.

18. The transcript of President Dwight D. Eisenhower's "Budget Message" to Congress was printed in the *New York Times*: "Text of President Eisenhower's Budget Message to Congress Covering Fiscal Year 1956," January 18, 1955, 14–19, esp. 14. "$3,000,000 Sought in War on Crime: President Acts to Aid States Curb Delinquency—Budget Also Helps the Aged," *New York Times*, January 18, 1955, 22; Fine, *1,000,000 Delinquents*, 7.

19. The title of this section is derived from a 1955 ten-article series, "Our Lawless Youth," on juvenile delinquency written by Margaret Parton of the *New York Herald Tribune*.

20. In an editorial printed by *Life* magazine, "What to Do about Juvenile Crime," New York, California, New Jersey, Wisconsin, and Massachusetts are considered among the most up to the task of facing juvenile delinquency. See "Editorials: What to Do about Juvenile Crime," *Life*, March 15, 1954, 24. For a more detailed account of the New Jersey and California efforts, printed in the same issue, see "Helping Bad Boys: A Plan Pays Off for New Jersey," *Life*, March 15, 1954, 97–105.

21. Estes Kefauver, "Letter to the Editor: 'Our Lawless Youth,'" *New York Herald Tribune*, June 21, 1955, 22.

22. Margaret Parton, "Our Lawless Youth: Behind the Statistics; Children in Conflict with Society—At 17 'You're Cryin' Inside All the Time,'" *New York Herald Tribune*, June 1, 1955, 1.

23. Parton, "Our Lawless Youth: Behind the Statistics," 1, 25.

24. Allan McMillan, "Youth Group Open Delinquency War," *New York Amsterdam News*, May 13, 1950, 9; Henry Epstein, *Perspectives on Delinquency Prevention*,

report (New York: Office of the Mayor, 1955), 12 (emphasis in original). On the "delinquency-hazard age bracket," Epstein points out, "If five seems a tender age to list as the lower limit, I might mention the fact that in the Gluecks' research, more than 44% of their 500 delinquents displayed clear signs of anti-social behavior between the ages of five and seven." Sheldon Glueck and Eleanor T. Glueck, *Unraveling Juvenile Delinquency* (Cambridge, MA: Harvard University Press, 1950), 226.

25. Parton, "Our Lawless Youth: Behind the Statistics," 1, 25, esp. 25. Epstein, *Perspectives on Delinquency Prevention*, 5, 6. The ten priority programs listed in Epstein's study were Recreation and Community Programs in Public Housing, Remedial Reading, Police Services and Juvenile Delinquency, Youth Board "Street Clubs" and Casework Services, Providing Comprehensive Youth Board Services in Three Additional Areas, Teacher Rotation, Parent Education, The Co-op Program and Guidance in Schools, Youth Board In-Service Training, and Planning and Coordination.

26. Epstein, *Perspectives on Delinquency Prevention*, 21–24, esp. 21, 24. Similar "successes" were achieved when the saturation experiment was tried in the Seventy-Third Precinct in Brooklyn and the 103rd Precinct in Queens. On the "saturation" of police surveillance, see Margaret Parton, "Our Lawless Youth: Why Isn't Something Done about Delinquency? Answer Is: A Host of Agencies Are Fighting It," *New York Herald Tribune*, June 7, 1955, 1, 25, esp. 25.

27. Epstein, *Perspectives on Delinquency Prevention*, 21–24; Parton, "Our Lawless Youth: Why Isn't Something Done about Delinquency?," 25.

28. New York City Youth Board Data by Residence of Offender, "Delinquency Rates by Area, 1954," map, reprinted in Epstein, *Perspective on Delinquency Prevention*, 22; Juvenile Aid Bureau Police Department Data, "Arrests and Police Referrals, 1954," map, reprinted in Epstein, *Perspective on Delinquency Prevention*, 23. For Youth Board figures on juvenile delinquency rates and trends in New York City by borough for the first half of the 1950s, see Parton, "Our Lawless Youth: Behind the Statistics," 25. On Harlem as the "Negro City," see Constance Curtis, "Harlem Diary: This Is Harlem, 1953," *Atlanta Daily World*, September 8, 1953, 2.

29. For an examination of the new settlement houses in New York City, see Michael B. Fabricant and Robert Fisher, *Settlement Houses under Siege: The Struggle to Sustain Community Organizations in New York City* (New York: Columbia University Press, 2002), esp. 15–61. Clifford R. Shaw belonged to a talented cohort of social scientists in the mid-twentieth century who were interested in systematic mapping and ethnographic study of community life among European immigrants and African Americans in the urban North. See Khalil Gibran Muhammad, *The Condemnation of Blackness: Race, Crime, and the Making of Modern Urban America* (Cambridge, MA: Harvard University Press, 2010), esp. 236–41, 266. On Shaw's area approach to juvenile delinquency, see Clifford R. Shaw, Frederick M. Zorbaugh, Henry D. McKay, and Leonard S. Cottrell, *Delinquency Areas: A Study of the Geographic Distribution of School Truants, Juvenile Delinquents, and*

Adult Offenders in Chicago (Chicago: University of Chicago Press, 1929); Clifford R. Shaw and Henry D. McKay, *Social Factors in Juvenile Delinquency: A Study of the Community, the Family, and the Gang in Relation to Delinquent Behavior for the National Commission on Law Observance and Enforcement* (Washington, DC: Government Printing Office, 1931); and Clifford R. Shaw and Maurice E. Moore, *The Natural History of a Delinquent Career* (Chicago: University of Chicago Press, 1931).

30. Malcolm Nash, "Juvenile Delinquency and a Cure! Part Three," *New York Amsterdam News*, November 6, 1954, 1, 8. Nash's article was part of a four-part series that the *Amsterdam News* ran on delinquency in the fall of 1954. On the current Hansborough Recreation Center, see New York City Department of Parks and Recreation, "Hansborough Recreation Center," accessed October 28, 2017, www.nycgovparks.org.

31. Nash, "Juvenile Delinquency and a Cure!," 8. Margaret Parton, "Our Lawless Youth: A Picture of the City's Social Agencies at Work Trying to Substitute for Defaulting Parents," *New York Herald Tribune*, June 8, 1955, 1, 25. For more information on Walter J. Weinert as the director of the Riis–Red Hook Community Center, see "Jimmy Murphy's Column: To Put Up Dukes," *Brooklyn Daily Eagle*, December 5, 1952, 19; and "Jimmy Murphy's Column: Funds for Christmas," *Brooklyn Daily Eagle*, December 1, 1953, 23, both in Series II: Administrative Files, 1894–1990, Jacob A. Riis Neighborhood Settlement Records, 1891–1990, Manuscripts and Archives Division, New York Public Library, Astor, Lenox, and Tilden Foundations, New York, NY.

32. Parton, "Our Lawless Youth: A Picture of the City's Social Agencies," 25.

33. In New York City, the Manhattanville Center joined the Community Service Society, United Neighborhood Houses, Henry Street Settlement, and the Hudson Guild as centers distinguished by a "social action" viewpoint that worked at integrating their programs with major redevelopment activities and housing projects that were changing the face of many areas in the city. See Murray B. Meld, "Housing and Planning: Today's Social Frontier," *Social Work* 2 (April 1957): 32–36, esp. 32. On similar developments reported in other major cities, see Daniel J. Ransohoff, *Survey of Youth Facilities and Programs in Certain Low-Rent Housing Projects of the Public Housing Administration* (Washington, DC: Housing and Home Finance Agency, 1955); Parton, "Our Lawless Youth: A Picture of the City's Social Agencies at Work," 25.

34. "Columbia U. Community Project: Integration at Work—While J.D. Declines," *New York Age*, May 24, 1958, 9. In the seventh article the "Our Lawless Youth" series, Margaret Parton investigated the Manhattanville Center. See Parton, "Our Lawless Youth: A Picture of the City's Social Agencies at Work," 1, 25, esp. 25.

35. Parton, "Our Lawless Youth: A Picture of the City's Social Agencies at Work," 25.

36. Parton, "Our Lawless Youth: A Picture of the City's Social Agencies at Work," 25.

37. The concept and authority of the parental state provided a cultural and legal framework for regulating child neglect, misbehavior, and crime. "Rooted in the

doctrine of in loco parentis," according to the criminologist Geoff K. Ward, "the framework defined the state as the surrogate parent of the nation." See Ward, *The Black Child-Savers: Racial Democracy and Juvenile Justice* (Chicago: University of Chicago Press, 2012), 25–29 (quote on 25). On the origins of the concept of juvenile delinquency, see Mary Carpenter, *Juvenile Delinquents: Social Evils, Their Causes and Their Cure* (London, 1853); E. C. Wines, *The State of Prisons and of Child-Saving Institutions in the Civilized World* (Cambridge, 1879); Philippe Ariès, *Centuries of Childhood: A Social History of Family Life* (New York: Penguin Books, 1962). Ward, *Black Child-Savers*, 23, 230; Parton, "Our Lawless Youth: A Picture of the City's Social Agencies at Work," 25.

38. Malcolm Nash, "Juvenile Delinquency and a Cure! Part Two," *New York Amsterdam News*, October 30, 1954, 1, 6. Founded in 1947 "because of the urgent need to meet an alarming and climbing juvenile delinquency wave," the New York City Youth Board was made up of thirteen nonsalaried persons appointed by the mayor. The Department of Welfare, the Department of Health, the police department, Department of Parks, the Children's Court, the City Housing Authority, and the Board of Education account for seven of the thirteen members, while the other six members were selected on the basis of their experience and interest in youth affairs. In 1954, the Youth Board had an annual budget, provided by both the city and state, of a little more than $2 million to work with; however, Ralph Whelan, the executive director of the Youth Board, and other officials believed "that sum [was] not equal to the task." With "such meager resources for so sprawling a city," the Youth Board was forced to decide on which areas in the city warranted the most attention. Among the areas with more than 900,000 people and at least 250,000 youths was Brooklyn's Bedford-Stuyvesant section and Central and East Harlem. For more background information on the New York City Youth Board, see the New York City Youth Board, *Reaching the Fighting Gang* (New York: New York City Youth Board, 1960), Kenneth Marshall Papers, 1951–1977, Schomburg Center for Research in Black Culture, Manuscripts, Archives, and Rare Books Division, New York Public Library, New York, NY. On the "detached worker" approach, see New York City Youth Board, *Reaching the Fighting Gang*, esp. 2–3.

39. The title of this section is derived from the tenth article of the "Our Lawless Youth" series. See Margaret Parton, "Our Lawless Youth: How Teen-Agers and Experts Appraise Delinquency and What Mr. and Mrs. Citizen Can Do about It," *New York Herald Tribune*, June 12, 1955, 14–17, esp. 17.

40. Constance Curtis and Chollie Herndon, "Know Your 5 Boroughs: Friends of Youth; Youth Workers Build Citizens of Tomorrow," *New York Amsterdam News*, February 26, 1949, 6, 22, esp. 6. Founded in 1929, the New York State Training School for Boys at Warrick was "a high profile program and housed hundreds of boys," removing them from "an environment of violence, gangs, and poverty." For more information, see "The Warwick Story: The Story of New York State Training School for Boys," *Times Herald Record*, 1957, accessed October 28, 2017, www.albert wisnerlibrary.org.

41. Among the many news items printed in the March 1957 issue of *Your Block Is Your Concern* was one on a local football player, Isaac Keyes, who was one of three black players on the Greystone football team; an ice cream parlor opened by Sidney Miller on 141st Street; a story about Joan Langford modeling party dresses in a fashion show given by the Aphrodites Girls Club of the Mt. Calvary Baptist Church. See Esther Stanley and Ann Langford, eds., *Your Block Is Your Concern*, ca. March 1957. "Some Harlemites Try to Make Harlem Clean Place to Live," *New York Amsterdam News*, March 30, 1957, 5.

42. Curtis and Herndon, "Know Your 5 Boroughs," 6, 22. For more on the increased activities and efforts of the Harlem YMCA under the directorship of Rudolph J. Thomas, see "Harlem YMCA Signs Jackie and Campanella," *Atlanta Daily World*, July 10, 1949, 7; "Harlem YMCA Gears for Biggest Campaign: Head Harlem Drive 100G Goal Is Aim of Met N.Y.," *New York Amsterdam News*, September 22, 1951, 1–2; "Harlem Branch YMCA Set for Campaign Homestretch," *New York Amsterdam News*, March 22, 1952, 6; Rudolph J. Thomas, "YMCA Thanks Us for Sammy Davis Promotion," *New York Amsterdam News*, May 28, 1955, 18; "Church Rally Tuesday: Dr. King Speaks for YMCA," *New York Amsterdam News*, February 23, 1963, 8; "Rudolph Thomas Quits Harlem Y: Resigns!," *New York Amsterdam News*, November 28, 1964, 1–2. The archival records of the Harlem Branch YMCA (1855–1989) are a part of the Kautz family YMCA Archives, housed at the Andersen Library at the University of Minnesota, Minneapolis, MN.

43. "What Shall It Be, Character or Delinquency? New York's Harlem 'Y' Holds the Answer," *Chicago Daily Defender*, March 15, 1956, 12–13; Curtis and Herndon, "Know Your 5 Boroughs," 22. Jackie Robinson was, arguably, the most active professional athlete involved in the efforts of the Harlem Branch YMCA. He also regularly wrote a column for the *Daily Defender* on juvenile delinquency in 1959. See Jackie Robinson, *Chicago Daily Defender*, October 1, 1959, 15; Robinson, *Chicago Daily Defender*, November 9, 1959, 11.

44. A "kangaroo court" is a judicial assembly that disregards recognized standards of law or justice. "Teen-Age Terror on the New York Streets: An Epidemic of Juvenile Violence Erupts in Three Senseless Deaths," *Life*, July 11, 1955, 33–35.

45. H. Taylor Jr., "Ticker: Confidential," *Jet*, April 5, 1962, 12.

46. Samuel Richardson's documented struggles with racial injustices in New York started in the late 1940s, when the Harlem businessman was banned from purchasing a home in Addisleigh Park, a mixed black-white neighborhood in Queens. See "Court Forbids Sale of Queens Home to Negro: Upholds Old Covenant in Mixed St. Albans Area; Case Will Be Appealed," *New York Herald Tribune*, February 14, 1947, 19; "Ban on House Sale to Negro Is Upheld," *New York Times*, December 23, 1947, 25. On June 21, 1947, the *Chicago Defender* printed a short article about a play written by Samuel Richardson, *Our Community*, based on the problem of juvenile delinquency. No other references to this play can be found; however, it is likely that this play was in fact written by the same Samuel Richardson. See "New Play Is Hit in New York," *Chicago Defender*, June 21, 1947,

10. On Richardson's involvement with the National Association of Negro Business, see "Hold Meet to Aid Business," *New York Amsterdam News*, August 4, 1951, 5. On the establishment of the Harlem Business Council, see "Small Business Group Formed in Harlem Area," *New York Amsterdam News*, August 27, 1955, 36. On the model-block program, see "Some Harlemites Try to Make Harlem Clean Place to Live," *New York Amsterdam News*, March 30, 1957, 5.

47. "Harlem Businessman Starts Drive against Delinquency," *New York Amsterdam News*, August 16, 1958, 3.

48. "Harlem Mothers Meet Sept. 11," *New York Amsterdam News*, September 13, 1958, 9.

49. "Mothers Conference Meets," *New York Amsterdam News*, September 27, 1958, 27. Richardson said he received a letter from US Senator Estes Kefauver commending him on his endeavor and wishing him success; however, he also stated that he wrote the Kefauver committee in May 1958 requesting information on the committee's plans to combat juvenile delinquency, to which, it is assumed, he received no response. See "Harlem Businessman Starts Drive against Delinquency," 3. On the letters that Richardson received from Harlem residents, see "Mothers Conference Meets," 27.

50. Samuel Richardson, "Pulse of the Public: We're with You," *New York Amsterdam News*, January 10, 1959, 6. Richardson also organized an antidelinquency committee among his Odd Fellows fraternal organization. See "Odd Fellows Name Committee on Delinquency," *New York Amsterdam News*, September 19, 1959, 10.

51. Allan McMillan, "Youth Group Opens Delinquency War," *New York Amsterdam News*, May 13, 1950, 9. For more on Allan McMillan, see "A. W. McMillan, 91, Longtime Columnist at Amsterdam News," *New York Times*, September 11, 1991, www.nytimes.com. Another youth-inspired organized effort against juvenile delinquency in Harlem included the Bethel Church Crusade Against Adult Delinquency, which stressed "the family as an important unit in any neighborhood betterment program." On the Bethel Church Crusade Against Adult Delinquency, see "Youth Crime Laid to 'Adult Delinquency' by Speaker for Church Crusade in Harlem," *New York Times*, July 18, 1955, 28. Through the 1950s, the New York City Youth Board established several organized efforts against juvenile delinquency in Harlem, and as stated earlier in the chapter, while effective to an extent, their most significant hurdle was obtaining the trust of the community. For more organized efforts founded by the Youth Board, such as the Street Club Project, see Jesse DeVore, "'High Hazard Area': Harlem Delinquency Problems Discussed," *New York Amsterdam News*, October 5, 1957, 16.

52. "Harlem Students Kayo Juvenile Delinquency," *New York Amsterdam News*, October 25, 1958, 27.

53. From September 1959 through February 1960, the *Chicago Daily Defender* periodically printed Jackie Robinson's untitled columns on youth crime and juvenile delinquency in New York City. On the organization Athletes for Juvenile Decency, see Jackie Robinson, *Chicago Daily Defender*, November 9, 1959, 11. On Robinson's

Hall of Fame announcement, see Jackie Robinson, *Chicago Defender*, February 10, 1962, 8. Robinson, *Chicago Defender*, February 10, 1962, 8. Robinson was inducted into the Baseball Hall of Fame on July 23, 1962. On Robinson's official Hall of Fame induction, see National Baseball Hall of Fame, "Remembering Jackie," accessed October 28, 2017, http://baseballhall.org.

54. In 1964, according to the Uniform Crime Reports, persons under twenty-one represented 30.3 percent, or 1,421,606 total, of all arrests in the United States (compared to 15.9 percent, or 269,831 total, in 1954). There were 1,697,050 people arrested in all age groups in 1954. Federal Bureau of Investigation, *Crime in the United States, 1964*, Uniform Crime Reports Online (Washington, DC: Government Printing Office, 1965). The years cited in this section (1949–64) are available at http://archive.org (accessed October 28, 2017).

CHAPTER 5. "IN ALL OUR HARLEMS"

Epigraph: James Baldwin, "A Report from Occupied Territory," *Nation*, July 11, 1966, 6.

1. William Craig was quoted in various newspaper reports of four of the Harlem Six being released after pleading guilty to the lesser manslaughter charges. See "'Hardest Day of Our Lives': Harlem Four," *New York Times*, April 8, 1973, 239; "Harlem 4 Freed after 9 Years," *Afro-American*, April 14, 1973, 21.

2. For Baldwin's description of Harlem, see Baldwin, "Report from Occupied Territory," 6.

3. On police as the "frontline soldier," see Lyndon B. Johnson, "Statement by the President Following the Signing of Law Enforcement Assistance Bills," September 22, 1965, American Presidency Project, accessed November 1, 2017, www.presidency.ucsb.edu.

4. Malcolm X referred to Harlem as "a police state" in his speech at the Militant Labor Forum of New York on May 29, 1964. See Malcolm X, *Malcolm X Speaks: Selected Speeches and Statements*, ed. George Brietman (New York: Merit, 1965), esp. 64–71.

5. The first print media report of the "Harlem Fruit Riot" was published in the *New York Times* on April 18, 1964. The headline described the incident as "75 in Harlem Throw Fruit at Policemen." The following day, two days after the incident, the *New York Times* carried a slightly different version: "four youths and a man, were involved in a free-for-all on Friday afternoon, after they allegedly overturned a fruit stand." The difference is important because it was the "four youths and a man" who went on to face the charges in lieu of the seventy-five. See "75 in Harlem Throw Fruit at Policemen," *New York Times*, April 18, 1964, 27; and "Lawyer for 5 Tells Court Police Roughed Up Clients," *New York Times*, April 19, 1964. Willie Jones from the Harlem Youth Opportunities Unlimited (HARYOU) conducted the tape-recorded statements of Wallace Baker and Daniel Hamm. They are quoted in Truman Nelson's *The Long Hot Summer* (Berlin: Seven Seas, 1967), 129n4, 129n6.

6. On "the policemen's inept handling of a minor situation," see Junius Griffin, "Harlem: The Tension Underneath; Youths Study Karate, Police Keep Watch and People Worry," *New York Times*, May 29, 1964, 13; "Harlem Unite: Let Us Defend Ourselves!," *Challenge: The New Revolutionary Weekly Paper*, n.d., Folder 17D, Box 4, Conrad Lynn Collection, Howard Gotlieb Archival Research Center at Boston University, Boston, MA.

7. Douglas Dales, "2 Bills Prepared on Police Search: Law Enforcement Aides in State Reach Agreement," *New York Times*, January 21, 1964, 18. On opponents of the two anticrime bills, see Martin Arnold, "N.A.A.C.P. and CORE to Fight Bills Increasing Police Powers," *New York Times*, February 29, 1964, 24; Douglas Dales, "Rockefeller Signs Bills Increasing Powers of Police: Bar and Civil Rights Groups Call 'Stop-and-Frisk' and 'No-Knock' Laws Illegal," *New York Times*, March 4, 1964, 1. I think it is important to note that although these two laws had become a subject of national concern in the mid-1960s, the police power to detain and question is "as old as the common law of England." For a long history of stop-and-frisk that was referenced in the 1960s, see Loren G. Stern, "Stop and Frisk: An Historical Answer to a Modern Problem," *Journal of Criminal Law, Criminology, and Police Science* 58, no. 4 (1967): esp. 532.

8. *Mapp v. Ohio*, 367 U.S. 643 (1961). For a more comprehensive history of *Mapp v. Ohio*, see Carolyn N. Long, *"Mapp v. Ohio": Guarding against Unreasonable Searches and Seizures* (Lawrence: University Press of Kansas, 2006). On police demands for a "stop-and-frisk" statute, see Memorandum of the New York State Combined Council of Law Enforcement Officials to the New York State Legislature in Relation to Temporary Questioning and Search for Weapons, cited in "The 'No-Knock' and 'Stop and Frisk' Provisions of the New York Code of Criminal Procedure," *St. John's Law Review* 38, no. 2 (1964): esp. 393. As written, the "stop-and-frisk" statute allowed a police officer "to stop any person abroad in a public place whom he reasonably suspects is committing, has committed or is about to commit a felony or a serious misdemeanor." Further, if the police officer "reasonably suspects that he is in danger of life or limb from the person he has stopped, he may search the person for a dangerous weapon." And if the officer finds a weapon or "any other thing, the possession of which may constitute a crime, he may keep it during the questioning." Thereafter, the officer must either return the item if it was lawfully possessed or arrest the person for possessing it. On the "stop-and-frisk" statute of 1964, see N.Y. Code Crim. Pro. § 180-a (effective July 1, 1964). The "stop-and-frisk" statute in New York was derived from the Uniform Arrest Act of 1942, which gave police officers the right to arrest any person whom they reasonably believed was committing or had committed a felony or misdemeanor. For more on the Uniform Arrest Act of 1942, see "The Uniform Arrest Act," *Virginia Law Review* 28, no. 3 (1942): 317. On the vote breakdown, see Layhmond Robinson, "Legislators Pass Anticrime Bills: Senate Sends Rockefeller His 'Stop-and-Frisk' and 'No-Knock' Measures," *New York Times*, February 19, 1964, 41.

9. On the "no-knock" statute of 1964, see N.Y. Code Crim. Pro. § 799 (effective July 1, 1964). For a more detailed description of the two anticrime laws, see "'No-Knock' and 'Stop and Frisk,'" 392–405. On the proponents of "no-knock" and the vote breakdown, see Layhmond Robinson, "Assembly Votes Anticrime Bills: Measures Would Ease Laws on Searches by Police," *New York Times*, February 12, 1964, 41; "Frisk-Law Advice Is Given to Police: City Warns against Hasty Use of New Powers," *New York Times*, June 28, 1964, 28.

10. Layhmond Robinson, "Bar Group Urges Crime-Bills Veto: Sees Threat of 'Police State' in Additional Powers," *New York Times*, February 12, 1964, 39. For a different perspective on the two laws, by members of the Progressive Labor Movement, see "Harlem Unite: We Have Come to Understand," *Challenge*, n.d., Folder 17D, Box 4, Conrad Lynn Collection.

11. Michael J. Murphy, *Civil Rights and Police: A Compilation of Speeches by Michael J. Murphy, New York City Police Department* (New York: New York City Police Department, 1964), 11, 9 (emphasis in original). For an example of how print media portrayed the strength of the police force surrounding the world's fair, see Theodore M. Jones, "Murphy Alerts Police for Fair: Emergency Duty to Cope with Stall-In Threat and Opening Events Police Put on Emergency Duty to Prepare for the Opening of the Fair," *New York Times*, April 18, 1964, 1, 16. For a concise history, and photographs, of the 1964 world's fair, see Bill Cotter and Bill Young, *The 1964–1965 New York World's Fair* (Charleston, SC: Arcadia, 2004).

12. On James Farmer's statement, see Richard J. H. Johnston, "Murphy Charges Attack on Police: Says 'Brutality Complaints Seek to Weaken Force,'" *New York Times*, April 29, 1964, 28. On Commissioner Murphy's stance against the brutality allegations, see Murphy, *Civil Rights and the Police*, 12, 13 (emphasis in original). Murphy's defense of his officers, especially from "outside pressure," was widely known. See Lynda Richardson, "Michael J. Murphy, 83, Dies; Led New York Police in 1960's," *New York Times*, May 18, 1997, www.nytimes.com.

13. On the roughly thirty youths marching and chanting, see "75 in Harlem Throw Fruit at Policemen," 27. Tape-recorded statement of Wallace Baker, transcribed in Nelson, *Long Hot Summer*, 20. Tape-recorded statement of Daniel Hamm, transcribed in Nelson, *Long Hot Summer*, 23–25.

14. Tape-recorded statement of Mrs. Baker, transcribed in Nelson, *Long Hot Summer*, 21–22; tape-recorded statement of Mrs. Hamm, transcribed in Nelson, *Long Hot Summer*, 25–27.

15. "Lawyer for 5 Tells Court Police Roughed Up Clients," *New York Times*, April 19, 1964, 47; "Cops Probe Brutality Cry in Wake of Fray," *New York Amsterdam News*, April 25, 1964, 55.

16. Baldwin, "Report from Occupied Territory," 5–6.

17. Youth challenges to racial inequality escalated in the 1960s, and as the historian Heather Ann Thompson highlights, they targeted numerous civic institutions, such as secondary schools, which embraced more punitive policies to respond. Thompson, "Why Mass Incarceration Matters: Rethinking Crisis, Decline, and

Transformation in Postwar American History," *Journal of American History*, December 2010, 710–11. On the CORE protest that included the bridge sit-down, see Leonard Buder, "Bridge Sitdown by CORE Blocks the Triborough: 6 Held after Demonstration on 125th St. Approach during Evening Rush," *New York Times*, March 7, 1964, 1, 52. For more coverage on this demonstration, see Leonard Buder, "CORE 'River Rats' Stress Militancy: Dramatic Civil Disobedience Is Tactic of Harlem Group," *New York Times*, March 14, 1964, 11. For a sampling of school boycotts, picketing, and other demonstrations in spring 1964, see Malcolm Nash, "The Boycott: Only 330 Report to Junior High 136," *New York Amsterdam News*, March 21, 1964, 51; Junius Griffin, "11 Are Arrested in Harlem Clash: Police Brutality Is Alleged after Traffic Protest," *New York Times*, May 20, 1964, 33; and "Demonstrators Adopt Hit-Run in New York," *Atlanta Daily World*, August 4, 1963, A4.

18. On the youths' account of pigeon keeping in Harlem, see Junius Griffin, "View in a Harlem Street: 'Whitey' Won't Give Me a Job; Teen-Agers Express Futility by Asking: Why Go to School?," *New York Times*, May 9, 1964, 13. In James Baldwin's "Report from Occupied Territory," he too makes mention of pigeon fanciers who "kept pigeons on the roofs" and argues that police were "especially afraid of the roofs, which they considered to be guerilla outposts." Baldwin, "Report from Occupied Territory," 5. On Daniel Hamm's description of police harassment after the fruit-stand incident, see Truman Nelson, *The Torture of Mothers* (Boston: Beacon, 1965), 63.

19. On the *New York Times*' first detailed account of the incident, see "3 Youths Seized in Harlem Killing: A Racial Motive in Recent Assaults Is Investigated," *New York Times*, May 1, 1964, 31.

20. On the arrest of Rice and Hamm, see Martin Arnold, "2 Held in Killing Admit Another: Will Be Questioned on 2 More," *New York Times*, May 2, 1964, 55. On Baker's prearrangement, see "Suspect Gives Up in Harlem Death: New Youth Is 3rd Accused in Shopkeeper's Murder," *New York Times*, May 5, 1964, 32. For media coverage of the search for Baker outside New York, see "Seek Negro, 19, Believed to Be in Racist Gang," *Chicago Tribune*, May 4, 1964, 3; "Police Claim Muslim Youth in Terror Gang," *Chicago Daily Defender*, May 6, 1964, 6; and "Young Racist Slaying Suspect in Custody," *Atlanta Daily World*, May 10, 1964, A1.

21. For a comprehensive history of the Scottsboro case, see Dan T. Carter, *Scottsboro: A Tragedy of the American South* (1969; rev. ed., Baton Rouge: Louisiana State University Press, 2007). For a comprehensive history on the Trenton Six, see Cathy D. Knepper, *Jersey Justice: The Story of the Trenton Six* (New Brunswick, NJ: Rivergate Books, 2007). Truman Nelson published two separate books in support of the Harlem Six. The first, *The Torture of Mothers*, was a detailed account of the media coverage and firsthand interviews with witnesses and the mothers of the six youths. His second book, *The Long Hot Summer*, was written in the autumn of 1964 and describes "without later revision" events and condition of the long, hot summer. It included various transcriptions of interviews with the

Harlem Six and their mothers. For the Nelson quote, see Nelson, *Torture of Mothers*, 43; Nelson, *Long Hot Summer*, 52.

22. Tape-recorded statement of Mrs. Craig, transcribed in Nelson, *Long Hot Summer*, 39–42. The "stop-and-frisk" and "no-knock" laws were set to be enforced beginning in July 1964. For a more thorough account of the police precinct actions, including transcripts, see Charter Group, "Fact Sheet in the Case of 'the Harlem Six,'" esp. 1–9, Folder 17D, Box 4, Conrad Lynn Collection.

23. Selma Sparks, *A Harlem Mother's Nightmare: The Story of Six Harlem Youths Who Face Possible Death for a Crime They Did Not Commit* (New York: CERGE, ca. 1965), 1, 5.

24. On the case of the Harlem Six as a racial incident, see Nelson, *Torture of Mother*, 1 (emphasis in original), 45. Correspondence between Truman Nelson and James Baldwin points to a tension between black leaders and white liberals on issues relating to race relations in the 1960s. Nelson acknowledged his racial outsider perspective; however, in so doing, he expressed resentment toward Baldwin's erroneous "white liberal Southerner" label. In a letter to Baldwin, Nelson wrote, "God how I abhor them and white liberal novelists. I am white . . . I am a revolutionary." In Baldwin's response to Nelson, he apologized for the mislabel though admitted, "[I am] not entirely sorry because I think my error taught me something and perhaps my error will help us to become friends." On the correspondence between Baldwin and Nelson, see Truman Nelson to Mr. Baldwin, May 2, 1966; and James Baldwin to Mr. Nelson, May 11, 1966, Folder: Harlem Six, Box 3, James Baldwin Papers, Sc MG 936, Schomburg Center for Research in Black Culture, Manuscripts, Archives, and Rare Books Division, New York Public Library, New York, NY. On the letter mailed to Beacon Press, see "Letter," n.d., Folder 17D, Box 4, Conrad Lynn Collection. On the torture of mothers, see Nelson, *Long Hot Summer*, 35–36.

25. James Baldwin, *The Price of the Ticket: Collected Nonfiction, 1948–1985* (New York: St. Martin's, 1985), 424. On the mothers forming their own defense committee, see Harlem Defense Counsel, *Police Terror in Harlem*, pamphlet (New York: CERGE, 1965), 4.

26. Tape-recorded statement of Mrs. Thomas, transcribed in Nelson, *Long Hot Summer*, 57; tape-recorded statement of Mrs. Hamm, transcribed in Nelson, *Long Hot Summer*, 57. For Nelson's take on why the community became skeptical, see Nelson, *Long Hot Summer*, 57–58.

27. The HARYOU researcher was never identified. Junius Griffin, "Anti-white Harlem Gang Reported to Number 400: Social Workers Says Its Members Are Trained in Crime and Fighting by Defectors from Black Muslims," *New York Times*, May 6, 1964, 1, 30.

28. Griffin, "Anti-white Harlem Gang," 1, 30.

29. According to Griffin's report, the NYPD reported leads on two adults, Orlando X and Hannibal, whom they suspected to be responsible for organizing and teaching the youth referred to as the Blood Brothers. Junius Griffin, "40 Negro

Detectives Investigate Anti-white Gang: U.S. Agency Studying Harlem—Civil Rights Groups Criticize Violence," *New York Times*, May 7, 1964, 28. Kenneth B. Clark, director of HARYOU, publicly stated, "There is nothing in the data collected by the HARYOU research staff which would support the contention that there exists in the Harlem community a group or groups of young people who are dedicated to organized anti-white violence. . . . And no such statement was made by a HARYOU staff member." Les Matthews and George Barner, "They Still Can't Prove That 'Blood Gang' Lie!," *New York Amsterdam News*, May 23, 1964, 1, 55. Conrad Lynn, a civil rights attorney, demanded that Griffin present the evidence, writing, "He hasn't appeared. I am still waiting. He is afraid to face me after what he has done." Nelson, *Long Hot Summer*, 67.

30. Griffin cited many reports of organization leaders who made the case for the gang's existence. In addition to Farmer, these also included Alexander J. Allen, the executive director of the Urban League of Greater New York, who wrote, "If it is true, upon reflection, it's an outcome of the long-standing alienation and rejection which Negro youths in Harlem and Bedford-Stuyvesant have faced for a long, long time—all their lives, in fact." On Malcolm X's address to the Militant Labor Forum on May 29, 1964, see Malcolm X, *Malcolm X Speaks: Selected Speeches and Statements*, ed. George Brietman (New York: Merit, 1965), esp. 64–71. See Griffin, "40 Negro Detectives Investigate Anti-white Gang," 28.

31. On black newspaper accounts that refuted the gang's existence and warned of problems that the allegations could spark, see Matthews and Barner, "They Still Can't Prove That 'Blood Gang' Lie!," 1, 55.

32. Statement of Wallace Baker, made to Robert J. Lehner, ADA, May 4, 1964, transcript, esp. 3753–54, Folder 17C, Box 4, Conrad Lynn Collection; statement of Daniel Hamm, made to Robert J. Lehner, ADA, May 1, 1964, transcript, esp. 5, Folder 17A, Box 3, Conrad Lynn Collection.

33. Nelson tape, transcribed in Nelson, *Torture of Mothers*, 70.

34. Harlem Defense Counsel, *Police Terror in Harlem*, 4; Nelson, *Torture of Mothers*, 76; Les Matthews, "A Closeup of William Epton," *New York Amsterdam News*, August 15, 1964, 46.

35. Nelson, *Torture of Mothers*, 77–78.

36. On Lynn's belief of the Harlem Six's innocence, see Sparks, *Harlem Mother's Nightmare*, 5. The 1901 ruling invoked was *People v. Fuller*, which states, "A destitute defendant, charged with murder in the first degree, can have no part in selecting the counsel authorized to be assigned to him by the Court and paid for by the County." *The People of the State of New York, Plaintiff v. John Fuller, Court of General Sessions of Peace in and for the County of New York*, May 1901, 35 Misc. 189 (N.Y. Misc. 1901). In the case of the Scottsboro trial, the defendants had court-appointed lawyers, but the Supreme Court ruled that Sam Leibowitz, a top criminal lawyer, could defend them and that they were not to be burdened legally with the errors they claimed were made by their court-appointed counsel. On Lynn's property-as-income defense, Lynn's transcribed statements appear in

Nelson's *Torture of Mothers*, 79, 81–83, 85. According to various CERGE reports, the average African American family earned $3,480 a year, compared to the city-wide average of $5,103, yet were charged $50 to $74 a month for a one-room flat that would rent for $30 to $49 in a white neighborhood.

37. In an interview with Fern Marja Eckman, Baldwin referred to the streets of Harlem as "the only human part of New York." Baldwin, interview by Fern Marja Eckman, personal Interview, New York City, June 21, 1966, in "Baldwin, James," at Columbia Center for Oral History, New York, NY. The Harlem riot of 1964 was ignited by the execution of a fifteen-year-old black Harlemite, James Powell, who was gunned down by an off-duty policeman, Thomas Gilligan. For a sampling of the print media coverage of the incident, see Theodore Jones, "Negro Boy Killed: 300 Harass Police; Teen-Agers Hurl Cans and Bottles after Shooting by Off-Duty Officer," *New York Times*, July 17, 1964, 1, 34; Theodore Jones, "Teen-Age Parade Protests Killing: 200 March in Yorkville as Police Watch—Shooting of Boy Being Investigated," *New York Times*, July 18, 1964, 1, 23. In addition to mainstream newspaper coverage, organizations such as CERGE published political pamphlets to expose police brutality. See Harlem Defense Counsel, *Police Terror in Harlem*, 4. For comprehensive coverage of the Harlem riot of 1964, see Fred C. Shapiro and James W. Sullivan, *Race Riots, New York, 1964* (New York: Crowell, 1964). For a firsthand account of the riot, see "Harlem: Hatred in the Streets," *Newsweek*, August 3, 1964, 50–51. For secondary literature that discusses the murder of James Powell and the consequential rioting, see Michael W. Flamm, *In the Heat of the Summer: The New York Riots and the War on Crime* (Philadelphia: University of Pennsylvania Press, 2016); Vincent Cannato, *The Ungovernable City* (New York: Basic Books, 2002); Michael Flamm, "The 'Long Hot Summer' and the Politics of Law and Order," in *Looking Back at LBJ: White House Politics in a New Light*, ed. Mitchell B. Lerner (Lawrence: University Press of Kansas, 2005), esp. 128–52; and Janet L. Abu-Lughod, *Race, Space, and Riots in Chicago, New York, and Los Angeles* (New York: Oxford University Press, 2007), esp. 159–96. On the assassination of Malcolm X, see George Brietman, Herman Porter, and Baxter Smith, *The Assassination of Malcolm X* (New York: Pathfinder, 1976). On James Baldwin's debate with William Buckley Jr., see Herb Boyd, *Baldwin's Harlem: A Biography of James Baldwin* (New York: Atria, 2008), 87–102, esp. 93–94. Baldwin, "Report from Occupied Territory." James Baldwin to David Baldwin, James Baldwin Files, Schomburg Center for Research in Black Culture, New York, NY, cited in Boyd, *Baldwin's Harlem*, 94–95. For other biographies that cover Baldwin's take on the Harlem Six, see W. J. Weatherby, *James Baldwin: Artist on Fire* (New York: Laurel Books, 1989); and David A. Leeming, *James Baldwin: A Biography* (New York: Arcade, 1994). On Baldwin's call to boycott, see "James Baldwin Calls for 'Massive Boycott,'" *New York Times*, August 25, 1967, 18. Baldwin also wrote two unpublished essays on the Harlem Six. See Baldwin, "Our Children: The Harlem 6," n.d., Folder 50: Essays, Box 43; and Baldwin, untitled essay, n.d., Folder 50: Essays, Box 43, Baldwin Papers.

38. Sidney E. Zion, "Convictions of 6 in 1964 Harlem Slaying Reversed," *New York Times*, November 30, 1968, 78. On the Harlem Six's refusal to talk to their court-appointed attorneys and their court protests, see "Charter Group for a Pledge of Conscience Join in the Appeal of the Harlem Six," Folder 12, Box 14A, James Weldon Johnson Community Centers, Inc. Records, Schomburg Center for Research in Black Culture, Manuscripts, Archives, and Rare Books Division, New York Public Library, New York, NY.

39. "Harlem Lawyers Back Judge," *New York Amsterdam News*, March 1, 1969, 42. On Judge Culkin's racial connotations, see Sidney E. Zion, "Judge Accused of Racial Slur against 'Harlem 6,'" Folder 17A, Box 3, Conrad Lynn Collection. Michael Newton, "Harlem Six," in *The Encyclopedia of American Law Enforcement* (New York: Facts on File, 2007), 150.

40. Joseph Lentol, Helene Weinstein, and Jeffrion Aubry, "The Death Penalty in New York: A Report on Five Public Hearings on the Death Penalty in New York Conducted by the Assembly Standing Committee on Codes, Judiciary, and Correction, December 15, 2004–February 11, 2005," 12. N.Y. Sess. Laws 1965, ch. 321. In 1967, the death penalty was amended to include intentional murder, depraved indifference to human life murder, and felony murder; see N.Y. Sess. Laws 1967, ch. 791. In 1968, the act of recklessly engaging in conduct evincing a depraved indifference to human life that results in the killing of another person was removed from the list of death-eligible crimes; see N.Y. Sess. Laws 1968, ch. 949. Lesley Oelsner, "One of 'Harlem 6' Guilty in Retrial: Other 5 to Be Tried in 1964 Murder of Shopkeeper," *New York Times*, April 11, 1970, 27.

41. On the Rice and Hamm confessions, see Conrad J. Lynn to Hon. John V. Lindsay, Mayor, New York City, January 31, 1972, Folder 17B, Box 3, Conrad Lynn Collection. The same letter was sent to Shirley Chisholm, congresswoman, and Hon. Percy Sutton, Manhattan borough president. Oelsner, "One of 'Harlem 6' Guilty in Retrial," 27; "Harlem Six Face Sugar Murder," *New York Amsterdam News*, April 18, 1970, 2; Charlayne Hunter, "3d Trial Begins for 'Harlem Six': Defenders' Backers Demand Removal of Prosecutor," *New York Times*, September 22, 1971, 28.

42. On the Harlem Four trials, see Oelsner, "One of 'Harlem 6' Guilty in Retrial," 27; "Harlem Six Face Sugar Murder," 2; "Awaiting Jury Verdict," *New York Amsterdam News*, March 20, 1971, 1; "Harlem Six Retrial in Hung Jury," *New York Amsterdam News*, March 27, 1971, 1; and Hunter, "3d Trial Begins for 'Harlem Six,'" 28. For Ossie Davis quote, see Hunter, "3d Trial Begins for 'Harlem Six,'" 28. The untitled, signed petition is in Folder 17B, Box 3, Conrad Lynn Collection.

43. Lacey Fosburgh, "4th Trials Opens for 4 Accused of '64 Store Murder in Harlem," *New York Times*, November 30, 1971, 50.

44. Lacey Fosburgh, "Trial Here of the 'Harlem Six' Interests Student Observers of All Age Groups," *New York Times*, January 9, 1972, 62; Cheryl Sanders to "Yo' Brothers," March 19, 1972, Folder 17C, Box 4, Conrad Lynn Collection.

45. On the juror deliberations, see Lacey Fosburgh, "Defense in Harlem Slaying Trial Rests after Calling One Witness," *New York Times*, January 18, 1972, 63. On

the decision to offer bail after a fourth mistrial, see Lacey Fosburgh, "Case of the 'Harlem 4' Ends in Hung Jury," *New York Times*, January 28, 1972, 1, 19.

46. On Craig's outburst in the courtroom, see Fosburgh, "Case of the 'Harlem 4' Ends in Hung Jury," 19. William Craig, "Power," poem, Folder 17B, Box 3, Conrad Lynn Collection. On Lynn's concurrence, see Lacy Fosburgh, "Harlem 4: When Is Justice Done?," *New York Times*, February 20, 1972, E10. On Justice Martinis's decision, see "Harlem Four to Get Word on March 8," *New York Amsterdam News*, February 19, 1972, A3.

47. "Harlem 4 Postponed," *New York Amsterdam News*, March 11, 1972, A2; Philip C. Cooper, "The Harlem Six: Justice on Trial," *New York Amsterdam News*, March 18, 1972, A5; Lacey Fosburgh, "Case against 'Harlem 4' Said to Be Based on Lie," *New York Times*, March 18, 1972, 1, 35; Fosburgh, "Conflict Is Denied in Harlem 4 Data: New Disclosure Backs Its View, Prosecution Says," *New York Times*, March 23, 1972, 37; Fosburgh, "'Harlem 4' Due to Be Released Tomorrow as Bail Is Reduced to $5,000 Each," *New York Times*, March 30, 1972, 28.

48. The twenty-five-year-old Robert Barnes Jr. decided to come clean in his affidavit "to right a terrible wrong" because it was the truth. He described his initial interrogation and explained the fear he felt to comply while in police custody. "I was afraid. They kept saying over and over, didn't you intend to kill [Mrs. Sugar], wasn't this a plan to kill white people, until I finally said yes." When the police mentioned the six, Barnes continued, "I included their names." Barnes was serving an eight-year sentence for armed robbery when he submitted the confession and was concerned that the admission may impact his chances for parole in 1973. Still, he wrote, "I've just now decided to tell the truth. I could never lie on the stand again." Some people believed Barnes's confession was a ploy to implicate specific officers on the police force; however, only one detective of the four Barnes identified was still active with the department at the time of the submission. Any other possible motivations were difficult to identify. "It appear[ed], from the document," according to the Harlem Six defense team, "that his desire to 'come clean' [had] been building within him for a number of years." Lacey Fosburgh, "Witness Recants in Harlem 4 Case: Asserts Those He Identified Are Innocent, and Reports Intimidation by Police," *New York Times*, July 7, 1972, 1, 35; "Harlem Four Facing Their Fourth Trial," *New York Amsterdam News*, July 8, 1972, C10; Lee Cook, "Harlem 4 Dismissal Is Now 'a Must,'" *New York Amsterdam News*, July 29, 1972, C10.

49. Lacey Fosburgh, "'Harlem Four' Are Freed after Manslaughter Pleas," *New York Times*, April 5, 1973, 1, 55; "Harlem Four: 'Hardest Day of Our Lives,'" *New York Times*, April 8, 1973, 239; "Harlem 4 Freed!," *New York Amsterdam News*, April 7, 1973, A1. For national coverage of the Harlem Four being released, see "Free 4 in Plea Switch," *Chicago Defender*, April 5, 1973, 7; "High Court Denies Delay for Retrial of Black Youths," *Jet*, April 12, 1973, 29. Lewis Steel, of Lynn's defense team, suggested that the prosecution was more amenable to a plea now because another trial might be political embarrassing for the incumbent district attorney.

50. Fosburgh, "'Harlem Four' Are Freed after Manslaughter Pleas," 55; James M. Markham, "Parole Is Granted but Then Revoked for a 'Harlem Six' Inmate: Packing to Leave Conviction Voided," *New York Times*, March 6, 1973, 45; newspaper insert, *New York Amsterdam News*, March 9, 1974, A11 (emphasis in original); William Worthy, "Last of 'Harlem Six' Inmates Victim of 'Compromise' Solution," *Baltimore Afro-American*, November 6, 1979, 5.

51. "Robert Rice, Harlem Six, Awaits Bail," *New York Amsterdam News*, August 11, 1973; "Murder Charge Dismissed against One of Harlem Six," *New York Times*, September 15, 1973, 35; United States Ex. Rel. Robert Rice v. Leon J. Vincent, 491 F.2d 1326 (2d Cir. 1974); Arnold H. Lubasch, "Ruling to Throw Out Conviction in 'Harlem Six' Case Reversed," *New York Times*, February 8, 1974, 38; "State High Court Upholds a 'Harlem Six' Conviction," *New York Times*, October 10, 1974, 57; newspaper insert, *New York Amsterdam News*, June 5, 1976, A10 (emphasis in original). H. Carl McCall, a *New York Amsterdam News* journalist, published an article, "A Perversion of Rehabilitation," in support of Robert Rice's release. He wrote, "The voice of Harlem has spoken in the past concerning the Harlem Six case. That same voice must be heard again, and now louder and more persistently than ever before." McCall, "A Perversion of Rehabilitation," *New York Amsterdam News*, June 12, 1976, A5. Worthy, "Last of 'Harlem Six' Inmates Victim of 'Compromise' Solution," 5. For the most recent status update on Robert Rice, see Department of Corrections and Community Supervision, New York State, "Inmate Information," http://nysdoccslookup.doccs.ny.gov.

52. William Craig to Wallace Baker, n.d., Folder 17B, Box 3; Truman Nelson to Conrad Lynn, n.d., Folder 17A, Box 3; and Craig, "Power," Conrad Lynn Collection.

AFTERWORD

The title of this chapter comes from the lyrics of a rap song, "Young Forever," by the hip-hop artist Jay-Z. See Jay-Z, "Young Forever," *Blueprint 3* (Atlantic Records, 2009). *Epigraph*: Ta-Nehisi Coates, "The Myth of Police Reform," *Atlantic*, April 15, 2015, www.theatlantic.com.

1. Rahiel Tesfamariam, "Why Jay-Z Has No Desire to Be Our Generation's Harry Belafonte," *Washington Post*, July 25, 2013, www.washingtonpost.com; "Jay Z Outraged over Trayvon Martin Verdict and the 'Mall Cop' Who Got Off: 'Magna Carta' Rapper Blasts George Zimmerman and Stand Your Ground Laws," *Spin*, July 24, 2013, www.spin.com. More recently, Jay-Z produced a six-part miniseries, *Time: The Kalief Browder Story*, on the life and untimely death of Kalief Browder, a Bronx youth who was jailed for three years for allegedly stealing a backpack. Browder killed himself in jail after spending two of his three years in solitary confinement. He was twenty-two years old.

2. Jessica Guynn, "Meet the Woman Who Coined #BlackLivesMatter," *USA Today*, March 4, 2015, www.usatoday.com, quoting Travis Gosa. On Stokely Carmichael and "Black Power," see Peniel Joseph, *Stokely: A Life* (New York: Basic Books, 2014). Several scholars, including the historian Khalil Gibran Muhammad and the

political scientist James Lance Taylor, have made the connection between Black Power and #BlackLivesMatter. On #BlackLivesMatter as the new model for civil rights, see Khalil Gibran Muhammad, "The Revolution Will Be Live-Tweeted: Why #BlackLivesMatter Is the New Model for Civil Rights," *Guardian*, December 1, 2014, www.theguardian.com. For a brief history of #BlackLivesMatter, see Christopher J. Lebron, *The Making of Black Lives Matter: A Brief History of an Idea* (New York: Oxford University Press, 2017). For a contextualization of #Black-LivesMatter, see Keeanga-Yamahtta Taylor, *From #BlackLivesMatter to Black Liberation* (Chicago: Haymarket Books, 2016).

3. The quote was tied to the case of the Harlem Six.

4. For the full transcript of President Barack Obama's White House speech on Trayvon Martin, see "Remarks by the President on Trayvon Martin," Obama White House, July 19, 2013, https://obamawhitehouse.archives.gov. Tierney Sneed, "A Year after Trayvon Martin, Who Is Leading the Race Conversation?," *U.S. News and World Report*, July 18, 2014, www.usnews.com. For more on the killing of Michael Brown and its aftermath, see Jelani Cobb, "Between the World and Ferguson," *New Yorker*, August 26, 2014, www.newyorker.com; "Chronicle of a Riot Foretold," *New Yorker*, November 25, 2014, www.newyorker.com; "Selma and Ferguson," *New Yorker*, March 8, 2015, www.newyorker.com; Niraj Chokshi and Sarah Larimer, "Ferguson-Style Militarization Goes on Trial in the Senate," *Washington Post*, September 9, 2014, www.washingtonpost.com; Carol Anderson, "Op-Ed: Ferguson Isn't about Black Rage against Cops. It's White Rage against Progress," *Washington Post*, August 29, 2014, www.washingtonpost.com. For a more in-depth analysis of white rage, as put forth by Anderson in the op-ed, see Carol Anderson, *White Rage: The Unspoken Truth of Our Racial Divide* (New York: Bloomsbury, 2016).

5. For President Barack Obama's comments about Freddie Gray and the protests in Baltimore, see Rebecca Kaplan, "Obama: 'No Excuse' for Violence in Baltimore," *CNN News*, April 28, 2015, www.cnn.com. For a list of unarmed people of color killed by police since 1999, see Rich Juzwiak and Aleksander Chan, "Unarmed People of Color Killed by Police, 1999–2014," *Gawker*, December 8, 2014, http://gawker.com. See also Simon Vozick-Levinson, "Black Lives Matter: 11 Racist Police Killings with No Justice Served," *Rolling Stone*, December 4, 2014, www.rollingstone.com. For an up-to-date database of police shootings compiled by the staffers at the *Washington Post*, see "Police Shootings Database," 2017, www.washingtonpost.com.

6. For a sampling of "die-ins" throughout the country, see Wesley Lowery, "'Black Lives Matter' Protesters Stage 'Die-In' in Capitol Hill Cafeteria," *Washington Post*, January 21, 2015, www.washingtonpost.com; "Arrests as Hundreds Protest at Mall of America," *USA Today*, December 21, 2014, www.usatoday.com; Yamiche Alcindor, "Demonstrators Stage 'Die-In' at NYC Apple Store, Macy's," *USA Today*, December 6, 2014, www.usatoday.com; Marina Koren, "A Brief History of Die-Ins, the Iconic Protests for Eric Garner and Michael Brown," *City Lab*, December

4, 2014, www.citylab.com. On athletes in support of Trayvon Martin, see "Heat Don Hoodies after Teen's Death," *ESPN.com*, March 24, 2012, www.espn.com. On athletes in support of Michael Brown, see "St. Louis Police Officers Angered by Rams' 'Hands Up, Don't Shoot' Pose," *Sports Illustrated*, November 30, 2014, www.si.com. On athletes in support of Eric Garner, see Chris Strauss and Nate Scott, "LeBron James, Kyrie Irving among Players Wearing 'I Can't Breathe' Shirts before Nets-Cavaliers Game," *USA Today*, December 8, 2014, http://ftw.usatoday.com. On athletes in support of Freddie Gray, see Mike Rose, "Carmelo Anthony, Marching in Baltimore, Urges Calm and Patience," *Newsday*, April 30, 2015, www.newsday.com. On Colin Kaepernick and why taking a knee during the anthem became an international protest, see Lee Siegel, "Why Kaepernick Takes the Knee," *New York Times*, September 25, 2017, www.nytimes.com. President Barack Obama condemned the "criminals and thugs who tore up the city of Baltimore on Monday night, after rioting and looting paralyzed the city and overwhelmed local officials." See Eric Bradner, "Obama: 'No Excuse' for Violence in Baltimore," *CNN Politics*, April 28, 2015, www.cnn.com.

INDEX

Adams, Francis W. H., 110

Additon, Henrietta, 23–24, 27, 181n25, 182n34

Alexander, Fritz, 142

Allen, Samuel, 17, 178n14

Alpert, Harry, 114–15

American Council on Education study, 43, 187n10

anticrime bills: "no-knock" laws, 12, 125, 126, 127–28, 131, 135, 140, 213n7, 214n9, 216n22; opposition to, 127–28; police and, 126–30, 213n8, 214n9; public protests and, 131; "stop-and-frisk" laws, 126–27, 128, 131, 135, 140, 213nn7–8, 216n22; support for, 126–27

antidelinquency, 11–12, 98, 118, 123

arrest statistics: black girls and, 66; crime wave discourse and, 70, 73–74, 85, 199n21; juvenile delinquency and, 12, 66, 103–4, 111, 123, 169n14; police surveillance and, 10, 20, 111; policy slips, 18, 127–28, 178n15; rural arrests, 104; "stop-and-frisk" laws and, 12; Uniform Crime Reports (UCR), 73–74, 103, 126–27, 205n12; use of data categories, 103, 197n13, 205n12; wartime rates, 66; youth crime, 73–74, 103–4, 205n12, 212n54

Ashburn, Arcelius, 121

Athletes for Juvenile Decency, 123

Baker, Wallace: arrest of, 133, 135; fruit-stand incident, 130, 133; gang relationships, 137; images of, 134, 147; release of, 14748; retrial of, 143, 145; Margit Sugar murder and, 124, 126, 129–30, 133. *See also* Harlem Six

Baldwin, James: on black youth, 68, 124–25, 218n37; on Harlem, 68, 124–25, 218n37; the Harlem Six and, 130–31, 136–37, 141–42, 216n24, 218n37; on policing of Harlem, 130–31, 215n18; on youth treatment facilities, 36–37

Baldwin, Joseph, 13

Baltimore uprising (2015), 154–55, 156, 222n6

Barnes, Robert, Jr., 146–47, 220n48

Barrow, Lionel C., 58

Bedell, Sister Minnie, 16–17, 178n12

black: use of term, 5

Black, Algernon, 62, 193n50

black crime discourse, 11, 70, 195n4. 94

black girlhood, 114, 167n10, 169n14, 175n19, 179n19, 185n14

#BlackLivesMatter, 153–54

black women: black girlhood, 114, 167n10, 169n14, 175n19, 179n19, 185n14; employment, 43, 179n18; Protestant Big Sisters of New York, 37; WAVES and, 46. *See also* Bolin, Jane Matilda

black youth: attitudes toward race relations, 43; black girlhood, 114, 167n10, 169n14, 175n19, 179n19, 185n14; Children's Court of the City of New York and, 30, 33–34, 87–88; racialized construction of youth criminality, 5–8

"Blood Brothers" of Harlem, 137–39, 216n29, 217n30

ABOUT THE AUTHOR

Carl Suddler is Assistant Professor of History at Emory University.